When the
Opposite Sex Isn't

When the Opposite Sex Isn't

Sexual Orientation in Male-to-Female
Transgender People

Sandra L. Samons

Routledge
Taylor & Francis Group
New York   London

Routledge
Taylor & Francis Group
270 Madison Avenue
New York, NY 10016

Routledge
Taylor & Francis Group
2 Park Square
Milton Park, Abingdon
Oxon OX14 4RN

© 2009 by Taylor & Francis Group, LLC
Routledge is an imprint of Taylor & Francis Group, an Informa business

Printed in the United States of America on acid-free paper
10 9 8 7 6 5 4 3 2 1

International Standard Book Number-13: 978-0-7890-3447-2 (Softcover) 978-0-7890-3446-5 (Hardcover)

Library of Congress Cataloging-in-Publication Data

Samons, Sandra L.
    When the opposite sex isn't : sexual orientation in male-to-female transgender people / by Sandra L. Samons.
        p. cm.
    Includes bibliographical references and index.
        ISBN 978-0-7890-3446-5 (hardbound : alk. paper) -- ISBN 978-0-7890-3447-2 (pbk. : alk. paper)
        1. Transgender people. 2. Transgender people--Identity. 3. Gender identity. 4. Male-to-female transsexuals. 5. Transgenderism. I. Title.

HQ77.9.S26 2008
306.76'8--dc22   2008021082

Visit the Taylor & Francis Web site at
http://www.taylorandfrancis.com

and the Routledge Web site at
http://www.routledge.com

Dedication

I dedicate this work to transgender people everywhere,
for your courage to be yourselves, and to your loved ones
and friends who have the courage to stand by you.

Contents

List of Tables

List of Figures

Foreword

I first met Sandra Samons when she became a member of the Harry Benjamin International Gender Dysphoria Association in 1993. She was, at that time, a master-level clinical social worker in private practice. While she was a frequent attendee at the biannual symposiums, she remained quietly in the background until the 1999 symposium, when she read three papers, demonstrating her philosophy and the seriousness of her commitment to working with the transgender population. She read another paper and gave a poster presentation at the 2001 symposium. She had become a familiar face, but I did not know her well. I did not know that the seriousness of her commitment had motivated her return to school to study for her PhD, which would lead her to write this book.

In 2005, I was a keynote speaker at the annual convention of the International Foundation for Gender Education. In that talk, I emphasized the tremendous need for more research on all aspects of transgender. Sandra approached me after my talk, saying she wanted to tell me about her research. To that end, we had lunch together and she described what she had done. I agreed to read her manuscript, although I did not have very high expectations. Her manuscript was based on her doctoral dissertation, and these are notoriously dry reading.

I was surprised and pleased to find that this work had been rewritten in an engaging style, and that is not easy to master—taking a dissertation and turning it into a book. While the research was sound, it was not presented in a dry academic manner. It included numerous digressions and anecdotal material that helped to hold my interest. While she included the standard review of the literature, definitions, and so forth, she also offered personal comments and a little humor here and there. She expanded on her subject matter in ways that went beyond the typical narrow focus of a dissertation and offered insights and observations from having worked with a large number of transgender clients.

Those of us who have worked in the field of transgender studies have been aware for some time that the sexual orientation of at least some transgender people undergoes a change at some point in the process of transitioning gender role, although there have been only a few research studies to help us understand this phenomenon, done with small samples. This book sheds much needed light on the how and why of it. In spite of the limitations, which Sandra has made clear she is well aware of, this research is a major contribution to our understanding of this subject and should be required reading for anyone who has a serious interest in gender identity or sexual orientation.

I particularly like the way she has addressed the issue of autogynephilia. I encouraged her to expand further on this topic given the controversies surrounding it and the paucity of research on the subject. She provides interesting data regarding fantasies and arousal patterns of her transgender participants, and her data challenge the notion that many transgendered individuals might be suffering from some type of paraphilic condition. She acknowledges that this condition exists, but that it is a rare phenomenon.

In short, I think this book is a great read for the professional as well as the educated layperson. It is important research that advances our understanding of the transgender phenomenon. It is written with compassion and sensitivity for the plight of people who are like the rest of us in most other ways, but are dealing with an extremely complicated problem. It is written in the same way that Sandra is as a person—and I am so glad that her personality has come through this book. I recommend it to any reader who would like to have a better understanding of transgender individuals, and in particular, their sexual attractions and orientation.

Eli Coleman, PhD
Professor and Director
Program in Human Sexuality
Department of Family Medicine and Community Health
University of Minnesota Medical School

Acknowledgments

I owe a huge debt of gratitude to a number of people who played various roles in this project. I mention them more or less chronologically and not necessarily in their order of importance.

Foremost among them is Sandra S. Cole, PhD, MHS, a professor at the University of Michigan (now retired) and a former president of the American Association of Sex Educators, Counselors and Therapists (AASECT). Sandra was the single most influential person in encouraging me to pursue a doctoral degree, which led to the research study that eventually resulted in this book. She also served as chair of my dissertation committee, devoting countless hours to guide and challenge me in this endeavor, and sharing without reservation her knowledge and experience.

Professor Barnaby B. Barratt, PhD, DHS, formerly of Wayne State University, also a former president of AASECT, and the founder and director of the Midwest Institute of Sexology, served on my dissertation committee as well, and was invaluable to me, giving me his guidance in the methods of conducting research and being a source of calm reassurance.

Ted McIlvenna, PhD, MDiv, the president of the Institute for Advanced Study of Human Sexuality in San Francisco, also served on my dissertation committee and encouraged me, but even more importantly, through his leadership at the Institute, he provided an arena for study that allowed me to pursue my chosen field of interest relatively unfettered by bureaucratic constraints and in a learning environment that enlivened rather than numbed my mind.

Although he did not assist in the writing of this manuscript, I feel the need to also mention Dennis P. Sugrue, PhD, yet another former president of AASECT. In providing consultations and second opinions for my clients, he helped me learn and grow in my understanding of transgender. All of these people have my enduring respect and gratitude.

Also very high on my gratitude list is Larisa McEachran Leader, MSW. While still a student herself, she served as my assistant in this research project, devoting countless hours to function as my sounding board, sharing her knowledge of research methods, patiently helping me with my woefully inadequate computer skills, and most of all, crunching numbers, developing charts and graphs to illustrate my findings, and helping with layout. She served as my labor and delivery coach as I gave birth to this project. Now she has finished her own degree and I welcome having her as a colleague.

Of course, there is Professor Eli Coleman, director of the University of Minnesota Medical School's Program in Human Sexuality and past president of the Harry Benjamin International Gender Dysphoria Association (HBIGDA), now known as the World Professional Association for Transgender Health (WPATH), who read my manuscript, offered additional editing suggestions, provided guidance in the publishing process, and helped me connect to Haworth Press, making the publication of this work possible. He took time out from his own busy career to support my work, and I am honored that he agreed to write the foreword for this book, thus earning an even more generous-sized place on my gratitude list.

Next on my gratitude list is Dallas Denny, editor extraordinaire (think *Chrysalis* and *Transgender Tapestry Journal*), who assisted me early on with the question "Now that it is been birthed, what do I do with it?" Without her editing assistance and publishing encouragement, this project might have gathered dust in some obscure corner, to be read by no one. I have benefited by her experience as an editor as well as her knowledge of the transgender world (not to mention my enjoyment of her quick and subtle wit).

There are many more people who have helped and encouraged me to go forward with this project. Outstanding among them is University of Michigan professor Emerita Lynn Conway, who patiently read my manuscript several times, offering her suggestions and helping me with tweaking after all the words began to look alike to me. Her insights and suggestions, and especially her validation, have been invaluable to me.

In acknowledging my appreciation, it would be unthinkable to leave out my husband, Doyle Samons. Since I view the current project as an extension of my work on my doctoral degree, I can only think in terms of his contribution to the entire process. For him, it meant altering the course of our life plan at the stage that included his retirement. He agreed to the revision of our financial plan and, early in the process, assumed responsibility for many tasks that had heretofore been in my province. His patience and faith in my ability to achieve my goals allowed me to pursue the initial phase of this work. My only regret is that he did not live long enough to see this book in print.

I also want to thank all those nameless clients, the subjects whose statistics comprise the basis for this study. I hope they will feel as if their contributions have helped their sisters and made the world a better, more understanding, and more hospitable place for transgender people to live. To quote for them from Desiderata, "You are a child of the universe and you have a right to be here." To them I say, I know that you have not always felt that you really did have a right to be here, and all too often you have felt that others thought you did not have a right to be here. Just like the rest of us, you have your struggles, and you certainly do make your contributions toward the world becoming a better place for everyone. Sometimes social prejudice and misconceptions have made your struggles needlessly more difficult and painful. I hope this work helps in some small way to alleviate this deplorable social condition.

Finally, there are the helpful people at Routledge and Haworth Press who have made it relatively easy for a novice author like me to make my work available to the interested public. I will not try to name you all, but I am very glad you are there! This is especially true of Dr. Terry Trepper, who was endlessly patient as life handed me many challenges that resulted in delays in the editing process, helping me continue to believe that humanity still exists within the professional world.

My thanks to all of you for the parts you have played in the development of this manuscript, and to all those others I have not mentioned, but who also gave me their encouragement and support.

Introduction

The Inception

As I accumulated experience in my clinical work with transgender clients, I made what I considered to be a fascinating and potentially useful observation. It seemed to confirm what I had already suspected. A change in self-identified sexual orientation was occurring for some of my male-to-female clients during the transition process. It came about as their female social role gradually became actualized. These changes were consistently and exclusively in the direction of increased attraction to male sex partners. I was able to find very little that had already been written on this subject.

This book grew out of that observation, as it led me to a more careful study of sexual orientation in a group of male-to-female transgender people who were or had been my clients. I followed them as they examined their gender identities, and as they addressed questions and made decisions about the possibility of transitioning from a male to a female gender role.

While the primary focus of this book is on the male-to-female transgender population, it is important to acknowledge that there is a sizable female-to-male population, equally deserving of professional attention. Their issues are unique, and it is simply beyond the scope of this book to address the perspective of this segment of the transgender population. I hope to see a work similar to this one that does have that specific focus. I think it would offer a truly fascinating contrast.

As indicated, the data I am using came from my private clinical files and are used with the permission of the subjects. The identity of each subject has been protected and the anonymity preserved (see Chapter 3 and Appendix C for details).

The scope of the research presented here is limited to members of the segment of the transgender population who live near enough to access my practice and who are in a position to be able to afford my services. I will be saying more about this at a later time as well.

If you happen to have a great love of statistics, including research methods and numerical values, you will find the details you seek in Appendixes C and D. If, on the other hand, you are a statistics-phobe, feel free to skim over these parts when you get to them, without even a twinge of guilt.

Although I had recognized all along that people in general are attracted to the same or opposite sex to varying degrees, prior to this study I had always considered sexual orientation to be constant within the individual range of each person. The exceptions, when they occurred, were under certain specific circumstances, such as when heterosexual men have no access to female partners for extended periods of time, as during incarceration; or in puberty, when people are just discovering and exploring their sexuality. I did not consider these to be true changes in sexual orientation, as they are attempts to make the best of a difficult situation or attempts to learn about one's self as a sexual being. My observations caused me to reevaluate my thinking on this subject.

I have always routinely explored the subject of sexual orientation with all of my transgender clients as they addressed their gender identity issues and options. Whenever a change in sexual orientation was observed, we would examine the possible reasons for this change. The observations I will tell you about do not tell us if the shifts in sexual orientation that were reported by some of these individuals have or will be proven to be lasting, or how much additional change might eventually take place for any of them. It tells us only of the shifts that occurred during the time studied. I mention this for the benefit of transgender people or their therapists who may read this, to remind them to keep this fact in mind and not jump too quickly to conclusions about feelings that may not persist or that may undergo further change.

A follow-up study might be able to offer more definitive conclusions about whether these changes in sexual orientation were transient or were permanently incorporated into the arousal templates of the individuals involved. We cannot be certain that a longer study would not show an even greater incidence of change in the same direction, that is, toward increased attraction to male partners. I suspect the latter would be true since it appeared to be the trend, but this is only speculation.

Without additional work, it would be risky to make generalizations about the transgender population as a whole. However, my
observations can offer a tilling of the soil from which further studies
may emerge, and hopefully they will inspire someone who is younger
than I am and better able to think in terms of longitudinal studies to
undertake a study of much greater breadth and length.

Some Context

During the decade of the 1990s, American society found itself in the
process of a gradual moderation in attitude, moving toward greater
acceptance of human diversity, including those of gender expression
and sexuality in a variety of its forms. Evidence of this may be seen
in the increased political advocacy for gay rights and in the increased
media portrayal of homosexual and transgender people in a sympathetic light. We can also note the greater visibility of public figures who openly acknowledge they are homosexual or are otherwise
different from the traditional norm. The advent of the Internet and
other electronic technology has played an important role in this and
other social changes.

Among members of sexual minorities, this trend has contributed
to a healthier level of self-acceptance, an increased sense of belong-
ing to the larger community, and a greater sense of entitlement to
equal rights. Society has begun to realize that minority populations
have the ability to make valuable contributions to society in general
and to their chosen fields of endeavor in particular, that they pose
no threat to the rest of us, and that we can all live harmoniously
together in society because in most ways we are all fellow human
beings who are not so very different from each other, especially when
we consider that we are—all of us—alike and different from each
other in many ways.

Despite a conservative backlash that has emerged with the dawn
of the 21st century, the increased familiarity of the average person
with the issues of sexual minorities makes these issues increasingly
obvious and understandable, or at least brings the issues to the fore-
front of awareness. Unless we would prefer to live as a society of
clones, diversity enriches society. Fortunately, more and more people
are recognizing this to be true. In this vein, I offer one of my favorite quotes, attributed to Frank Zappa: "Without deviation from the

norm, progress is not possible." Please take a few minutes to consider the profound implications of this thought.

Diagnosis—What Purpose Does It Serve?

Among transgender people in particular, there is an increasing level of social acceptance, and along with it a higher level of personal self-acceptance. Some people may argue that a diagnosis of gender identity disorder is necessary in order for insurance to cover needed medical services. However, many insurance plans already exclude any services, including mental health services, related to gender identity disorder. In the eyes of some others, its classification as a mental disorder invalidates the need for any related medical services.

It seems to me that we might work toward having gender identity–related medical services covered under a medical, rather than a mental health, diagnosis. As for mental health services, because of the distress typically associated with issues related to gender identity and social role, there is nearly always another diagnosis that could be used. When a diagnosis of depression or anxiety does not apply, that of adjustment disorder would certainly fit most cases where the person is struggling to decide what to do about gender identity and expression, in coming out to loved ones and friends, and incorporating changes into his or her daily life. This might be viewed as analogous to someone who is diagnosed with diabetes and experiences depression, anxiety, or problems with adjustment when faced with the implications this medical diagnosis has for his or her lifestyle.

In its current diagnostic form, only a small minority of transgender people benefit from the mental health diagnosis of gender identity disorder. Only a very few have insurance that will pay for any kind of treatment, whether mental health or medical treatment, of dysphoria related to gender identity. Those few who do benefit by having insurance to help defray the cost also pay a price for being able to use this diagnosis. It is a dubious benefit that only a few receive but for which the entire population of transgender people pays the price: the social stigma that results from this labeling of transgender as a mental illness through the existence and use of this diagnosis. This kind of labeling hinders the transgender person in being able to perceive himself or herself as a mentally healthy person. It also serves to perpetuate that perception in society at large. Thus, the entire population of transgender people pays a cost in stigma for the existence of this diagnosis, while only a few of them receive any compensatory benefit. It hardly seems to be fair or worth the price.

The Impact of Social Change

Despite the influence of the current diagnosis of gender identity disorder, perceptions are changing. So far, we know little about the impact social change may be having on self-identified sexual orientation within this population. Among professionals whose services are most often sought out by male-to-female (MTF) transgender people, and who therefore tend to be the ones who have the most contact with this population—especially psychotherapists, speech therapists, primary care physicians, endocrinologists, urologists, plastic surgeons, physicians who specialize in reproductive medicine, and people who specialize in electrolysis and laser hair removal—there was formerly a widely held but problematic assumption that, to some extent, still persists today.

This belief, which was initially based on limited knowledge in the absence of scientific research, was that MTF transgender individuals were of only two types: crossdressers (transvestites), for whom dressing en femme was eroticized, and transsexual women, who had lost any emotional attachment they might ever have had for their male genitals and who avowed having a female identity or wanted to become and live full-time as women, including the desire to have genital reconstruction surgery (GRS; American Psychiatric Association). This belief has kept many people, including transgender people, from thinking about the possibility of a broader variation of transgender identities.

All too often, gender-variant behavior has been interpreted as symptomatic of some underlying psychopathology. Of course, whenever a therapist sees a new client, this is something that must be ruled out, since it certainly can be such a manifestation, but just as it does not give automatic immunity from psychiatric disorders, being transgender should not be considered an automatic indication of underlying psychopathology. In my clinical judgment, the presence of a comorbid condition is relatively uncommon, or at least no more common than in the general population. The one qualifier I would make to this statement has to do with the more frequent presence of depression and anxiety, the result of not being able to be one's self without fear of reprisal or of feeling or being treated like a social outcast. These are conditions that are reactive rather than intrinsic, and often remit spontaneously when the person comes to terms with his or her transgender issues. Self-acceptance provides insulation from social rejection—up to a point.

Also all too often, gender-variant behavior has been attributed to some flaw in the parenting of the child, an attribution to which I take great exception. No one has perfect parents, so if therapists search for flaws in parenting, they will most certainly find them. However, my extensive clinical experience with transgender clients and non-transgender clients in the larger general population confirms that the parents of transgender people are no better or worse than those of anyone else. Nor do I observe any common thread in their parenting styles that might be construed as a causative factor for the transgender feelings in their children. However, parents are profoundly affected in many ways by having a transgender child, a subject that I will address in more depth at a later time.

The Therapy Game

The process of the transgender person who is trying to make sense of her own feelings and decide what, if anything, to do about them is made significantly more complicated by the difficulty in finding a therapist who is knowledgeable about transgender. In the past, attributing a certain mystique to the professionals who claimed expertise with transgender issues, and believing these professionals had special knowledge about the transgender condition—and although I refer to the past, this is still true to some extent—many transgender people have accepted and believed what professionals have told them about themselves, especially about the categories of transvestite or transsexual, and they have attempted to understand themselves within this context and to conform to these definitions.

Others, in the hope of improving their chances to obtain desired services, conformed simply as a means to an end. This is especially true with regard to obtaining hormones and genital surgeries, which require letters of approval from mental health professionals. This behavior was not so much devious or deliberately manipulative as it was a creative attempt to survive in a world where they were often

misunderstood and where service providers were often not responsive to their needs (Stone, 1991). As knowledgeable and sympathetic
therapists are becoming more widely available, this gamey approach
to therapy seems to be diminishing, as it is less often perceived as
being necessary to obtain responsive help.

Avoiding Identity Theft

As the political and social climate evolves, increasingly transgender
people are claiming the right to define their own gender identity
in their own way, rather than looking to others for this definition.
The result, which is decidedly edifying for the rest of us, has been
the emergence of a broader spectrum of gender diversity within
the transgender population. It has generated freer thinking about
gender identity in general and a greater sense of freedom for transgender individuals to explore options for gender expression. Many
people within the mental health profession are coming to believe
that this acceptance results in individuals having a greater sense of
freedom to also question and reevaluate their sexual orientations in
light of their transitioning gender role. Consequently, a truer picture
of sexual orientation may now be emerging.

Young people of today often prefer to refer to themselves with
some other term, such as *gender queer*; there are even some who
entirely reject the terms *transgender* and *transsexual*. They may use
the term *gender queer* defiantly or proudly, wanting others to just
get over it. They may view some of the terms that I am using here as
both stigmatizing and passé. Their philosophy is often that diversity
is a normal part of everything and should not be labeled, as labels are
divisive and constricting. I have to say that I think they have a wor-
thy point that all of us can learn from, but in their youthful idealism
they may not fully appreciate how slowly the rest of society is likely
to change. So, my apologies to youth as I persist in using terms that
some segments of society still consider new, even if they do not.

Throughout this book I have used examples to illustrate points.
Some of them are vignettes from my own personal life, and these
are true stories. However, in examples that appear to be descriptions
of clients or other transgender people I have known, I did not use
real people. Instead, I created composite people, drawing bits and
pieces from many transgender people I have known. Quite a few

transgender people have written and published their personal stories. Often, I have a client ask me if I have read this or that book, written by another transgender person, telling his or her supposedly unique personal story. The client asks because he or she then says to me, "This person told *my* story." My transgender clients see themselves in the story of this other person. They marvel that another person has felt and experienced so many things that they too have felt or experienced. This happens because many transgender people do share common feelings of shame and fear. They also have in common many of the same behaviors that were used as attempts to conceal or eradicate their transgender feelings. They share many of the same internal struggles with what their transgender feelings mean and what to do about them. They share many of the same experiences of rejection by family, friends, co-workers, and employers. They also share many of the same feelings of joy and liberation when finally allowing themselves to be themselves, when discovering that they are not alone, that there is a name for what they feel, that there are others who have felt this same way, and that there are ways to make it possible to live in peace with themselves. As is true in all of life, while all people are individuals, there are common patterns that repeat over and over.

So, it is quite possible that someone who reads what I have written will see herself in one of my examples and even wonder if I am talking specifically about her. I am not. However, if that happens, I will consider it an indication that I have done a good job in creating a true-to-life example, but I want to be very clear that I have not used any particular individual as an example. If it sounds like you, then that should tell you that you are not the only one who has had the feelings and experiences I describe.

By the same token, when creating examples, I have tried to remain true to life, so the reader who thinks an experience I describe seems far-fetched should interpret my use of such an example to mean that it is not—that what I describe is simply not unusual for transgender people.

1

Beyond Vocabulary

The primary focus of this book is sexual orientation of MTF transgender people. It is intended for the therapist who is still establishing a foundation of experience while working with transgender clients. It might be possible to address this topic without providing context, but the result would not only lack heart, but also probably not be an accurate reflection of the population we seek to understand. Therefore, the reader will find digressions related to things such as the process of transition or how to talk with a child about someone who is transgender. But suppose a child asks innocently, "But, who will she marry?" and suddenly, talking with a child about transgender has implications related to sexual orientation. Without some basic understanding, the reader may not know how to answer the child.

To provide another example, if an inexperienced therapist is working with a couple where the husband is transitioning to the female social role, the focus might be entirely on whether the wife will decide to stay in the marriage. But in so doing, another very important question might be overlooked: What if the transgender person thinks "he" wants to preserve his marriage and goes to great lengths to do so, only to discover that now, experiencing herself as female, "she" is attracted to men? How will this possibility be dealt with, with the couple? Unless there is a frank discussion of all possible outcomes, "she" might stay and feel cheated, while "he" might feel enormous guilt for having persuaded his wife to do something that "she" now wishes she had not done.

Well-intentioned transgender people have been known to work their way out of one dilemma only to find that they have stepped into another one. Part of the job of a therapist is to help people avoid doing these things. A transgender person experiences only one transition. An experienced therapist, however, experiences many secondhand.

And while no two transitions are exactly alike, these experiences can benefit the client and save her from reinventing the wheel.

So, awareness of the larger context of the transgender person becomes essential to true understanding. This kind of discussion involves the risk that is inherent in the use of generalizations. The only way to avoid this, short of avoiding the topic altogether, would be to treat each person as a completely separate case. Certainly there is some validity in this, as each of us is a unique individual, but it is also inefficient. Generalizations exist because they provide a picture that is true for many people, and as long as we keep in mind that *many* is not the same as *all*, we can benefit from the use of generalities. I ask the reader to keep this important distinction in mind.

Words Are Meaningful

The terms and phrases used here are part of the lexicon of the transgender world. None of them are meant to be rigidly interpreted, and when referring to the status of an individual person, they carry no implications for whether the individual has or will make changes in his or her body or gender role at some future time.

In the research presented here, rather than attempting to place individual people in specific categories such as crossdresser, transgenderist, or transsexual, the broader term *transgender* has been used to refer to all people with gender identity variance, since specific categories might prove to be an inaccurate reflection of the individual throughout the course of this study and may not prove to be accurate throughout the lifetime of the individual. Sometimes the shortened version of terms, like *trans* or *TG*, has been used, either alone or as part of another word, such as *transwoman*. This is efficient, and is also part of the standard usage among transgender people.

Choice of words is meaningful for transgender people. With the choice of a pronoun, you can validate a transgender person, stab her in the heart, embarrass or deeply offend her. This is not so very different from the rest of us. Try referring to your brother as "she" and see what happens! When it comes to the vocabulary of gender, transgender people can become political and sometimes militant in their insistence that other people get their gender right, particularly when it comes to pronouns.

To the novice in the world of transgender, vocabulary can seem like walking through a minefield. Once a person has established himself of herself as transgender-friendly, members of the transgender community usually allow a little more latitude for the assumption of well-meaning intent. This is due to the fact that nearly everyone, including transgender people themselves, struggles with vocabulary and pronouns to some degree. This is unavoidable in a situation where thinking, and therefore vocabulary, is evolving. There are still a number of terms about which no consensus has been reached. An example of this is in the use of the term *transgender* itself. When a person has extensive contact with the world of transgender, whether through the written word or face-to-face, he or she observes considerable vacillation between referring to someone as a transgender person and a transgendered person. I have chosen to use the former here, but the latter is also common.

Exactly What Do We Mean by *Transgender*?

As indicated above, for present purposes I have used the term *transgender* or *trans* in its broadest sense, to include all individuals who fall anywhere within the spectrum of gender-variant identity, whether in feelings or behavior, and whether or not the person publicly or privately crosses or transcends traditional boundaries of gender expression. The reader may have to expand his or her way of thinking to realize that there is as much individual diversity within the transgender world as there is in the nontransgender world. Think for a moment about the wide range of feminine appearance and expression that exists among heterosexual natal females (individuals who were born with female body parts). This variation includes things the person has no or little control over, such as height, body type, and facial features. It also includes body movement and choices such as how to wear one's hair and how to dress. Even among heterosexual natal males there is a wide range of masculine characteristics despite the fact that, unlike the reverse with natal females, any degree of femininity is taboo. The same wide range of expression and appearance is true for transgender people.

Among MTF transgender people there is a wide range of diversity that extends from the man who often fantasizes about himself as female and does nothing more, to the occasional crossdresser, to the transsexual woman who not only lives full-time as a female, but has had all of her legal documents changed to her female name and who has had genital reconstruction surgery. This is said with apologies to those in the latter group who often bemoan the fact that it seems as if they can never quite get beyond the label of being transgender. Often, all they really want to do is fit in as women, which they see as having always been their true gender identity, and to get on with their lives. They do not wish to forever be considered "transsexual" women, but simply as women, which feels so right and accurate to them.

There are other MTF transgender people who embrace their gender-variant history in its totality, including the years spent in the male role. They try to extract what is positive from that experience and recognize that, for loss or gain, their bodies were, at one point, masculinized and that this cannot be completely reversed. Some have become proudly out as transpersons. There is no right or wrong here; it is but one of the many manifestations of diversity within the transgender population.

Especially the middle ground of the transgender spectrum is widely diverse in gender feelings, self-identity, and forms of gender expression. Many aspects of this diversity can be described, but due to the variability and fluidity of transgender expression, do not have specific labels. There are those who, were it not for the constraints of society, would simply consider themselves a third gender, or at least a gender different from either male or female. Some rebel against rigid gender categories, finding them to be artificial constraints. Others just try to fit into the slots available and get along in the world without making too many waves.

Even among the rest of us there is fluidity in how we define masculinity and femininity and how we express our gender from day to day. In the 1960s and 1970s there was a great deal of social controversy about the appropriate length for a man's hair. Many young men grew their hair long in defiance of social norms. Sometimes they were called "fag" or "sissy-boy" or some other pejorative epithet when, in fact, the length of their hair usually had more to do with a social statement than it had to do with their gender or their sexual orientation.

Using myself as an example, there are days, especially in cold weather, when I am most comfortable wearing jeans, sweatshirts, and tennis shoes, but in warm weather I simply love wearing summer dresses and sandals. I very much enjoy the feel of both. Would you say that I am more masculine in the winter and more feminine in the summer? I encourage the reader, whether male or female identified, to set aside personal biases and consider your own range of gender expression.

Crossdressers

Among those transgender individuals who limit gender-variant expression to occasional crossdressing, this activity can vary in frequency and form, and may or may not be eroticized. The degree of eroticization may change over time or in context. These individuals are typically lumped together and referred to collectively as crossdressers. They are the people who were once referred to as transvestites, but that term has acquired so many negative connotations that it has been disavowed by the greater numbers of transgender people. The term is still used in the *Diagnostic and Statistical Manual of Mental Disorders* (DSM-IV-TR; American Psychiatric Association, 2000), where it is called transvestic fetishism. No account is made by the DSM for those individuals (probably the majority) for whom the erotic aspect of crossdressing was never present or has or would fade over time. Furthermore, no account is made for those individuals who achieve self-acceptance and no longer feel significant distress about their crossdressing.

Typically, crossdressers live their daily lives in the male role, which they do not wish to abandon. However, they also feel a strong, even a compelling urge to express the female component of their personalities periodically through partially or fully crossdressing. This may occur only in private or may take on a variety of public forms of expression. For example, consider a young man who worked as an auto mechanic and appeared very masculine in all outward respects. However, he wore female underpanties and panty hose under his jeans and men's socks. He never fully crossdressed, but he wore these things to work every day and no one knew. This helped him feel both masculine and feminine at the same time, and that was what he wanted. It was not eroticized for him (except on those occasions when he would have felt sexually aroused anyway), but rather, it helped him feel like his masculine and feminine parts were integrated. This illustrates a form of crossdressing that might not occur to the reader who is unfamiliar with the world of transgender.

Some who call themselves crossdressers consider their crossdressing to be a sort of hobby, except that this is a hobby that is fairly compelling, perhaps in a way that is analogous to runners. Some runners enjoy occasional running. Others can be seen out running in all kinds of weather. For some crossdressers, this is one of their main social outlets, or perhaps their only social outlet. They find dressing up and going out with "the girls" fun and even euphoric. This can, but does not necessarily, involve flirting or even more overt sex play with men, but these individuals do not usually define themselves as gay.

The Middle Ground

Also included under the broader umbrella term of *transgender* are those MTF individuals who consider themselves transgenderists. These individuals live part or even all of their daily lives as female, but do not deny or reject their initial male socialization and the masculinization of their bodies. These individuals identify more strongly with the female gender than do crossdressers, but still have no aversion to their male physical and personality components and, even if living nearly full-time as female, have no immediate intentions of having facial or genital surgeries, nor are they typically using hormones with the intent of making permanent physiological changes to their bodies. They may or may not have facial hair removed. They may or may not shave their legs or arms. They may or may not eventually reconsider and take further steps to feminize themselves.

Some individuals make only partial changes—perhaps to a greater degree than a transgenderist—but still fall short of full social or surgical transition from male to female. For these people, the identification with being female appears to be stronger than is consistent with only crossdressing, but they would not consider themselves transsexual because they have no desire for radical and permanent physiological changes, such as facial or genital surgery, that would preclude them from periodic returns to the male role. Others may use hormones to develop breasts or have breast augmentation surgery. They may have extensive electrolysis or laser hair removal from the face and other parts of the body if appropriate for their esthetic or cosmetic needs, but still may not wish to have GRS.

There are transgender individuals who simply reject the concept of gender categories to varying degrees. Some present themselves as gender-neutral. Some deliberately defy and confound conventional norms of gender role or expression (chest hair and ruffled blouse, for example), and others live a life divided between male and female gender roles. For example, an individual might work as male but live most or all of her personal life as female.

The Other End of the Spectrum

Then, of course, there are MTF transsexual women, the individuals who do not identify at all with their male natal sex—nor do they relate at all to their socially assigned male role. When someone like this contacts a therapist, she may still be living as a male but already clearly know what she wants to do about it. Or, she may have already fully transitioned to living in the female social role, possibly even including hormonal and surgical transition. What precipitated the scheduling of the appointment and what are the therapy goals and the life goals of the individual will determine the work that client and therapist will be doing together.

There are therapists who seem to take offense at the idea of a transgender person transitioning without the help of therapy, reacting as if a transition done without the help of a therapist is not valid. This is analogous to a medical doctor who becomes defensive when a patient comes in with a self-diagnosis and a request for a prescription. On occasion, the patient actually can figure out what is going on in his or her own body. She may have experienced this before; she may be right and actually know what's best for herself! This kind of situation requires a high level of maturity and objectivity on the part of the therapist so that the therapist's own ego will not interfere with the best interest of the client.

There are some MTF transgender individuals who are "hidden in plain sight," as others may know and interact with them routinely as women without any awareness of their gender history. However, many people would be uncomfortable and not know how to relate to another human being if they were not certain about the gender of that other person. Especially if she had not had GRS, it might be difficult for a transgender person to maintain gender privacy in a situation that called for communal showers (a swim class), if she was imprisoned, if she was hospitalized for some reason, or if she became very old and in need of care from others. Otherwise, when you come to think of it, unless we are anticipating having sex with someone, why should it matter to us what is between the legs of another person? Shouldn't we be able to simply relate to that person as another human being?

Square Pegs, Round Holes

There are a variety of reasons why a transgender person might live entirely as female but not have genital surgery. Perhaps the person is simply terrified of surgery. Perhaps she feels constrained from taking this step as long as an elderly parent is still alive because she is protective of this fragile elderly parent. Some individuals may indeed be transsexual but may also have complicating health problems that make them ineligible for GRS. They may be required to lose a certain amount of weight to reduce the difficulty and risk of complications before they can have the surgery. Perhaps there is some other medical condition, such as diabetes, that could make the risk of surgery too high. Perhaps they are in the midst of a trial period of living cross-gender while making a final decision or trying to meet the readiness criteria for this surgery. Perhaps they simply do not have the money to pay for surgery. It would be a mistake to make assumptions about a transperson's gender identity based on whether or not they have had genital surgery.

One of the difficulties with the term *transsexual* is that there are MTF individuals whose life circumstances preclude the external expression of their true feelings and the internal reality of their gender identities. This would give the person the outward appearance of matching her natal male sex while not reflecting her true internal gender identity. Thus, a person could be transsexual, but hide it from everyone or from certain individuals in certain parts of her life. For the sake of a marriage, for other loved ones, or for a career that represents a tremendous personal investment, perhaps for the perceived lack of options, the person may live most or all of her life in discomfort and grief at having to always live a lie, playing a part that does not feel congruent with who she is, never being able to be fully herself. Such a person should be considered just as truly transsexual as the person who has fully transitioned, because the term accurately reflects the internal reality of the person, independent of external appearance.

Degrees of Intensity of Transgender Feelings

When a person elects to transition despite such constraints, it is usually not a simple matter of choice. There are individuals who appear quite literally to be incapable of indefinitely sustaining a presentation in the natal gender role, regardless of what they may lose or how much they may love certain people who would be affected by their transition. It may have taken heroic effort to conform for the early part of their lives, and they may simply be unable to endure it any longer. Their emotional energy may have become depleted to the point that they are no longer able to sustain this facade.

There are also significant numbers of people who have managed their transgender urges fairly easily up to a certain point in time, but for whom the intensity of these feelings appears to increase in the middle years of their lives. I don't think anyone can explain this, except to say that it seems to coincide with other internal physiological changes that are typical of all people in this age group, but which only precipitate these kinds of reactions in predisposed individuals. When this happens, the person may feel enormous confusion and distress. He may feel both exhilarated and joyful about the experience of being en femme and, at the same time, torn apart and terrified about what is happening to his life. The risk of suicide may become a matter of concern for the individual, as it may seem like the only means of escaping from this dilemma. Therapists need to be alert for signs of this risk.

Conversely, there are some transgender people who would be considered truly transsexual by all other diagnostic criteria, but who do manage to live without transitioning as long as they are able to accommodate some measure of feminine expression into their lives. For some, this is a source of comfort and an outlet that allows them to maintain their male roles. For others, the more they express their femme side, the more the urge to do so grows. For now, all we can do is accept these responses as part of the diversity of transgender.

The Ability and Need to Pass

To a large degree, we are all stuck with our physical appearances, but some of us are more stuck than others. There are individuals whose feelings and internal reality match one gender definition (e.g., female) but whose physical appearance has been so masculinized by testosterone and genetic traits that no amount of transitional hormones or surgery or facial and body hair removal can ever give the person anything more than the appearance of a visibly gender-variant woman.

This may or may not constrain the individual from transitioning from living as male to living as female, but certainly, when she does not have the physical attributes that make it possible for her to "pass" (go in public en femme without notice) as female and fit easily into the social mainstream, this has implications for the quality of life she can have as a woman.

While the term *pass* is distasteful to many, it is useful for the present, since knowing whether someone is male or female seems to be important to most people in our society. Thus, passing is often important to both the transgender person and family members and friends, as well as others who are relating to the transgender person in social situations. One could ask rhetorically, "How can you pass as yourself?" The point would be to draw attention to the fact that if a person is just being herself, to say she is or is not passing would be inappropriate. Why is it so important for us to know the genital body parts of another person in order for us to know how to relate to that person? As was so wisely expressed by Martin Luther King Jr. in a somewhat different context, in the best of all worlds we would not judge a person by his or her outward appearance but by the content of his or her character. In such a world, passing would become a moot question. How long will it take for us to become that civilized?

Some transgender individuals insist that passing is not important to them, either out of social defiance or from indifference born of self-confidence or from resignation to the reality of their appearance. For others, passing is a matter of great importance, sometimes so much so that it can be the determining factor in their decision as to whether they will transition. For some, if there were only enough money available for one surgery, either facial or genital surgery, they would choose facial surgery. And there are certain physical characteristics that no surgery can correct. A case in point is the very tall person who cannot be made shorter.

Interestingly, this issue is one in which FTMs and MTFs often differ. For the FTM person, when he takes testosterone, his voice will change and he will grow facial hair (among other things). When that happens, very few people will question his male gender. For the MTF person it is an entirely different matter. Her breasts may develop under the influence of estrogen, but this will not make her voice change back to become more feminine, and her facial hair will still have to be removed by laser and electrolysis. Even if she is able to train her voice to a more feminine speech pattern and timbre, her body may have become too masculinized to ever firmly categorize her as female in the eyes of others. Testosterone is, for the most part, a one-way street. Once it has induced changes, they are pretty much there to stay. In such a situation, society can be cruel, if only with humor. Cases in point are our former attorney general Janet Reno and even our much loved TV chef Julia Child (now deceased), both of whom were born female (we assume) but whose bodies and outward appearances were nontypically masculine, often making them the objects of unkind jokes.

This is not to imply that transition is easier for FTM people than it is for MTF people. Neither is easy. There are difficulties and challenges that are unique to each group and some that are shared in common. The way hormones act on the body illustrates one area of difference.

Being Transgender Is Only One Part of a Larger Picture

When passing is of great importance to a transgender person, it may be because she has her own internalized transgender phobia. To the extent that she sees others who do not conform to typical gender phenotypes as objects of disgust or ridicule, she may have these same feelings toward herself. When present, this is an issue that will probably need to be addressed in therapy. But there are also differences in personality among all of us that influence the extent to which we are social conformists or are comfortable being different from our peers. The transgender person is influenced not only by her own personality characteristics, but also by the personality characteristics of the people who are most important to her. If the people she loves the most are very conformist in nature, they will find it harder to accept her transgender because it forces them to also be more visibly different by having a loved one who is outside the norm.

In addition to the above-noted constraints, lack of money for things such as facial hair removal; hormones, which includes not only the cost of the hormones themselves, but the cost of the doctor visits and especially the necessary lab work that must be obtained to monitor the hormone levels and liver function, to avoid putting excessive strain on the liver; and surgeries may make it difficult for the transgender person to transition to living as female, since all these things are expensive. It may also be that feminizing changes in appearance could result in loss of a career that would leave the individual with no means of support. Or the person may be constrained by a real risk of abandonment by her entire support system, her circle of family and friends.

The person may simply be too early in the process of self-exploration to have made a determination about the nature of her transgender feelings and the direction in which she wants to go with regard to gender expression. When a person has been brought up and acculturated to think one way but feels another way, this can create internal confusion that requires time and effort to resolve. This is one of the ways that therapy can be helpful to the transgender person.

Everyone Has a Personality

Occasionally, in conversation, we hear someone described as having no personality whatsoever. The concept appeals to my imagination and sense of humor. What would such a person be like? In fact, it is impossible to have no personality, short of being indefinitely comatose. It may have been while watching *The Odd Couple* that we first heard someone referred to as an *inane drone*. Being an inane drone is probably as close as possible to having no personality whatsoever. I am saying this to encourage the reader to think about what constitutes a personality. For the transgender person, in addition to body type, personality is one of several factors that, to one degree or another, may be beyond the control of the individual but which plays a significant part in making decisions about transgender expression. Just as is the case with aspects of body type, components of personality are factors that influence the options that are available to the transgender person.

Personality differences make some individuals better able to cope with stress than others. Some individuals are more able to tolerate rejection or loneliness. Some actually require a certain amount of time alone for personal serenity, while others are uncomfortable being alone for any length of time. We see all kinds of personality differences in all people, not just in transgender people. These personality differences are part of what makes each person unique. Many psychiatric diagnoses are simply exaggerated versions of certain clusters of personality traits. The distinction is when a cluster of personality characteristics becomes exaggerated to the point where they interfere with the ability of the person to engage in stable and meaningful relationships, to function as a productive member of society, or when they create a significant amount of psychological distress for the person. There is a fine line between normal variations in personality and when differences rise to a diagnostic level.

Some people are more introverted, while others are more extroverted. Some take in stride the milestones of life, such as births, marriage, divorce, death, children growing up and leaving home, changes in employment, or moving to a new house or a new town, whereas others do not enjoy change and struggle with it. Some people are more adventurous than others. Some prefer staying within a predictable routine. Some feel stifled by routine. Some people are more outgoing and social than others. It is a typical part of the individual human search for self-definition to struggle between the need for connectedness (being alike) and the need for individuality (being different) from others.

The same is true of the push-pull between independence and dependence. We all need other people, and we all need a certain amount of autonomy. None of us like to be burdened by too much dependency on the part of someone with whom we are in a relationship, whether a friendship or a romantic relationship, but how much is too much? We all have to find our balance.

As long as these personality characteristics do not interfere with the person's ability to function, they are neither good nor bad. They are simply the components that make each personality unique. These personality differences have implications for how a transgender person will deal with transitioning. This is true not only for the transgender person, but also for those with whom she seeks to remain connected. They too have their own personalities that influence how they will deal with her being different. These differences also contribute to the difficulty we have with vocabulary, labels, and terms.

Labels—Sometimes Efficient but Never Without a Cost

Some transgender people are flamboyant or histrionic or exhibitionistic, just as nontransgender individuals may have these personality components. (Entertainers offer some examples. So do politicians.) As such, some gay males and some transgender individuals may be considered drag queens, either because they like being theatrical in their presentation or because they are using flamboyance as part of a theatrical career or to make a social statement. Sometimes similar to an attention-seeking adolescent, some will mature out of this behavior if they are only doing it for personal satisfaction. Female impersonators, on the other hand, are natal males who make their living portraying females on stage. A female impersonator may or may not be transgender. He may or may not be gay. Some, but not all, individuals who dress primarily for theatrical reasons also experience secondary gratification related to self-identity by being in the female role.

Still other transgender people perceive and present themselves as androgynous and may even reject the concept of gender categorization altogether, viewing themselves as genderless or nearly so. Some are simply gentle souls who prefer the female role only because it more closely matches their personality, while still thinking of themselves as genderless.

Many MTF transgender individuals who choose an androgynous presentation do so because that is the kind of female they identify with most closely. The variation in presentation is similar to the gender styles of some nontransgender people, especially natal females who choose gender presentations across a wide spectrum, from fairly masculine to extremely feminine.

Some are confused and ambivalent about their transgender feelings because of internalized social taboos, religious conflicts, passive and conformist personalities; because they simply lack information; or for various other reasons. Some may adopt an androgynous presentation temporarily, as an initial means of reality testing in the process of transition. Some may be too fearful to make drastic changes, preferring small incremental changes instead. Some transgender persons may choose to challenge conventional gender-related norms by adopting an incongruent combination of male and female cues (e.g., breasts and beard or feminine hairstyle and men's clothing, a style known somewhat facetiously as gender fuck).

Trying to understand and accept one's self when one has a nontypical gender identity is further complicated by our rigidly binary societal system, in which everyone is expected to be clearly either male or female. Completely aside from transgender, and in spite of the recent movement toward more relaxed norms, our society has only limited tolerance for diversity in appearance and expression. This includes expression of masculine and feminine characteristics, but also applies to other forms of nontypical appearance and behavior. This is true even among natal males and females who are comfortable with their socially assigned gender roles and who find their assigned role congruent with their body phenotype and internal sense of self. People who do not conform to the stereotypical male or female image are often the butt of jokes and may be subjected to the same ridicule, harassment, and possibly even physical violence as transgender people. These are some of the issues transgender persons need to address in order to make objective determinations about their gender identity and how they want to live their lives. Society's need for labels makes this task more difficult.

There is also the question of whether the person who has fully transitioned and has had genital reconstruction surgery should forever be labeled as transsexual, or whether the term should be applied only to those people who have not yet had GRS. Doing the latter would allow those who have had this surgery to finally move beyond the transsexual label and live simply as women. From a medical standpoint, that may never be entirely possible for various reasons. For example, current approaches to GRS do not include removal of the prostate gland. Scientific inquiry would want to preserve the entire history of the person, but that is another matter altogether.

As already mentioned, some MTF transgender people seek to pass, while others are either indifferent to passing or cannot pass because of body type or voice. Testosterone is indeed a one-way street. Without it, the fetal phenotype develops as female. Once certain testosterone-driven changes have taken place, they cannot be reversed. For example, estrogen will not produce a voice reversal, nor will it completely reverse hair loss in the natal male (although these are oversimplifications).

The Beginning of Gender Self-Discovery

For most MTF transgender people, the awareness of transgender feelings emerges at an early age, often from first memory. Less frequently, this awareness may develop later in life. It is nearly always present by the onset of puberty, yet occasionally emerges at an even later point in life. All the people who participated in the study presented here had some awareness of their transgender feelings by age 14, but clinical experience outside of this study informs us of exceptions. Because many factors contribute to the timing of when a transgender person will first become aware of her transgender feelings, it is important to recognize that these feelings are equally valid, regardless of the age of onset or first awareness.

If we could take a large sample of the general population, it is likely that we would find the same is true for all people. Can you think of a time when you became keenly aware of your gender identity? I can, and there is a story about this that I sometimes tell to clients, especially those who are concerned that a child could become confused about her own gender if she knew about the existence of transgender people.

Before telling this story, I have to tell you a story about something that came before, because it illustrates the flexibility of a child's body as well as the capacity for magical thinking, both of which are necessary to understanding the story about my own gender awareness. When I was in fourth grade, a fad got started among my classmates. We wanted to be able to bend our wrists in a sort of limp-wristed position so that the tips of our thumbs would touch our inner arms. If I tried to do this today, I would break a bone or at least certainly sprain my wrist. But, at the age of 9, most of us could come close to doing it, so it was easy to believe we could stretch enough to achieve it. This well-behaved group of children would sit in class, eyes forward, paying rapt attention to our teacher, except that our right hands would be pulling our left thumbs ever closer to our left arms (or visa versa), gradually stretching whatever needed to be stretched to accomplish this feat.

I don't recall our teacher ever commenting on our behavior. She didn't laugh. She didn't become impatient and tell us to cut it out. But she must have felt like it. Maybe she thought that as long as we appeared to be giving her our undivided attention, she should let well enough alone. By the end of the school year nearly every one of us could touch our left arms with our left thumbs and our right arms with our right thumbs. I was among those who could do this.

And now for the real story. I was an only child (at least for most of my childhood), and during most of my younger years my family lived on the outskirts of town, where the number of neighborhood playmates was limited by who moved in or out of the area. The summer after fourth grade must have stretched out very long for my mother as she sought ways to keep me entertained or out of her hair. Always having a whimsical streak, one day, apropos of nothing that I recall, she said to me, "Did you know that if you kissed your elbow you would turn into a boy?" I remember giving this long and careful thought. The fact was that I could almost do it. Given the experience with thumbs, I was sure that if I kept stretching and working at it, I would eventually be able to achieve it. But would I want to?

I thought of all the possibilities. I knew the story of the fisherman and the three wishes. Could this be anything like that? Did you only get to do it just so many times, or could you switch back and forth as much as you wanted? What if you only got one shot at it, and if you switched, you would be stuck there? What if you did it, and then had no memory of your former life, and didn't remember about kissing your elbow to go back? I was curious about what it would be like to be a boy, but I was very sure that I didn't want to spend the rest of my life as a boy. I liked being a girl. It felt right and good to me. I had absolutely no doubt about that. Maybe it was because of this that I couldn't sustain the thought to practice stretching, like we had done with our wrists. While I remained certain that I could eventually do it if I kept working at it, I kept getting diverted with other thoughts and activities. But I returned to think about it off and on in idle moments.

There was a neighbor girl who was three years younger than me. Because of this, I didn't play with her very often, but one day we were playing together and I asked her, "Did you know that if you kissed your elbow you would turn into a boy?" She said she didn't want to be a boy. She liked being a girl. But I persisted, saying, "Wouldn't it be fun just to see what it would be like? You could change right back again." I was trusting that this would turn out to be true, and I reasoned that I could act as a guide of sorts. If it worked, and she didn't remember to change back, I would make sure she did. At first she stubbornly resisted, but she finally gave in to my pressure. Only, she couldn't quite reach to kiss her elbow either, and was not too interested in working on it.

So, at the age of 9, I knew clearly that my gender was right for me, and once it was brought to her attention, apparently so did my neighbor at the age of 6. Without an incident like this, other children might not think about their gender until they are older. Maybe not until they had passed the age of magical thinking (to the extent we ever fully do so—as is so well illustrated by superstitions and a belief in wishful thinking that persists into adulthood for most of us). If you were past the age of magical thinking when you questioned your gender, you would probably feel as if it was a moot question, since there would be nothing you could do about it anyway.

It is a common theme for clients to tell me about going to bed every night wishing or praying that they would wake up as a girl (or as a boy for FTMs), and of course being disappointed over and over. Mostly, it was when the physical changes of puberty became evident that they were faced with the grim reality that it was not going to happen. When magical thinking ends, it sometimes leads to depression.

Sexual Orientation and Gender Identity

Both sexual orientation and gender identity are fundamental aspects of human sexuality. Because they are so closely intertwined, the distinction is frequently confusing, not only for the transgender person, but also for the mental health therapist and others who provide treatment for that person, as well as for the public in general. Even though these traits are interdependent, it may be helpful to begin by thinking of them as separate and independent of each other.

Sexual orientation typically refers to whether one has erotic attractions and sexual desires for males or females—whether in fantasy or in reality—and usually includes whether or not one engages in sexual behavior with them. The terms *homosexuality* and *heterosexuality* simply designate whether the attraction is toward the same or opposite biological sex. These terms are based on the idea that there are only two sexes, that all beings are either male or female. This is a commonly held misconception that is belied in nature (Roughgarden, 2004) and in human beings at the very least by the existence of intersexed people (Dreger, 1998, 1999). *Gay* is also commonly used when referring to homosexuals and homosexuality, especially in reference to males.

Even though they are now taken for granted, the words *heterosexual* and *homosexual* are actually terms of relatively recent origin. Although their origin is obscure and not well documented, it seems these terms were first seen in print in the late 1860s in Germany. Subsequently, the usage of these terms gradually spread around the Western world. We may eventually find that these terms are not useful when discussing transgender individuals. We might even find it more useful for all human beings to discontinue the use of such terms and to simply designate the specific individuals to whom one is attracted.

Who Has Been Paying Attention to Sexual Orientation?

Sexual orientation is considered by many experts to be constant (Colapinto, 2000; Hamer & Copeland, 1994; LeVay, 1996; Weiss, 2001; White, 1994). Despite the evidence that sexual orientation in the general population can shift over the life span, individuals are typically defined as being either heterosexual or homosexual, only sometimes allowing for bisexuality. The way transgender people view their sexual orientation appears to vary from one individual to another, and for some individuals, self-defined sexual orientation varies over time. The 0–6 scale devised by Alfred Kinsey to define the degree to which an individual is attracted to the same or opposite sex is still widely used today (Kinsey, Pomeroy, & Martin, 1948). It should not be construed to imply that a number value is given to attraction toward one sex over the other. Instead, at one end of the continuum is exclusive attraction to the same sex, and at the other end is exclusive attraction to the opposite sex, with most people being located at least a little inside of the extremes.

What does the DSM have to say about it? Although it would be preferable to see gender identity disorder redefined and viewed as a medical problem rather than as a psychiatric problem, at the present time it is still listed as a psychiatric disorder (gender identity disorder [GID]) in the DSM. However, the DSM does acknowledge that individuals with gender identity disorder may vary in their sexual orientation, indicating the need for specifiers for "sexually attracted to females, sexually attracted to males, or sexually attracted to both or neither" (American Psychiatric Association, 2000). This is a recognition of the fact that not all people with GID have the same sexual orientation. However, it does not show any recognition that sexual attraction may vary in a given individual over time.

Some MTF transgender people report unvarying exclusive attraction to females, regardless of the gender role in which they are appearing and functioning. When in the female role, these individuals may define themselves as lesbians. However, society and especially academia would typically continue to consider their partner selection as heterosexual, using their natal sex as the point of reference. This is an area of contention between the transgender community and traditional academia. Some transgender people find this way of defining their sexual orientation offensive, since they identify themselves as women who are attracted to women. Would that not make them homosexual? And when they are attracted to men, would they not be heterosexual? In a culture such as ours, with our rigid binary system of sex labels, the language of sexual orientation is often confusing, inadequate, and even contradictory. Still, it could be argued that both points of view have a degree of merit for defining same and opposite sex and are appropriate from their different perspectives. As increasing numbers of transgender people who are academics or professionals in related fields step forward, it will be interesting to observe how their contributions influence the evolution of language and definitions of terms.

Alice Dreger, in her writings about intersex, offers a thought-provoking discussion of how the medical profession has historically debated the best way to define the sex of a person. The debate centers around the question of whether there should be a single or multiple points of reference in defining sex, what these points of reference should be, and what relative weight should be assigned to each. This is especially relevant to the present discussion because with an intersexed person, it is not a simple matter of defining a person's sex by genitals at birth, since their genitals are so often ambiguously formed (Dreger, 1998, 1999). Of course, for an intersexed person, defining the opposite sex can also be an illusive and perhaps unnecessary proposition. For the sake of brevity, only a few of the most noteworthy examples of those who have studied and written about variation in gender identity have been mentioned here. There is no intent to slight other, equally noteworthy examples, but only an effort to offer the reader a sample of what is available.

It is commonly believed that chromosomes are the definitive indicator of sex, that all females have an XX sex chromosome and all males an XY chromosome. While this is typically the case, it is not always true, so we cannot rely on this as the definitive indicator of gender. Neither do we rely on this as an indicator on a routine basis since chromosomes are not readily visible. Most of us have no idea which sex chromosomes we have, since chromosome typing is usually only done for research or diagnostic purposes.

Neither can we base sex determination on the role the individual plays in reproduction. Would a male still be a male if he did not produce sperm? Would a female who is infertile or who has had a hysterectomy still be a female? Be very careful! How one answers these questions could have astounding repercussions. A person might wake up to find people with placards picketing their premises! Clearly, there does not appear to be any single reliable determinate of gender, except for the fact that most people seem to have a clear internal sense of self that includes gender. It appears that the closest we can come to the truth is to allow individuals to define their own gender.

Asking the Experts

No one can potentially know another person as well as that person can know himself or herself. Of course we all have blind spots regarding which we can benefit from the observations of others, but no one can see into the core being of another person. So, if we want to know something about another person, who is the first person we should ask? It seems clear that the first person should be the individual in question. If there is some reason to question the response we get, well, we can go from there.

There are some MTF transgender people who are consistently attracted to males but who may not consider themselves homosexual at any time because they also consistently define their own gender identity as female, regardless of their genitals or whether they are sometimes functioning in the male role. They define their gender identity by an unchanging internal sense of femaleness, and therefore consistently view males as the opposite sex.

Some transgender individuals report attraction to both males and females, either dependent upon or independent of their own gender role at a given time. Some report that they were always aware of an attraction to males, but could not imagine acting on it until their bodies were feminized, because male-to-male sex was not attractive to them. Some were even surprised by what appeared to be the spontaneous emergence of a new sexual orientation as they transitioned their gender role.

Is It a Question of Morality?

Public debate and research into whether sexual orientation is inborn, learned, influenced by hormones or other biological factors, or chosen—which is for some people a moral issue—has been primarily focused on homosexuality, and remains controversial (Burr, 1996; Besen, 2003). There are factions of both the left and right wing who are resistant to research that attempts to find an innate cause. Some advocates for the rights of sexual minorities fear that the ability to identify homosexuality in utero could lead to the aborting of potentially homosexual fetuses in a sort of calculated genocide (Gore, 1998; Kirby, 2000; Leland & Miller, 1998; Savage, 2000). Conservatives seem to fear the possibility that proving homosexuality is inborn could eliminate the question of its being a learned or chosen behavior, thus removing it from the realm of immorality and making it innate and "incurable," which could lead to its greater social acceptance.

As long as homosexuality is viewed as a choice, the implication is that the individual could choose to conform to what social conservatives consider more acceptable behavior. To imply that homosexuality can be cured implies that it is a treatable illness or mental aberration and in some way the result of a faulty or distorted learning process. In fact, it may be a normal part of the variation that can be seen in all aspects of both plant and animal life (Roughgarden, 2004).

Like homosexuality, gender identity appears to be innate. It relates to the perception of oneself as either male or female. It is a mental function independent of the physical form of the body, and is a basic aspect of the individual identity of most people. Regardless of how an individual is perceived by others, most people have an internal sense of self that includes identification as male or female. It is a core construct of the personality and may be thought of as how one perceives oneself with regard to gender, and how the continuum of masculinity and femininity is experienced by self, rather than how one is perceived and experienced by others. Since the term *homosexual* is based on a determination of same and opposite sex, determination of gender identity is a prerequisite to determining sexual orientation.

For most people, gender identity is consistent with the body form and genitals. It is not specifically about eroticism, although most people are more inclined to feel erotic when they see themselves as appearing attractive in the gender role that matches their self-perceived gender identity. It is the discrepancy between gender identity and body form or socially assigned gender role that troubles the transgender person.

The Debate Goes On

As with sexual orientation, there has been and continues to be much debate and theorizing within scientific circles and also within the transgender community itself as to how gender identity is formed. Is it inborn or learned? Can an individual choose? No one can say with absolute certainty. Most people play it safe by saying that it appears to be a combination of inborn and learned factors that are not yet well understood. However, we can certainly say that neither sexual orientation nor gender identity appears to lend itself readily to change, in the sense that an individual can turn them on or off at will, or that a therapist can "cure" the individual of these feelings. In fact, clinical observations suggest that it may be more accurate to say gender identity does not change at all, even in the transgender person, but rather that the true self is discovered or allowed to emerge or be outwardly expressed. What the transsexual person does change is gender role, about which more will be said soon. The sexual orientation of transgender persons appears to be an evolving process that is not specifically sought or brought about by identifiable influences other than increased transgender self-acceptance and, for many, gender transition.

The terms *homosexual* and *heterosexual* are dependent on the view that all people are either male or female. They do not take into account the fact that some individuals may be intersexed or transgender or may prefer not to define themselves with a gender designation. Neither do these terms take into account that some individuals may be autosexual, that is, specifically interested in solo sex without a partner, or asexual, with little or no interest in sex in any way.

Social Gender Role, as Opposed to Gender Identity

To clearly understand the distinction between the concepts we have been discussing, it is important to consider the additional concept of gender role, which has to do with presenting oneself to the world as a man or as a woman, functioning in social roles associated with a particular gender, and with how a person prefers to have his or her gender perceived by others. A closeted transsexual person may prefer to be publicly perceived by others as one gender while privately identifying as the opposite gender. In just this way, a social gender role other than natal sex can be played in life as it can be played on the stage. Indeed, many MTF transgender people report feeling as if they have played the role of a man for many years before embarking on a search for their true gender or allowing themselves to express it.

For most of us, gender role, gender identity, genitals, and natal sex are all in agreement. A transgender person does not appear to initially have that congruence—often from earliest memory and possibly from birth or before—but is usually taught from birth by well-meaning and unquestioning parents and others to conform to a gender role that is congruent with their genitals but incongruent with their core gender identity. This explains how the transgender person may be hidden in plain sight, and also explains how the transgender person may not be conforming with the specific conscious intention to mislead others, but rather is initially conforming unquestioningly to the role that has been assigned to her. Questioning the accuracy of this role is usually a gradual process. The individual often finds the incongruence confusing and increasingly difficult to sustain over time. That is why the person may eventually choose to transition, perhaps even in the face of enormous obstacles (Samons, 2001). So we can say that whereas for most people gender identity is congruent with gender role and with the genitals that were noted at birth, the transgender person is striving to achieve that congruence.

Are Transgender People Just Trying to Get Attention?

People have raised this question, wondering if this could explain transgender behavior. Isn't it enough to question gender identity? Does someone always have to bring up a new monumental issue such as erotic attraction? Once the transgender individual begins to examine the incongruencies of her feelings around her gender, the related question of sexual orientation eventually emerges. Due to both external and internal homophobia, this often means there is yet another difficult issue for the person to face and resolve. Helping professionals have frequently assumed that sexual attraction would remain constant in the wake of transition, and therefore have not always encouraged the transgender person to explore his or her attractions.

The transgender client may infer from the silence of the therapist that the therapist either does not consider the question of sexual orientation important or is uncomfortable with the subject. The client may assume that the therapist is taking the constancy of sexual orientation for granted, and therefore may assume that no one but herself has these feelings, making her reluctant to draw attention to herself as different in yet one more way. The client, being aware of the therapist's role as gatekeeper, may be reluctant to initiate discussion of a topic that could be viewed as thorny and which could possibly complicate or delay the process of reaching her goals—particularly access to hormones and genital reconstruction surgery. As a result, the transgender client may avoid the topic in therapy. She may simply be embarrassed to talk about sex, and not inclined to take the initiative to bring it up. Or, due to her own homophobia, she may be reluctant to address the issue, and will not bring it up unless the therapist does so. The way in which the therapist frames the subject will determine how willing the client will be to discuss it.

The Search for a Definition of Self

When individuals with transgender concerns first present themselves to a mental health professional, a certain percentage will not know how to define their own transgender identity. When gender identity is not clear at the beginning, it will need to coalesce in the therapy process. Some individuals will define themselves one way at the start of therapy but modify the way they define themselves during the course of therapy, as they obtain more knowledge about transgender and develop more insight about themselves and their feelings, and as they reach a higher level of self-acceptance. When initially unclear about the distinction between being gay and being transgender, the person may wonder if she is gay, or even assume she is gay. The person may even prefer to be gay, because this does not necessitate coming out in all areas of life. If you are transgender and decide you must transition, people in every one of the domains of your life are bound to notice.

As would be the case in any therapy situation, it is important that the therapist not lead the client, or get caught up in what may be a passing enthusiasm of the client. After years of being closeted, it can be quite euphoric to come out and be one's self. There is often a pink cloud or honeymoon period in which the client may think there could never be too much expression of her femme self. This could level off as the honeymoon wanes. The therapist must remain neutral so the client can take responsibility for reaching her own conclusions about her gender. In such a situation, it is usually indicated for a therapist to caution a client not to burn any bridges too quickly. While it is usually wise for the client to hold off on telling other people until she is more certain about herself, ultimately the client will do what seems right to her. Once the therapist has pointed out the possible pitfalls, the choice remains with the client because it is the client who must live with the outcome.

Yet, there are exceptions to the neutral stance of the therapist, for example, when the client is stuck between feeling she must move forward and being immobilized by fear. This dilemma can prevent the client from making progress and can drag her into severe depression. It may require a nudge from the therapist in order for her to get past being stuck. This is an area in which a therapist must use extreme caution to be sure the best interests of the client are being served. If a therapist identifies too strongly with a client, she might be tempted to nudge the client just to assuage her own anxiety or impatience. Therapist self-awareness is essential in deciding if a nudge is in order.

To illustrate this point, consider the case of a MTF client who found it impossible to move forward with his life because it meant increased investment in the male role, which the person simply could not do. But at the same time, the person was terrified of exploring the female role. In this example the person got a nudge from someone other than the therapist. The therapist suggested that he attend a transgender support group, but go as male, since going anywhere as female seemed overwhelming. The support group that was suggested met once a month in a very nice hotel.

So, the client went, but could not make himself get out of his car. He sat there in the hotel parking lot and watched people going in and out of the hotel, some of whom he was able to recognize as transpeople. Each month he went and sat in his car in that parking lot, immobilized by fear. This went on for three or four months. Apparently one of the regular attendees observed this, because one day this person walked over to the car and asked, "Are you here for the transgender support group?" My client choked out an affirmative. "Well, come on, then!" the other person said, and they walked in together. Attending this group was a turning point for this client in being able to evaluate what he wanted to do about his gender, but there is no way of knowing how long he would have remained immobilized if he had not gotten this nudge.

The Standards of Care

Before 1977, there were no formal protocols offering guidance or direction to professionals who provided services to transgender people. There was no venue that helped interested providers to connect with others who shared their interest in transgender people and to offer them opportunities to discuss their observations and experiences and learn from each other. As a matter of fact, many providers were reluctant to even try to help transgender people because they risked taking on the stigma of their clients and loss of professional standing in the eyes of colleagues.

It was at that time and in that climate that the Harry Benjamin International Gender Dysphoria Association (HBIGDA) was established. HBIGDA (which in 2007 was renamed the World Professional Association for Transgender Health [WPATH]) was named for an endocrinologist who pioneered in the early study and treatment of transsexual people. Its purpose was and is to offer a way for interested professionals to confer with each other, and thus to mutually benefit by their collective experience and keep abreast of the latest research. To that end, HBIGDA provided a forum for professionals to share knowledge and observations about the transgender condition and to explore approaches to treatment. Initially, it also lent legitimacy to those professionals. However unsophisticated many of the approaches were at first, and in some respects still are, the organization provided a venue for learning from each other and improving knowledge and abilities. The level of sophistication that has been achieved is based on the still primitive understanding of the origins and determinates of sex and gender, and remains limited to some extent by the tendency of a few to cling to outdated concepts.

Through the collective efforts of the members of WPATH (then HBIGDA), standards of care (SOCs) were developed in the late 1970s as guidelines for providing psychological and medical treatment for transsexual people. These standards of care are now in their sixth revision and continue to be recognized throughout the world as the official guidelines for professionals providing services for this population (http://www.hbigda.org/soc.html). Although not always appreciated as such, these SOCs have also lent legitimacy to the transgender condition by establishing a recognized protocol for treatment, however in need of further refinement.

The standards of care, in their present form, define eligibility and readiness criteria for certain irreversible medical interventions, particularly hormonal sex reassignment and some of the surgeries employed to change certain physical sex characteristics. They include requirements that the individual obtain mental health evaluation and therapy and have written support from a therapist in order to begin hormone augmentation. They also require that a candidate for genital reconstruction surgery experience a minimum of one year living full-time in the gender role with which she identifies and that she obtain supportive letters from both the primary therapist and a second mental health professional in order to be approved for this surgery. This period of living in the desired gender role is termed the real-life experience (RLE). HBIGDA formerly called this trial period the real-life test (RLT), by which name it is still sometimes referred.

The intention of this HBIGDA/WPATH requirement is that the person will experience life as a woman (for the MTF person) while still being able to retreat from that role if it does not prove to be what the person hoped it would be. It is typically during the RLE that the MTF individual begins to examine sexual orientation in the new gender role.

The Standards of Care as a Focus of Controversy

Some members of the transgender population believe transgender people should have the right to unfettered medical self-determination, including unrestricted access to any medical and surgical services that play a part in the transition process. They are resentful of the HBIGDA/WPATH standards for limiting this freedom. They perceive them as unnecessary obstacles, as paternalistic gatekeeper functions, and believe they contribute to the general perception that transgender people are less than competent mentally. Some believe that the requirements are self-serving on the part of providers, who profit financially from transgender people who are essentially held hostage to these required services. They believe the actual issue is that parts of their bodies are in need of correction. As mentally competent people, these transgender persons believe they should have the right to make their own decisions about changing their bodies, and that this matter should be between them and their physicians or surgeons without the constraint of mental health professionals or any professional organization, no matter how well intended. They see this as analogous to someone being able to have elective facial cosmetic surgery. They still sometimes refer to the RLT (*test* rather than *experience*), when being sardonic about this perceived paternalism of WPATH, as a means of emphasizing the aspect of having to pass a test to gain access to services.

Conversely, HBIGDA deliberately changed the term to the real-life experience in order to emphasize that it is not a test. The naysayers then say that a rose is still a rose. As another step in the ongoing process of self-examination and discussion of how best to serve the transgender population, including the fact that the term *gender dysphoria* has specific mental health connotations (as opposed to medical), and to shake off the negative connotations that had become associated with its name, in 2006 HBIGDA began the process of changing its name to the World Professional Association for Transgender Health.

Although lacking in malevolent intent, there is a valid basis for some of the negative reactions to HBIGDA within the transgender community. Although the SOCs did and do serve a constructive purpose and were and are well intended, and while the revisions have certainly brought improvement, subsequent revisions can be expected to reflect our growing understanding, through research and experience, and a more sympathetic approach to the transgender dilemma. We anticipate being able to provide better answers to our questions about how best to serve this population. The name change to WPATH serves to more accurately reflect the perceived mission of its members, to emphasize this perspective to the members, and to convey it to the people it serves.

Included in this professional growth should be the treatment of transgender children and youth, as well as easier access to certain surgeries for adults (i.e., orchiectomy for MTFs and top surgery for FTMs). The most recent revision in the SOCs (sixth version) recognizes that chest reconstruction surgery for FTMs is often a first step toward being able to live successfully in the male social role. In fact, for a large-bosomed person, it is critical to a successful RLE and needs to be available early in the transition process. In recognition of this, the criteria have been removed from the former categorization of this procedure with genital surgery, and it now carries the same criteria as hormonal augmentation, which is a more realistic expectation. This is an example of improvement in the SOCs. Still, it is pointed out by some that natal females who are not transgender can have breast augmentation or reduction at will. No one requires them to obtain a supportive letter from a therapist to certify they are competent to make the decision to undergo these procedures.

On the other hand, there are problems that can arise in the course of providing services to the transgender population, problems of which many transgender individuals are unaware. For instance, many people do not know there are individuals who may appear to be normal to the superficial observer but who have insipient psychoses or who seek repeated surgeries on healthy body parts in a sort of self-destructive kind of compulsion. With a pseudo-transgender presentation, such individuals may be showing symptoms of an underlying psychological problem and may present themselves as being transgender as a means of obtaining surgeries. Surgeons rely on the mental health evaluation to identify such individuals and to help them in ways that do not involve self-mutilation, as would be an accurate term for these surgeries when performed on such people.

Some individuals who are genuinely transgender lack insight as to what their lives would be like in transition and may be ill-equipped to cope with such a life in the present social climate. The object is to improve the quality of life, not to create bag ladies. Such individuals may need help in preparing for the challenges of a new life. This is what the readiness criteria are all about, as opposed to the eligibility requirements. The latter speaks to validity of the diagnosis, and the former to preparedness. However, it is also true that the help of a mental health professional could simply be made available upon the request of the transperson, or at the recommendation or requirement of a physician or surgeon when specific concerns are present.

Transgender People Need to Have Hope

Transgender people also fear rejection from their churches and other community sources of social, emotional, and spiritual support. Human beings are social creatures, and to thrive, we need the companionship and support of others. We also have a spiritual core, whether expressed and nurtured through a religious faith or by some other means. It has been said that two of the features that distinguish humans from other creatures is that we can appreciate beauty for its own sake, and that we will die for an idea. We all need to believe in something. We all need beauty in our lives. We all need hope. We all need to be inspired by an idea and to value something above our own small selves. These things are part of what gives meaning to our lives.

As this research sample bears out, the risk of being ridiculed, ostracized, and rejected is a real influence on the transgender person, often resulting in the person spending many years attempting to suppress transgender feelings before seeking professional help. Taking this step requires that the individual first acknowledge to herself the existence of the issue and become willing to take the risk of addressing it. Although this may appear to be a simple matter of choice, it is more often a simple matter of physics, in which pressures in this direction reach sufficient magnitude to effect movement.

Once the transgender individual faces her own feelings, she will usually need to give consideration to the impact her transgender will have on her loved ones if she decides to act on her feelings in a way that cannot be concealed from them. The feelings, attitudes, and possible reactions of all these other people have profound implications for the transgender individual. One consideration is the question of whether the transgender person has the moral right to pursue gender congruence when it is not only her life that will be affected, but when it will upset the lives of loved ones as well. Many of the subjects reported struggling painfully with this question.

This dilemma is not so very different from others we all may encounter in life. Does a grown child have a right to accept a job offer that would require him or her to move away from aging parents? Does any person have a right to get a divorce unless the other party also wants it? Does a family have a right to move when a child does not want to change schools or neighborhoods? Does a son or daughter have the right to pursue a college career choice that is different from what the parents want for the child if the parents are paying for the education? Do parents have a right to choose what they are paying for, or would it be too controlling and a form of emotional blackmail to threaten loss of financial assistance if the child does not pursue the course of study chosen by the parents? Do parents have the right to spend what they have earned even if it means there will be no inheritance for their children? All of us are faced with this kind of dilemma on occasion. We make decisions that affect the lives of others and which sometimes displease them or make them unhappy, even though that may not be our intention and even though we may regret causing them distress. Where is the point beyond which we do not have the right to do so?

The Transgender Person May Be Possessive of Her Closet

At times, the participants in this study reported going through a stage in which they possessively guarded the secret of their transgender, not wishing to come out to anyone. Aside from fear, I believe this feeling is driven in part by the fact that coming out to another person represents an even higher level of facing and accepting the existence of the transgender feelings than is required simply to acknowledge those feelings to oneself in the privacy of one's own mind. There may also be a part of the person that experiences possessive feelings similar to those felt by a child who does not want to share his candy or a toy: "This is my special thing and it would be less special if I shared it with someone else." Coming out may also represent a certain loss of autonomy for the transgender person, as loved ones may try to interfere, to influence or place restrictions on the person's transgender expression.

It amuses me to recall a client who, as a teen, got a night job stocking shelves in a large discount department store. Sometimes he worked alone. He always looked forward to those occasions because he would dress in women's clothing off the racks, do his work in them, and then put them back at the end of the shift and go home. When we try on clothing in a department store, we all assume that other shoppers may have tried on the same clothing, but this is probably not what we think about. Since that client, I can never try on clothing in a department store without smiling to myself as I wonder who else has tried it on.

He May Hold on to the Hope That He Will Outgrow It

If the MTF transgender person recognizes the significance of his transgender feelings and his impulses to express contragender behavior while he is yet a child, he will often suppress them or keep the feelings carefully hidden from family and friends. He will quickly realize these are considered undesirable feelings for a boy, and he will not want to risk incurring the disapproval, wrath, ridicule, or rejection of adults or other children by divulging that he has these feelings or by being caught acting on them. To the extent the child is open about these feeling and behaviors, he may be punished or overtly discouraged by adults, and teased or harassed unmercifully by other children. At the very least, he may not be taken seriously. Sometimes, the child's feelings may be viewed as something he will outgrow if it is not made into a big issue. Sometimes that is actually what happens. Most important is whether the parents handle it in a way that will not harm the fragile self-esteem of the child or indicate that he cannot be himself. Being told "That's not for boys, that's for girls," conveys a clear message of prohibition to the child.

Some male children are severely abused or humiliated for expressing transgender feelings (Burke, 1996; Rottnek, 1999). Needless to say, other children can be cruel to a transgender child in ways that range from teasing to ridicule, to rejection, or to overt physical abuse. But other children are not the only ones who may behave in these ways toward a transgender child. Even his or her own parents may do so. In that situation, the child has nowhere to turn for help and reassuring support.

Even very young children are often keenly sensitive to subtle or indirect cues. They observe other children and the ways male children are viewed and treated by others if they exhibit femininity in any way. They observe conversations between other children, especially children a little older than themselves. They also observe conversations among adults and listen to what is portrayed on television. Because of these many influences that are outside the control of the parents, the transgender child needs more and ongoing affirmation of his worth than do other children. Unfortunately, boys are less likely than girls to be complimented for being gentle or compassionate, for sharing, for acting affectionately, for showing an interest in babies, or even for expressing appreciation for beauty. Instead, they may be labeled as sissies.

The expectations of masculinity are often the theme of situation comedies on television, and crossdressing is often used in comedy routines. As previously noted, there are very few of our great comedians and comic actors who have not used crossdressing in their acts at one time or another. Older children say, "That's so gay!" They may not even know what this means, or if they do, they may be using it as teen slang rather than intending to be literal. Adults tell gay jokes that children overhear. They whisper about neighbors or relatives who are viewed as different. The child gets the message that it is not acceptable for boys to be feminine and that being identified as feminine can result in rejection or being the butt of jokes.

Most parents never consider the possibility that one of their children could be transgender. Just having a child who is or might be gay would probably be a matter of concern. Unless they are knowledgeable and accepting, many parents would try to discourage behavior that they perceived as a tendency toward being gay. Having a transgender child would seem even less likely to most parents, but probably of even greater concern. After all, if your child is gay, you may not have to tell anybody, and the child will certainly not have to change the way he looks. But if your child adopts a female appearance and gender role, it is certainly noticeable to others. Some parents would be concerned that having a gay child would be an indication of poor parenting on their part, or that others would view it that way. Some parents would feel embarrassed, or be concerned that being gay would make life harder for their child. Some might simply be concerned about not having grandchildren to enjoy or to carry on a family name. Any concern parents might have about their child being gay would tend to be magnified if they thought their child was transgender.

The Meaning of the Terms *Masculine* and *Feminine*

How we define these terms is arbitrary and socially driven. It may vary slightly from one geographic location to another. The distinction is often subtle, but is certainly recognized. There is a *Far Side* cartoon showing several cowboys sitting around a campfire. One of them says to another, "Roy [or whatever his name is], don't do that!" You have to look at the picture for a minute to see what it is that Roy is doing wrong. It is the way Roy is crossing his legs! Are we picky about what is male behavior and what is female?

It is to be expected that a range of gender behaviors can be observed among natal male children. Some may prefer female friends or may engage in typically feminine play or behaviors at various points in their development. Some of these children will grow up to be gay, and some may even grow up to be transgender, while others will grow up to be garden-variety heterosexual men. This makes us hesitant to jump to conclusions about what a child will grow up to be. And rightly so. A child needs room to explore and discover self, but the child also needs safety and freedom to do so. These are things we are not yet very good at providing, as we often have our own agendas for our children.

Transgender feelings and behaviors in a child have often been misinterpreted as gay by parents and the professionals they may have turned to for help. In fact, even among professionals who specialize in such matters, it is difficult and at times impossible to make the distinction between a child who is homosexual, one who is transgender, and one who is on the feminine side but no less a young heterosexual male. Early on, there may be a significant amount of overlap in behaviors considered indicative of being gay or transgender, or these behaviors may simply mean nothing at all. In some cases these are only experimental behaviors the child will outgrow. The challenge for a parent is to let a child become who he is—not who we would like him to be—to help him become his best self, and to feel good about himself as he is. Or, as she is.

Being Different Is Difficult

It is never easy for a child to be different from other children. Even an exceptionally bright or gifted or beautiful or even a very tall child may experience difference as uncomfortable. As parents, we celebrate these gifts of difference while acknowledging the difficulty they can include. We try to help the child cope and feel good about his or her difference. Children with disabilities or who are physically unattractive or mentally slow, who are different in less desirable ways, must also learn to cope. This same approach can be used by parents when they have a child who is different in ways related to gender.

Have we stopped teaching our children that it is unacceptable to be cruel to others? Have we stopped teaching our children that it is not OK to tease other children because they are different in some way? Have teachers become afraid to censure this behavior at school? Do we support them if they do? Do we teach children to be sensitive or at least courteous to others, but at the same time think it is acceptable for us, as adults, to belittle others who are different from ourselves? Do we honestly think it makes sense to tell children to do as we say, and not as we do? All of us have a role to play in making the world a better place for children, and when it is better for children, it will be a better place for us all.

When I was in fourth grade I had a secret crush on a boy in my class. One day he committed a very minor infraction, but was asked by the teacher to stay after school. As the rest of us were leaving at the end of the day, I walked past him, still in his seat, and said, very quietly, "Nah, nah, nah, nah, nah." The teacher overheard me and immediately detained me. She took me aside (being careful not to make a spectacle of me) and simply said, "I'm disappointed in you. You know it isn't OK to make fun of someone else's misfortune." That's all she said. It's all she had to say. I was very ashamed of myself. I had been taught better. I never forgot it. Do you have a similar example in your life? What do you teach to people you can influence? Nowadays we are concerned about massacres in our schools after some kid has been teased mercilessly for years. I don't mean to say that parents and teachers can nip every instance of teasing or bullying in the bud, but I am certain we could be doing a better job than we are. Life doesn't have to be so hard for transgender children.

Learning From Martin Luther King Jr.

In the absence of clear and discrete diagnostic criteria, it is difficult for even an experienced professional to distinguish between the ways of being different regarding sex and gender (Rekers, 1988, p. 44). I hope to see the day when we are able to make clear differential diagnoses. We could then laugh with our children as they experiment with gender-related behaviors as part of their self-discovery. We could support those children who are destined to be gay, helping them to understand and accept themselves as they are. We could intervene early with hormones for those who are transgender, preventing their bodies from going through unwanted changes at puberty that would reduce the quality of their adult lives. For those children who are somewhere in between, we could help them find ways to be themselves without making irreversible changes. We just do not have reliable methods of doing these things yet, although research in the Netherlands is pointing the way (Cohen-Kettenis & Pfafflin, 2003). At the very least, we could learn from Martin Luther King Jr. to judge these children and their adult versions, as well as everyone else, by the content of their characters, not by superficial and ultimately harmless qualities such as how they like to dress or wear their hair and by which pronouns they prefer us to use in reference to them.

Along those same lines, we might think of another person named King, a young black man named Rodney King, who achieved notoriety several years ago because his needlessly brutal arrest for drunk driving was videotaped by a bystander, throwing him into the limelight of public debate and making him the object of nationwide controversy and sparking riots. This everyday man made a simple but profound plea when he asked, "Why can't we all just get along?" This is a question that should echo in the minds of us all when we consider our attitudes toward others. We could apply this question to living in a world of gender diversity as well as racial diversity.

The Loneliness of a Transgender Child

Transgender adults tell us about the ways they learned about transgender as children. Transgender children do not automatically have context or vocabulary to describe their transgender identities. This ability is often acquired as a result of the individual becoming aware of another transgender person. From transgender adults, we learn that the way this information is acquired has a profound effect on how the child deals with this information. Reading or seeing something on television is often reported as a way of acquiring the ability to define a transgender identity and the vocabulary to discuss it. Judging from the stories of transgender people, Christine Jorgensen and Renée Richards have offered positive role models to other transgender individuals, more than anyone can count. Lynn Conway has a wonderful section on her website called "Success Stories," where such role models now abound. These success stories can save lives.

If the first transgender role models are presented as objects of ridicule, such as one might find on a sleazy television talk show or as the result of an unfortunate chance personal encounter, or even by overhearing negative comments by adults, this may lead to conflicted feelings about self, to fear sometimes combined with the hope that goes with knowing that other transgender people do exist, a sense of connectedness combined with loathing. What is reported most often by transgender adults, when speaking about their childhood feelings, is a sense of being different in a way that is not acceptable, of never feeling free to be fully one's self, of always feeling separate rather than connected to others, a profound sense of loneliness. Not only is this very sad, but it can also contribute to difficulty in adult relationships, as the transgender person continues to feel unable to be fully open about herself with others. When the pattern of being closed about transgender feelings becomes deeply ingrained, it is difficult to change. This can become especially problematic in an adult primary relationship.

When and How Does Awareness of Transgender Identity Emerge?

The majority of people in the research study at hand first began to become aware of their transgender feelings between the ages of 3 and 14 years. This age range may be contrasted with that of 26–68 years, which was typical for entering therapy. The sharp discrepancy between age at first awareness of being transgender and age when first seeking therapy highlights the length of time required for most transgender people to become ready to address the issue.

The majority (90%) of the participants reported being aware of their transgender identities well before reaching their teenage years, with 100% reporting awareness by age 14. However, I can report anecdotally that there are others not included in this study who reach awareness at a later time in life. The fact that there were none in a study of this size only serves to emphasize how far outside the norm such late emerging awareness is. Sample bias could also be a factor. Regardless of age of first awareness, the transgender feelings appear to be no less valid.

In this study, the older the individual when becoming aware of transgender issues, the more likely she was to describe herself as a clueless or isolated child who spent a lot of time in her own little fantasy world, not attuned to the outside world and generally unaware of her own feelings. She sometimes reported feeling genderless or detached from the larger world. These things can be the artifacts of living in a rural area, or of being an only child, or even of being a child who is very creative. Creative children sometimes have such rich fantasy lives that they are almost disassociated from the larger world in early life, spending an inordinate amount of time daydreaming or engaging in fantasy play. Of course, for some children, this kind of detachment can be a defense as well.

Professional Self-Monitoring

Unrelated to transgender, there have been instances of excessive or needless surgeries being performed by surgeons who were overly eager or too accommodating. Examples of this include the too routine removal of tonsils, uteruses, and appendixes. To monitor practice, medical ethics in general frowns on the removal of healthy body parts. In addition, insurance coverage requires justification for any procedure a doctor performs. Sometimes physicians and surgeons are uncomfortable with altering healthy bodies because it is contrary to usual practice. Medical response to the needs of transgender people requires an approach from an opposing perspective. The SOCs, when applied at their best, chart a middle ground that makes ethical provision for the needs of transgender people.

The SOCs Do Not Offer Guidance for Every Case

So, what about the transgender person who does not plan to transition? Does that automatically mean the person is not transsexual in the truest sense of the word? If the person has no intention of making any permanent changes to the body, does not plan to come out to anyone who is important in her life, or at least to only a very limited number of carefully chosen people, does that mean the person is probably a crossdresser? How would a therapist best define such a person and what kind of help might be offered? Certainly, each case needs to be considered on its own merits, using differential evaluation.

Knowing About Alternatives

Suppose for a moment that you were a natal male who had strong transgender feelings from early in life, but assumed your situation was hopeless, that anatomy was destiny, and that you had to make the best of life as a male. Suppose you met and fell truly in love with a young woman who was a devout Christian. To your great joy, she returned your love, and you were married. The euphoria of being in love dimmed your transgender feelings for a while, and you even began to think they might be gone for good, so you never mentioned them to her. You hoped, and convinced yourself, that it would never be necessary to tell her. Suppose this young woman came from a large extended family, all of whom were members of the same fundamentalist Christian church. It was the hub of her social life and that of her family, and it was her heart's desire that you join this church with her, and you did, thinking this too would help suppress your transgender feelings. Periodically they reemerged, but you pushed them down. You joined the social circle that your wife and her family already had among members of their church.

Time went on. Babies were born, and you discovered a new kind of love, but of equal intensity. You wanted to give these children all the best that life could offer. When the transgender feelings pushed their way up to the surface, work also helped distract you. So, you worked hard and became very successful in your career. Your children were raised in the church and grew up with the beliefs that were taught there, that if God made you a man, it would be sinful to attempt to change that. Even wearing any item of female clothing was considered a perversion. Because of the religious beliefs they were taught, you didn't think you could ever tell your children about how you felt, even after they were grown.

Your wife was a full-time homemaker, and she lived in a world circumscribed by home and family and church. You, on the other hand, had this same world of home and family, and also the world of your work, which included travel and many colleagues and friends all over the country. As much as you fought it, as time passed it seemed like your longing for the female role intensified. Or maybe you were just emotionally exhausted from so many years of trying to suppress it. Maybe you just didn't have the energy you once had, to keep it at bay. While out of town on business, you bought a few items of female clothing and began to dress in your hotel room sometimes. It was such a wonderful relief to finally be yourself! The more you did it, the more you wanted to do it. One of your travel bags became your femme bag. You bought makeup and a wig and began to develop some skill in dressing.

One evening, while in your hotel room dressed en femme, a battery died. It was essential for a computer presentation you would be making first thing in the morning. You knew you could buy one at a drug store just half a block from your hotel. You decided to try it. With your heart pounding, you walked out of your room. The lobby was deserted and the clerk at the desk didn't even look up as you walked by. You went out the door and down the street in the dark, relieved that there was no one else walking, just the cars zipping by, apparently paying no attention to a lone pedestrian.

Now you were at the drug store. Hardly able to breathe, you pushed through the door and into the bright lights inside. You tried to make yourself invisible as you found the batteries you needed, and you made sure you had the cash in hand when you walked to the checkout. No one seemed to pay any attention to you. You put your purchase and your money on the counter in front of the clerk and kept your eyes down. Fortunately, you didn't have to speak. The clerk handed you your change and your purchase in a bag and said, "Have a good evening." You nodded your head but made no reply.

Your heart nearly pounded out of your chest until you were safely back in your room, where you sank into your chair and heaved a huge sigh of relief, followed by a flood of euphoria. You did it! And the sky didn't fall! You replayed the entire scene over and over in your head all night, hardly able to sleep.

After that, you experimented more and more with going out in public. If anyone noticed, and you were quite sure they sometimes did, they were too polite or unconcerned to show it. Your confidence grew. Pretty soon the anxiety was almost completely gone. What remained was a sense of well-being like nothing you had ever felt before. Now, being en femme began to seem natural to you.

You decided you would try to talk with your wife about it. Over and over you made a plan and rehearsed it in your head, only to have something come up to delay you. One time, just as you were about to open your mouth, the phone rang. It was for your wife. She talked for a long time. By the time she was free, you had lost your nerve. Another time, you were ready to talk with her when one of your kids, now grown, stopped by to visit. Then there was the time when you built up your resolve and were determined that this time you would not back down, and that was when her father went into the hospital. Obviously you couldn't bring up your crossdressing when she was already so worried about him.

But one day you finally found the right time, you told her you needed to talk, and you began to tell her about the femme feelings you had struggled with all your life. She was horrified. She put her hands over her ears and began to sob uncontrollably. You tried to calm her, but it only seemed to make matters worse.

Finally, she said she never wanted to hear another word about this. She would forget you ever said it, and she was not going to talk about it. She ran to her room, slammed the door, and cried loudly for a long time. You felt awful. What had you done to her? It was probably a terrible mistake to have brought this up. She was silent and distant for some time after that, but gradually your life and your relationship returned to "normal," and although you were sure she could not have forgotten, she seemed to have succeeded in achieving some sort of denial about it, and you were relieved.

Finding Creative Solutions

So, you went back to your former pattern. But you spent more and more time en femme when on the road. You made friends with shop-keepers and waitresses, and eventually you took the risk of coming out to a woman colleague who lived halfway across the country. She and her husband were both supportive and understanding. You were invited to their house for dinner as your female self. It felt so wonderful! This must be what it felt like for someone who had been held hostage and then set free.

Little by little, you created a whole world for your female self. But as much as you longed to make this a seamless part of your life, you now knew that it could never be. You realized that even if your wife could be made to listen, she would never understand or accept this part of you. And think what an impossible position she would be in if she did. Even if she could understand, no one else in her world would. Not her parents, siblings, and extended family, none of her friends, her pastor, not even your own children. You should have seen this all along. She was as trapped as you were.

So, as true to self as you felt yourself to be while en femme, you knew that you would lose everyone you loved if you tried to transition to live as female. It tore you apart, but you knew you could never do it. You did the only thing you could do. You made the best if it. You lived a double life, in part as male and in part as female. Both had their rewards, but it was such a split that you never could have sustained it if you had not been such a strong person and had not loved your family so much. The only thing that would have been worse would have been to give up the part of your life where you were able to be female. You couldn't do that either. There was nothing else for you to do but make the best of it, but then that's what you had been doing all your life. It took its emotional toll, but you knew how to do it. You had a lifetime of practice.

This scenario illustrates what has been said about transition and GRS, and the fact that deciding not to do these things is an unreliable indicator of being transsexual. It also illustrates what many transgender people face in their lives, and one possible solution, although not ideal, for the MTF person to accommodate her female identity into an otherwise male existence.

Living One Day at a Time

Most of us have heartbreak in our lives at some time or other. Some of us live with it on a daily basis. It can be done, at least by some people. Some others, for a variety of reasons, simply cannot. They will give up everything else in their lives just to feel whole. This story is an example of why it is important for a transgender person to think carefully about the choices he or she makes. In the midst of the first euphoric blush of finding your true self, the thrill of the amazing feeling of really being yourself for the first time in your life, a person is at risk for taking precipitous actions that she could later regret. For this reason, it is an integral part of the therapy process to encourage clients to slow down and consider carefully the magnitude of this decision.

Many transgender people initially go from the extreme of being closeted to the extreme of wanting to come out too fast, before they and the other people in their lives are sufficiently prepared for what may ensue. The closet that was once a safe haven for the transgender person can become a prison, and when the door is opened, they often come bursting forth before looking to see what's out there. Understandably, when a person first comes out of the closet, the feeling of liberation can be extremely euphoric. He or she may experience a honeymoon period of sorts, during which some individuals are at risk of harming their lives by taking precipitous actions or going farther than they would later be happy to have done.

2

Sex and Gender

Evidence can be found in the historical, anthropological, and socio-logical literature indicating that various cultures at different points in time have recognized more than two genders (Bolin & Whele-ban, 1999; Bullough & Bullough, 1993; Coleman, Colgan, & Gooren, 1992; Feinberg, 1996; Garber, 1992; Williams, 1986). Examples of this include the Hijras of India, the Acault of Myanmar, the Mahkee of Thailand, and the Native American Berdach, or two-spirits. Although this broader form of conceptualizing gender continues to exist in some cultures, it is not prevalent in present-day Western culture.

Western Culture—Too Smart for Its Own Good?

In the West, there has been ongoing debate as to how gender iden-tity and sexual orientation are formed (Benjamin, 1966; Blanchard, 1985; Blanchard, Clemmensen, & Steiner, 1987; Burr, 1996; Diamond & Sigmundson, 1997; Hamer & Copeland, 1994; LeVay, 1996; Tully, 1992). These arguments have centered on the influences of nature versus nurture—biology versus biography. Although some theorists (e.g., Money, 1986; Money & Ehrhardt, 1973) have emphasized the learned aspects of gender and sexual orientation, others have seen them as biologically determined (Burr, 1996). John Money, who was extremely influential in defining these concepts, saw gender as a product of a combination of biological and social influences, with critical periods in development when one of them plays a stronger role and periods when the other factor is dominant (Money, 1995). The difficulty in reaching consensus revolves around the complicated task of agreeing on concrete criteria for defining gender, sexual ori-entation, and related terms (Dreger, 1998; Weiss, 2001).

For example, in looking for a definitive marker for gender, should we rely on genitals at birth? This would be problematic for intersex individuals, whose genitals at birth may not be exclusively male or female. And if we rely on genitals at some later point in life, how would we define a person who did not identify as transgender but who, as a result of either an accident or a disease process, had lost all or part of his or her genitals? Would this person no longer be able to claim his or her previous gender? Then what gender would they have? Completely aside from transgender, it seems that reliance on genitals to define gender is to rely on a complicated and illusive indicator.

Western society has been persistent in its tendency to dichotomize and simplify issues such as gender, using the concepts that feel most comfortable to the general population. Of course, there are individuals who consider this a matter of morality (White, 1994)—and these people do not tend to concern themselves with scientific inquiries (Besen, 2003). Thus far, no definitive conclusions have been reached, except to say that most experts do not consider transgender a matter of choice or a moral issue. For now, we can only assume that both biological and psychological components are at work (Bem, 1993; Colapinto, 2000; Fausto-Sterling, 2000; Money & Ehrhardt, 1973; White, 1994).

Sex Designation

As mentioned earlier, in scientific inquiry the sexual orientation of transgender individuals has traditionally been defined with reference to natal sex designation, which is in turn determined by a visual inspection of the genitals at birth (Beach, 1976). This is problematic for transwomen, for example, who, as part of their transition process, may have been hormonally feminized, may have had genital reconstruction surgery, may even have lived for many years in a gender role different from their genitals at birth, but who would forever be condemned (as it would probably feel to them) to be defined by their gender at birth. This approach disregards the fact that it is contrary to the way in which they define themselves and how they are defined by others. That means, by such a definition, a transgender woman who identifies and lives fully as female, and is identified as female by others, would still be defined as male in scientific and academic circles and would be defined as homosexual if she were attracted to males. An analogous situation would prevail for transmen. This is disrespectful and offensive to transgender people. Neither is it likely that any homosexual man would be attracted to a transwoman because, by definition, his preference would be for a male-bodied sex partner, which she is not.

As mentioned before, neither does this traditional method work well for intersex individuals, who are born with genitalia, gonads, and chromosomes that make it difficult to fit them into the rigid binary system of sex categorization to which our society persists in clinging (Dreger, 1998). At the time of birth, intersex babies often have ambiguous genitalia that are intermediate between male and female. Often, one sex appears dominant, but this may not prove to accurately reflect the gendered reality of the individual over time, and in some cases the apparent physical dominance will change at puberty. (For an interesting fictionalized account of such a case, see Eugenides, 2002.) I hope to live long enough to see a revision in the academic standards for designation of gender and sexual orientation, to see acceptance of standards that will be based on improved knowledge and reflect a more compassionate and scientifically accurate understanding of both sexual orientation and gender designation, standards that will not cause stigmatization, confusion, and human suffering.

Reasons for Conducting This Research Project

To understand the research project we will be discussing, the reader needs to know exactly what was studied, who was studied, and how the study was carried out. Of equal importance is understanding the reasons for the study. Some people believe that we already understand gender. They believe that people (and other living creatures) are either male or female. What more is there to understand? However, it is not quite that simple, not for humans and not for other living things (Roughgarden, 2004).

Even within the medical community there is no consensus and there are no reliable objective scientific determinates for either gender identity or sexual orientation, no consensus about the criteria on which to base gender. And, without being able to agree on a way to define gender, how can we talk about who is or is not the opposite sex? There is incontrovertible evidence about the existence of more than two genders; yet we persist in using the terms *homosexual* and *heterosexual*, which essentially refer only to same or opposite sex. Consequently, when professional service providers are examining these topics with clients, it is best to rely on their own self-reports, as was done with the people who participated in this research. Although there are limitations to the objectivity any person can have about her own self, essentially each person is the best available expert on self.

In the past, there have been good reasons for transgender and homosexual people to emphasize the differences between each other. Each group had their own stigma to live with and deal with. Understandably, neither group wished to take on the stigma of the other group in addition to their own. When the wife of a heterosexual crossdresser finds out about her husband being a crossdresser, typically one of her first questions is: "Are you gay? Have you been having sex with men?" Heterosexual crossdressers have made strenuous efforts to dispel this image of being gay. They did not consider it accurate, and many marriages failed because of this misconception.

Conversely, gay men usually like their masculinity, and while some may play with gender at times, they do not want to become female. Neither do they desire female sex partners. If they did, they would no longer be gay or fit in as gay men.

In a similar way, while crossdressers certainly enjoy female expression, they also do not want to give up their masculine selves, which is their dominant gender identity. Like gay men, they like being men. Unlike gay men, although they may be flattered by the attention of men while they are en femme, they are typically attracted to women. At least, if they were not gay before they put on a dress, then putting on a dress would probably not suddenly make them become gay. Changing the basis of sexual attraction is just not that simple. This is an oversimplification that will suffice for now. More will be said about this at a later time.

To exacerbate the situation, in the minds of some therapists any suggestion of same natal sex attraction on the part of a transgender person has raised the possibility that the transgender person might not be a "true transsexual," but instead a homophobic homosexual trying to make a same-sex attraction more acceptable to himself or others. This observation is based on the personal reports of numerous members of the transgender community. It is especially true of the reports of older members who can tell about the way things used to be. A change in thinking is gradually taking place, and this concept appears to be less prevalent.

Because of the confusion and social pressure that has, in the past, surrounded the treatment of individuals with transgender concerns, therapists were also sometimes reluctant to support the transition of a MTF transsexual woman who was, and who they believed would remain, attracted to females. The argument was that this would be like creating a lesbian, which was not always considered an acceptable outcome in a day when homosexuality was stigmatized more than it is today. As can readily be seen, for the transgender person this created a damned-if-you-do, damned-if-you-don't situation.

In fact, many professionals were, in the past, reluctant to work with this population under any circumstances because they feared that they too would be stigmatized if they did so. Dr. Harry Benjamin was esteemed for his courage to champion the cause of transgender, even though by today's standards many would find his approach patronizing. This statement is not intended to imply that there is no longer any stigmatization of any of the parties, but only that it is not as widespread and usually is not of the former intensity. There are still times and places where the stigmatization of the past persists.

A Transition Story

I had no idea, when she came to her first appointment with me, whether she was MTF or FTM. On the phone, she sounded like a woman. She simply gave me her name (female) and said she needed to talk with someone who knew about transgender. She looked like a woman when she arrived for her appointment. I obtained some preliminary information, told her about her privacy rights, and tried to think of some way to get a clue about her gender history. I couldn't. She might have been a natal female who identified as male and was considering transition to the male social role, or a transwoman who blended in well as female.

Finally, somewhat sheepishly and with a touch of self-deprecating humor, I was forced to ask. She was bemused and, thankfully, not offended. One can never be sure when meeting a client for the first time how they will react to such a question. In fact, she had transitioned from male to female five years earlier, as a senior in college. She had gone to college right out of high school, only a couple hours away from her hometown, which was a few hours away from my office in the opposite direction, across the state line. She had never seen a therapist. She had dated a few women while still living as male, but never got serious because she knew she wanted to transition and thought it would be unfair to create false expectations. She didn't want to risk getting involved and end up hurting another person or being hurt herself.

She had done her own research on the Internet and knew more about hormones than I did. While in her second year of college, she persuaded her family doctor to prescribe hormones, and she still went back to him for yearly visits and prescription renewals. She had gone to an electrologist and had her facial hair removed, and just before graduating from college she had her name legally changed to its current form so it would be reflected on her diploma. She applied for jobs all around the country, and found one in my town.

All her family members and the people where she grew up knew about her transgender status. Although some had struggled with it more than others, all the people back home now accepted her. But no one in her new location had any idea she was transgender. They just accepted her as a woman. She reported that once she had settled into her new gender role, she had gradually become aware of finding certain young men attractive, but she had never acted on it. She had never dated a man. Other than that, she was living quietly but happily ever after.

So, why was she there in my office? Well, three things had happened recently. Up until now, she had felt that genital surgery was out of the question due to cost, but she had reached a point in her career where she could actually afford it. Even so, she really had seen no point in having this costly surgery until the past couple of months. After all, how likely was she to find someone who would love and want to share his life with her, a transwoman?

But she had been in communication via the Internet with another transwoman who lived across the country, and who, like my client, was living successfully as a woman but had not had genital surgery. This woman told her about a recent experience in which she was in an automobile accident and ended up in the hospital. When the doctors and nurses upon whom she was dependent for care became aware that she was transgender, the way they acted toward her became strained, and she felt that some of them were indifferent to her needs. This made my client begin to think about the possibilities in terms of herself, even wondering what might happen to her when she became an old woman. Suppose she became unable to care for herself and had to be in a nursing home? How would people react to her in such a situation?

Then something happened that proved to be the clincher, something she had not anticipated, something that got her to pick up the phone and call me for an appointment. She met a young man and they were mutually attracted to each other. She had gone on three dates with him! She felt like a schoolgirl with her first crush! But she hadn't even allowed him to kiss her yet. What was she going to do?

So, now she wanted several things from me. She wanted a referral to have her hormones reviewed by an endocrinologist, as she was still getting hormones from her old family doctor, who had never seen another transgender person except her. She wanted a referral to a surgeon who was experienced with genital reconstruction surgery (including my help in getting the second mental health opinion required for this surgery), and she wanted help in how to discuss her gender history with this young man. The average therapist, however good, would probably be at a loss as to how to help such a client.

Therapy for People Who Do Not Have a Diagnosis

All people experience personal problems and difficult times in their lives, and they often resolve these problems or muddle through these difficult times without the assistance of a therapist (although many would benefit from some professional help to get through such things). But having a personal problem does not equate to having a diagnosis. Otherwise, we would all be diagnosable, and such a broad generalization would make mental health diagnosis meaningless. In the same way, many transgender people are capable of managing their own transitions if they have access to competent medical care. The above vignette illustrates this point.

However, without a diagnosis, no insurance plan will cover the cost of therapy. Even with a diagnosis, some insurance policies specifically exclude any treatment related to transgender as a covered service. Insurance plans can do this; as a cost-cutting mechanism they can exclude coverage for diagnoses they do not consider cost-efficient, or which they see as being less valid than some other conditions. They fail to recognize that allowing the transgender person access to treatment may be more cost-effective than, for example, treating that person for a hospitalization after a series of suicide attempts.

An experienced therapist who is knowledgeable about transgender issues can make transition a little or even a lot easier by helping the transgender person sort out whether or not to transition, and by being helpful in working out ways to deal with some of the challenges of life that are unique to transgender people. Such a therapist is worth her or his fee.

Many transgender people, like the young woman in this vignette, seek out therapy for guidance, but would not qualify as having a mental health diagnosis other than gender identity disorder, except perhaps for an adjustment disorder, which implies a brief period of instability when met with an extraordinary life problem. And even when transgender is covered, would it still count if the person is no longer feeling distress or "dysphoria" about their gender? Many people, transgender and otherwise, go to a therapist for help with life problems when the amount of distress they are experiencing does not rise to a level that would qualify as diagnostic. Sometimes they pay out of pocket for the service, and sometimes therapists stretch the parameters and use the closest diagnosis, although the use may be somewhat questionable. After all, diagnosis is often a matter of the degree to which the person feels distress (subjective) and how much that distress interferes with the ability of the person to function in one or more domains of life. It is a judgment call that is arbitrary and imprecise. This is a fact that no one likes to talk about because to deliberately falsify a diagnosis in order to qualify for insurance coverage is fraud. Even when operating in good faith a therapist may be walking a fine line.

Some transgender people resent having to come to a therapist because they do not see themselves as being in need of therapy. Sometimes they are right. It can be helpful to be candid about this with such clients, but to also point out that two heads can be better than one, asking them if there were a harder way to transition (i.e., without the benefit of a therapist), would that be their first choice?

The vignette about the transwoman who transitioned on her own and later sought therapy was used because it illustrates several things: that it is possible to transition successfully without the help of a therapist; that it is never too late to come to a therapist for help; that transgender people may seek help for many reasons other than the most obvious, that is, because of confusion about gender or for help with transition. They may do so at many different points in their transition, as the challenges of coming out appear to be lifelong. The vignette also illustrates that a decision to forgo having GRS may be reconsidered at a later time, which has implications for a researcher who may be quick to draw conclusions about where a client will be in the future based on present intentions. Above all, it illustrates how it was possible that the people represented in the current research study were at such different points in their transgender process.

The Effect of the Gatekeeper Role

Standards of care, while serving a useful function, have also placed therapists in the role of gatekeepers because of the required letters of approval for hormones and certain surgeries. The two opposing points of view that were formerly sometimes espoused by therapists, that is, that a MTF transsexual might be a homophobic homosexual male, or that she could become a lesbian if attracted to females, made the transgender person fearful of being caught in this damned-if-you-do, damned-if-you-don't situation. Therefore, some MTF transgender people have been reluctant to consider the possibility of a sexual attraction to males, or to explore it even in the most private way, in their own minds. Among those who have given sexual orientation serious thought, they have been understandably reluctant to risk reporting such thoughts and feelings to professionals who had gatekeeper authority. They have had good reason to be afraid of discrediting their transgender goals in the minds of the providers from whom they were seeking services. Too often, they have been reluctant to engage in any discussion of sexual attraction because of the fear of being further pathologized, no matter what they said.

This deplorable situation has been and still is exacerbated by the fact that many medical and mental health care providers are uncomfortable discussing matters related to sexuality with their clients/patients. Although sexuality is fundamental to all creatures, it is rarely taught in schools of higher education and is not an integral part of professional training for medical doctors or mental health therapists, although it is sometimes offered as an elective course or integrated briefly into some other course. Because of this, a therapist may either overlook this topic in the course of therapy or feel a little relieved if it does not come up.

Some transgender people have become adept at anticipating what a therapist wants to hear and complying with it. The recent increase in social acceptance, in combination with an increased sense of entitlement within the transgender community, has made it more possible for transgender people to think objectively and speak more candidly about this topic. This is said while remaining aware of the risk from a conservative backlash. The gains that have been made could easily be lost. This progress needs to be guarded as carefully as possible if we are to continue to grow in knowledge and insight in this area of study.

The God Complex

Experienced gender therapists, being mindful of the dilemma created by the role of gatekeeper, have had to become skillful in addressing this issue with their clients so as to make it safe for clients to think and speak freely and openly about their sexuality. However, this is simply a matter of honing skills that a good therapist should have anyway. It means being sensitive to the concerns of the client, building a good therapeutic alliance, being respectful of the client's right to self-determination, and having good ego boundaries and the associated ability to recognize that the client is not the same person as the therapist, that the client has his or her own reality and may choose to live a different life than the therapist would choose. A good therapist will not be threatened or pull rank if the client does not agree with him or her, but rather, will work collaboratively with the client to find a solution that will be acceptable to them both. If this cannot be accomplished, it may be time for the therapist to refer that client to another therapist.

There are therapists who become upset by clients who do not accept their direction or who do not comply with some aspect of therapy. There are clients who insist on self-determination and who become manipulative if the therapist is perceived as an obstacle that they don't know how else to deal with. Sometimes, because of past experiences, the client will be manipulative from the start of therapy. Instead of the therapist working with the client to understand what might be contributing to this situation, the client may be labeled as uncooperative. While this can happen with any client, it is sad but true that transgender clients in particular have been reputed to be this way and have been treated accordingly. Many times in the past, it has been the only way the transgender person has succeeded in gaining access to services. In the transgender community, there was a time when specific ways to get around gatekeeper obstacles were freely shared and recommended as a first line of defense.

There certainly are individuals who are basically manipulative. It can be a style that has been adopted without even recognizing it as being manipulative, but only as a normal approach to life. However, more often than not a client may behave this way for some identifiable reason. This might include a disappointing history of seeking help that did not prove to be helpful. It might originate in a childhood of not being listened to or taken seriously, establishing a pattern that persists into adulthood and may extend to include all authority figures. It might involve a former or current therapist not exploring far enough into the feelings of the client to understand what is really going on, or trying to bend the client to the will of the therapist. If a client feels at an impasse with a therapist and sees the therapist only as a means to an end, then finding a way around the therapist may seem to the client like the only expeditious course of action. When a constructive therapeutic relationship is developed, the client and therapist will work as a team toward the mutual goal of helping the client achieve the best possible quality of life, including gender satisfaction.

The above is not intended to sound like a harsh judgment of therapists. It is true that there are times when the shoe fits. It is also true that there are times when a client may have a limitation in his or her personality that prevents that client from being objective or whose reality testing ability is impaired. The client may have emotional problems that result in behavior that is not in her own best interest. In such a case, an impasse with the client may be reached. If the therapist believes it would be a disservice to the client to endorse a certain course of action and the client refuses to acknowledge the concern of the therapist, if attempts to reach a mutually agreeable solution fail, it is advisable to recommend that the client find a more compatible therapist. If the therapist is correct, perhaps hearing this concern from more than one therapist or hearing it stated in a new way by a different therapist will prove helpful to the client.

The bottom line remains that it is wise for a therapist to remember that he or she is a therapist—not God. A little humility is good for everyone to have. And as any good experienced therapist will acknowledge in all humility, there will have been times when the therapist expressed concern to a client about some course of action the client was proposing but, beyond expressing that concern, decided to allow things to unfold as they would and assumed that it would be what we so kindly refer to as "a learning experience" for the client, only to have the outcome prove to be perfectly satisfactory. It was the therapist who had the learning experience, a reminder of the importance of humility.

Illustrating this point is the example of one of my clients (actually a composite of several similar examples) who came out at work in a way that was different than I recommended. This client was in a gradual process of changing to living full-time as a woman. She had come out to everyone in her personal life, where she spent nearly all of her time in the female role. All that remained was coming out at work. Conventional wisdom would have dictated that she talk with her boss and make a plan for announcing her change to her co-workers, all of this assuming that she would not lose her job. But she kept delaying this talk, and instead she gradually began to make some small changes without discussing it with anyone at work. First, she began to let her hair grow. Then she got her ears pierced, but only wore tiny studs in them. Gradually, she chose more androgynous clothing to wear. Then she tried wearing clear nail polish. Next thing you know, her androgynous clothing all came from the women's department. She wore loafers with her women's slacks. If anyone noticed, they were too polite to comment.

As her hair grew, one day she informed me that she had worn a simple brown plastic headband at work, just to keep her hair from falling in her eyes. Now, sometimes a guy will let his hair grow, but I had seen this headband and, while it was indeed simple, it was still definitely not the sort of thing you would expect a guy to wear. I took a deep breath and held my tongue.

I kept asking her when she was going to talk with her boss. I even suggested that she choose her most trusted co-worker and talk to him, to begin building a base of support at work. But she had other ideas. She wore a bracelet, but still a fairly androgynous one. No one thing she wore was completely femme (other than the headband), but the combination was certainly adding up. Eventually, her clothing selections, while always conservative, were becoming more and more unmistakably feminine.

One day, a friendly co-worker asked her point blank, "What's the deal with you? Are you becoming a woman?" And she replied, "Well, yes, I am." And the co-worker said, "Well, we've all been wondering when you were finally going to get around to telling us!" And it was as simple as that! She never did make a formal announcement. One day she went to her boss and told him she had legally changed her name and asked how to go about integrating that into the payroll records, and he matter-of-factly told her what she had to do. That was all. Except that I sat back in awe and tried to decide whether to tear my hair out or just laugh. I chose the latter.

The Health Insurance Portability and Accountability Act (HIPAA)

This law, passed in 1996, and the acronym for it with which we are most familiar, reinforces the rights of the patient to both privacy and self-determination in the management of his or her own medical care and medical records. It represents a milestone for the rights of the consumer of medical services. This includes the consumer of mental health care. Written to be implemented in increments, it means that the provider can no longer be as patronizing as in the past, but must include the informed consent of the client or patient in the decision-making process regarding his or her own care. It is not without flaws, but if it does some of what it is intended to do, it will begin to change the way we think about provision of health care services. It is a benchmark in the shift from the all-knowing provider, who can use the "because I said so" approach to making decisions about the care to be provided, to informed consent that includes making the client aware of the options and the pros and cons of each, and leaving the final decisions in the hands of the client, the person who will be the one to live with those choices.

When People Are Too Young to Speak for Themselves

An interesting extension of the question of the rights of the consumer is the case of intersex babies, who have traditionally been socially and surgically assigned a gender by medical professionals, either at birth or early in infancy. Parents make these decisions for their minor children, usually based on medical recommendations. However, a significant number of adult intersex individuals have reported that genital surgery in infancy resulted in gender incongruity for them as adults. Some of these individuals experienced permanent loss of sexual sensation or response in their genitals. Consequently, the Intersex Society of North America objects to routine genital surgery for intersex infants. These intersex adults and their advocates would prefer that medical professionals assign a functional social gender role to intersex infants at birth, while limiting surgical procedures to those that are essential for necessary bodily functions, and waiting until the person is physically and psychologically mature enough to be able to participate in the decision-making process before final and fundamental decisions are made about surgical reconstruction of genitals. By so doing, the individual will have a voice in the decision and can be certain of achieving the correct sex and gender identity designation (Kessler, 1998; Rottnek, 1999).

This would include the choice to take no action at all, as some intersex people are quite content to remain as they are. They may define themselves as having a gender other than simply male or female, or they may see themselves as not having a gender at all in the traditional sense of the word. The belief is that surgical intervention without the informed consent of the individual should be reserved for situations that are critical to healthy functioning of body parts, or to preserve basic health. This approach seems to be the most sensible and respectful of the individual and is in keeping with greater respect for recipient rights.

We could definitely complicate the picture if we were to broaden the definition of intersex to include what may eventually prove to be a less visible but nonetheless equally valid extension of intersexuality—transgender. Although there are significant differences in the way intersex and transgender people develop and experience their sense of gender, the origins of their conditions may be related. They may be like a tree with two main trunks but one common root system.

The Basis for Defining Sexual Orientation

Who has the right to define a person's sexual orientation? Most transgender people prefer to define their sexual orientation based on their presenting gender role. In a world where this were the norm, it would be left to each person to decide who he or she is attracted to, independent, to some extent, of genitals. Even for those whose sex and gender are congruent, being heterosexual does not imply attraction to all members of the opposite sex (for which we can all be thankful). Each person will find only certain physical and personality types attractive within the narrower confines of male or female. However, in a world where people would have to decide about physical attraction without foregone certainty about the other person's genitals, we would all have to rethink our perceptions about sexual orientation. Each of us would have to think through the relative importance of sex for pleasure versus sex for procreation, and clarify to what degree this is driven by religious conviction, since all of this would vary from individual to individual.

The Importance of Genitals

For pretransition MTF transgender individuals who are married or are in committed relationships with natal females, there are other important concerns. The natal female partners have usually perceived themselves as heterosexual women who have entered sexual relationships with heterosexual men. They usually have not identified themselves as homosexual, which appearances would suggest to be the case if the couple remained together when the partner had transitioned to the female role or when she and her nontransitioned but crossdressed husband appeared together in public. Neither have these females wished to be in a sexual relationship with a partner who had a female body. This is a critical consideration for most wives in deciding whether to try to preserve their marriages with MTF husbands (Boyd, 2003). They have been concerned not only about social appearances, but also about the kind of sex partner they find attractive.

At the same time, these women have usually been concerned about the possibility of their husbands being homosexual, that is, sexually attracted to men. If that were the case, the MTF husband might eventually no longer find the wife attractive, or might possibly be at risk of exposing the female partner to a sexually transmitted infection after engaging in unsafe sexual activity with a male partner. He might even eventually decide to leave the marriage to pursue a committed relationship with a man.

Concern about the reaction of the female partner and the risk of putting the marriage in jeopardy, including the possible loss of the relationship with any children, may cloud the MTF transgender person's ability to think objectively about her own gender identity as well as its possible implications for her sexual attractions. She may exercise poor judgment as she feels increasingly compelled to find answers. Some MTFs experiment with new sexual behaviors in an attempt to find answers to their own questions about their sexual orientation. They may do this experimentation in secret, hoping to discover that they prefer the life they have. At the very least, they hope to find the answer to this question before saying anything that might jeopardize their current relationship by prematurely raising questions that could prove to be moot. They fail to recognize that the experimentation itself may jeopardize the relationship. They count on no one finding out. Of course, it doesn't always work out that way, but even if it does, the secret itself creates an invisible barrier to intimacy with the wife. She may not know what the barrier is, but she usually senses that it is there.

What Does the Literature Say About Sexual Orientation in Transgender People?

Many authors have written about what they may term transgenderism, but typically they do not mention the subject of sexual orientation. When it is mentioned in modern-day literature, it is usually in passing, with only brief comments. For example, Erwin Haeberle (1978) makes reference to transsexualism in historical context, but does not address sexual orientation in those individuals. In *Human Sexuality in Four Perspectives*, several of the authors, especially William Davenport (Beach, 1976, chap. 5, p. 115) and Robert Stoller (Beach, 1976, chap. 7, p. 206), recognize transsexualism, but treat it either as a sexual deviation or as an alternative sexual identity without addressing the implications for sexual orientation, or they give it only brief mention while defining transsexualism as a variant manifestation of homosexuality in primitive cultures. Many transgender people object to the "ism" of transgenderism because they find it pathologizing. For that reason, it has not been used routinely herein.

Except for the work of a few groundbreaking scholars, the literature contains virtually nothing more than brief mention of shifts in sexual orientation accompanying the physical, psychological, and social changes associated with gender transition. The exceptions specifically include the work of Eli Coleman, Walter O. Bockting,

C. D. Doorn, Arlene Istar Lev, and a few others (Bockting & Coleman, 1992; Coleman, 1987; Coleman & Bockting, 1988; Coleman et al., 1992, Coleman, Bockting, & Gooren, 1993; Doorn, 1997; Lev, 2004), each of whom recognizes the same identity and attraction problems we have been discussing, and each describes several different ways these can become manifest (Bockting, 1999; Daskalos, 1998; Denny, 1999; Doorn, 1997; Stuart, 1991). Even leaders in the transgender community have not said much about it, at least not publicly.

In large part this may be due to a desire within the transgender community to minimize the confusion that already exists in the minds of the general public regarding the distinction between being gay and being transgender, as well as the efforts of each group to avoid taking upon themselves the social stigma associated with the other group. Denny and Green (1996) depart from this tradition by offering a frank discussion of bisexuality within the transgender population. Although their observations are not based on scientific research, these authors have extensive experience within the world of transgender people and are credible sources of information in this regard.

Transgender People Prior to 1948

Alfred Kinsey (Kinsey, Pomeroy, & Martin, 1948) and his associates devoted many years to conducting and documenting in-depth interviews and sexual histories with thousands of subjects from all walks of life and all geographic sections of the United States. He and his associates used a carefully constructed format for gathering and coding these sexual histories and practices as they were obtained from a broad cross section of the population. They then performed comprehensive analysis of the data. In order to gain access to so many segments of the population, Dr. Kinsey had to gain the confidence of community leaders (meaning not only civic leaders, but also leaders in church groups, social organizations, social subcultures, etc.), and his work was widely endorsed by these leaders—many of whom were themselves conservative even by the standards of their day. Through the endorsements of these group leaders, this team of researchers gained access to these groups. These are endorsements we cannot ignore.

One might view Alfred Kinsey as a funny little man, nerdy by most standards, compulsive in his approach to his work and attention to detail. How else could anyone have devoted so many years to an in-depth study of the gall wasp? He also had a damn-the-torpedoes regard for the truth and the search for objective facts. When asked to teach about a topic that he did not consider himself to know enough about (sex), he set out to remedy the situation. And he brought these same qualities with him in his search for truth and understanding of human sexuality.

Kinsey's research was done at a time when scientific methods for studying large populations were not well defined. In his book on sex and the human male, he discusses at length the methods he used, explaining the advantages and drawbacks of various approaches and his reasons for selecting among them (Kinsey et al., 1948). Even with its limitations, his work provides the foundation for methods of modern-day research with large populations and is the baseline against which other researchers compare their own results. However, reflective of the lack of social awareness of the day, Kinsey failed to ask his subjects about gender identity. He did, however, develop a sexual orientation scale that is still used today, basing the degree to which a person is attracted to males or females on a scale of 0 to 6.

Outliers

Statistically speaking, outliers are those people or objects who lie far outside of the area where most of the data are clustered. On a bell curve, these would be at the extreme outer edges, where the numbers are fewest. A Kinsey finding that has significant bearing on the study at hand is that only a few humans are clearly and exclusively either heterosexual or homosexual, only a few who would be counted on his scale as purely 100% 0 or 6 values. Based on reported feelings, fantasies, and practices over the span of a lifetime, the majority of people, both male and female, would be considered bisexual to at least some small degree. Moreover, their attraction templates can change over the course of their lifetimes. If this is true, and Kinsey presented overwhelming evidence that it is, then one might expect it to be true of transgender people as well. It is nonetheless an unfortunate truth that, in spite of this finding of Kinsey's research, society continues to cling to strict binary standards of gender and sexual attraction except when confronted with individual cases of medically diagnosed pathology. It would seem that all people have a remarkable capacity for ignoring information when it challenges established beliefs or makes them feel uncomfortable.

When working with people who are resistant to the idea that sexual attraction can change over time in the same individual, I sometimes find it effective to use myself as a humorous example. Being a woman of mature years, and one who has only been aware of being sexually attracted to males, I point out that it is certainly a good thing that attraction templates do change over time. Otherwise, I would still be attracted to adolescent boys. Almost without exception, people are able to see the humor in this, and can more readily accept the idea that evolving attraction preferences are, and should be, the norm. Some of us just vary over a wider range than others.

Along these same lines, Devor (1989) discusses the genetic, biological, and social influences that combine to support her theory of gender as a social construct distinct from biological sex. (Formerly Holly Devor, he has now transitioned to live as Aaron H. Devor. His writings can be found under both names, but it is the same person. The present use of female pronouns in reference to him is done to reflect the name and gender role at the time of a specific publication.) Her specific focus is on natal females who live so close to the male-female gender line as to be mistaken at times for men. She presents the lives of 15 natal females who represent a spectrum of gender blending, and discusses the influence of gender role presentation on choice of sexual partners. She discusses transsexualism as one way of examining gender, saying of FTMs:

> Around the time of puberty they usually develop sexual and romantic interests in persons who are of the same sex as themselves but of a different gender. (Devor, 1989, p. 20)

The findings of some professionals whose work focuses on MTFs differ from Devor's, just as the experiences of MTFs tend to differ from those of FTMs. This is an important distinction since her findings do not fit within the prevailing views of the MTF transgender community. However, this too may be changing. Nevertheless, her discussion of the interplay between gender role and sexual orientation offers a point of view from which to consider the findings of the research being presented here.

Richard Docter (1988) has done extensive research with the transgender population, primarily by self-report survey. Originally reflecting primarily the dichotomous, either-or perspective of transvestite or transsexual, his work foreshadowed a broader perspective with his concept of the late emerging or secondary transsexual. His thinking has evolved (personal dialog), along with the general increase in social openness about transgender, to encompass an even broader spectrum of transgender identities. His 1988 work was current with its time, but anticipated the later trend for transgender people to define their own gender identity as somewhere in the middle ground between these two extremes. As explained in one of Docter's later works, some of these individuals have called themselves transgenderists, a term coined by Virginia Prince, a community pioneer in modern transgender history (Docter, 2004). While offering valuable and still timely perspectives, Docter confined his 1988 work to a focus on gender identity and social role and did not address the question of sexual orientation.

While Leslie Feinberg has addressed the issue of gender identity from a sociological perspective, and Walter Williams has done so from an anthropological point of view, neither focuses specifically on sexual orientation, much less how it may change over time (see also Feinberg, 1996; Williams, 1986).

Autogynephilia: A Concept That May Have Been Carried Too Far

Ray Blanchard studied the sexual orientations of a group of transsexual women (Blanchard, 1985). He placed the sexual orientations of these transsexual subjects in five arbitrary categories, offering little discussion of his basis for using these categories. He did not discuss how he selected the subjects for his study from the presumably larger pool offered by his case files, or why other potential subjects were excluded.

Blanchard used what might be viewed as a modified Kinsey scale. He coined the term *autogynephilia*, in which a natal male is primarily sexually aroused by the act or fantasy of self-appearing as female. He considered a significant number of his subjects to be in this category, while others identified themselves as attracted to males, to females, to both, or as being asexual. More recently and among a handful of others, Anne Lawrence has been studying and advocating for the validity of the autogynephilia concept (Lawrence, 1998, 1999).

Autogynephilia is one of several hypotheses that remain controversial. I will explore it further in subsequent chapters. For now, I will say that it is questionable as to whether autogynephilia should be considered a sexual orientation or simply a part of the individual's arousal template—a part that appears to be transient for many transgender people.

Other Points of View

In an article in the SIECUS Report, Walter O. Bockting discusses the relationship between transgender and sexual orientation (Bockting, 1999). On the basis of his extensive clinical experience, he describes a wide range of sexual attractions and practices within the transgender population. He points out that even in the larger population, sexual attraction is not consistently linked to the degree to which an individual has masculine or feminine personality traits. Although he implies that he has observed change in sexual orientation over time in some transgender people, that is not the focus of his article.

In the same SIECUS Report, Dallas Denny writes about transgender in the United States. In this article, she devotes a paragraph to the question of sexual orientation, in which she states, "This orientation may or may not change after transition." Denny also questions the recent promotion of autogynephilia as a major factor in the sex lives of transgender people (Denny, 1999). However, as is the case with Bockting, she does not go into the topic of sexual orientation any further.

Christopher Daskalos reports on a retrospective study of the sexual orientations of 20 transsexual subjects, 16 of whom were MTF and the remainder FTM (Daskalos, 1998). Following Blanchard's example, the subjects were not grouped by natal sex, but rather by sexual orientation in reference to natal sex (Blanchard, 1985; Blanchard et al., 1987). This overlooks fundamental differences, both biological and social, between these two groups, and since the social issues of the groups are quite different, this weakened the validity of the outcome. Half (10) of the subjects were planning to have genital reconstruction surgery, and the other half had already had this surgery. The time since surgery varied.

The information in the Daskalos report was presented in a confusing manner, making it difficult to assess. After introducing information about the 20 subjects, the author chose, without explanation, to focus only on 6 subjects who reported a change in sexual orientation

from attraction to females to attraction to males. No consideration
was given to the possibility that at least one or more of these subjects
might have been either bisexual or in the process of reevaluating
sexual orientation, with no way of knowing if this would represent
lasting change. Daskalos does not offer any conclusions regarding
the sexual orientations of the subjects.

In her book *The Uninvited Dilemma*, Kim Elizabeth Stuart devotes
a section to the topic of sexual orientation in transsexual people
(Stuart, 1991). Based on interviews with 75 transsexual people, their
family members, and their medical and mental health providers, she
looks broadly at the transgender condition. Stuart was impressively
ahead of her time when she wrote this book. In spite of the rapidly
changing landscape of the transgender world, her work remains
timely more than 10 years after its publication.

Stuart recognizes that transgender people may shift sexual orientation with their shift in gender role, and identifies some of the factors that may influence this change. She does not specifically indicate
whether she considers the shift to be temporary or permanent, but
implies that it is permanent. She also identifies the need for additional research (pp. 55–62). Her findings are compatible with the
hypothesis presented here.

In her seminal work that has given truth and hope to countless
transgender people and their families, Mildred Brown explains
much of what it is like to be transgender (Brown & Rounsley, 1996).
She does not base her work on specific research, but rather on extensive and sound clinical observation. Brown's sensitive and insightful
portrayal is a valuable contribution, but addresses sexual orientation
only briefly and specifically from a mental health perspective.

Brown's work has been followed by that of Randi Ettner (1996,
1999), several works by Eli Coleman and Walter O. Bockting (Bockting & Coleman, 1992; Coleman, 1987; Coleman & Bockting, 1988;
Coleman et al., 1992, 1993), and more recently by that of Arlene
Istar Lev. In her book *Transgender Emergence*, Lev provides us with
the most comprehensive work to date on the subject of transgender (Lev, 2004). Although Lev sometimes uses vocabulary different from mine, with a few minor exceptions we are in agreement
on all essential points. Whereas both Brown's work and that of
Randi Ettner are geared to both the professional and the educated
lay reader, thus making them ideal for both the therapist who is
new to transgender and to transgender individuals and their family

members as well, Lev's work is more challenging and geared primarily to the clinician who seeks to develop expertise in the subject. Lev does address sexual orientation at various parts in her text, at one point saying:

> Sexual orientation is not malleable and cannot be changed through force of will. Sometimes, however, people's sexual orientation appears to "spontaneously" change during or after their transition process (e.g., males that had once been exclusively attracted to women find themselves attracted to men once they are living as women). This can be emotionally difficult for the transgender person but even more so for the spouse. Very little research has been conducted on the impact of sexual orientation confusion in relationships with a crossdressing or transsexual partner, but one study revealed that wives of transsexuals struggle less with their own identity than do wives of crossdressers (Hunt & Main, 1997). Clearly this is an area in which greater clinical and research attention should be drawn. (Lev, 2004, p. 301)

This is exactly my own observation.

Different Is Only Different, Not Necessarily Better or Worse

There is a paucity of academic work that does not pathologize the transgender person or place that person into a bifurcated paradigm of sexual orientation as heterosexual or homosexual, and gender identity as male or female, where one must be either a crossdresser or transsexual, either gay or straight. In fact, I am sometimes disappointed, confused, embarrassed for the writer, and even appalled at what passes for legitimate research among certain (here to be nameless) academics when it comes to topics related to transgender. Because of this, we, the consumers, should examine any research we read with a critical eye.

When the literature (even the really good literature) does mention sexual orientation in transgender people, no reference is made, beyond what has been cited here, to the possibility of change in sexual orientation in the course of transition. The usual assumption appears to be that there will be no change. For example, the DSM defines transvestic fetishism as occurring specifically in heterosexual males (American Psychiatric Association, 2000). In the diagnosis of gender identity disorder, the DSM-IV requires the sexual orientation of the individual to be typed as toward males, toward females, toward both, or toward neither (American

Psychiatric Association, 2000). There is no mention of a possible shift in orientation. By the way, the term *transvestite* has become out of favor among the transgender population because of the negative connotations associated with it. *Crossdresser* is now the preferred term, although the academic literature has been slow to keep pace with this.

My own clinical observations suggest that, for some portion of the transgender population, sexual orientation is more fluid, more tied to gender role or self-perceived gender identity, than has previously been believed, or, at least, that different sexual attractions may emerge under different circumstances. It seems possible that sexual orientation cannot become fully defined in the transgender individual until gender identity has been consolidated. Perhaps it is possible that when gender is ambiguous to varying degrees, so is sexual orientation.

On a Personal Note

I first began working with transgender clients in 1991 or 1992. I did not clearly note the date because I did not anticipate that it would lead me into a new area of specialty. However, I took the challenge seriously, including the coincident obligation to educate myself on the topic of transgender. I read and sought consultation from knowledgeable people. As time went on, I attended professional conventions that would bring me into contact with other therapists who shared my interest. In addition, I attended numerous transgender conventions to learn from that perspective as well. This brought me into contact with a broader cross section of the transgender community than I would have encountered simply in my own practice. I met transgender community leaders and professionals in my own and related fields from other parts of the country. I consider myself fortunate in regard to timing, because the transgender community was changing rapidly during those years. I was able to see some of what the world had been like for transgender people in the past, as well as being able to observe changes as they evolved and contributed to what it has become today. And since society continues to evolve, staying current is a process in which none of us can rest on our laurels and assume we have become knowledgeable and that our task is finished.

The Minnesota Model

This would be a good time for me to digress further by saying more about my purpose in going to transgender community conventions. Earlier in my career, before the thought of a transgender client had even crossed my mind, I found that the incidence of substance abuse–related problems was so high among my clients and their family members as to be one of the most frequently occurring factors in human unhappiness. The range extended from an overt and current addiction problem in a client or the loved one of a client, to the adult who suffered from a residual anxiety disorder because of growing up in a chaotic alcoholic environment. It included people who had poor personal boundaries and an exceedingly high tolerance for inappropriate behavior in others, which also appeared to be the result of growing up with an alcoholic parent, in a family where this kind of tolerance was the norm. In order to serve my clients better, I began to study addictions and eventually became certified in that field, working for a time in both inpatient and outpatient substance abuse treatment settings.

Prior to the advent of managed care for insurance plans, there was a proliferation of substance abuse treatment programs, and the Minnesota Model (developed in Minnesota, then considered to be the national leader in this field) became the gold standard for how such programs should be structured. Among other things, this model included a recommended staff ratio of recovering lay paraprofessionals to professional staff. Sometimes it included professional staff members who were themselves recovering alcoholics or addicts. This method of staffing recognized the valuable contribution that could be made by people who had personal experience with the problem at hand. It helped prevent a holier-than-thou mentality on the part of the professional staff. It bridged the potential gap between helper and helpee, and provided role models and hope for newly recovering people, for whom the ability to regain some measure of self-esteem was critical to their successful recovery.

I learned a great deal from my recovering colleagues. Also, sometimes my duties included accompanying a group of patients to an open meeting of Alcoholics Anonymous. Subsequently, I attended many such open meetings ("open" meaning open to the public, as opposed to a closed meeting where attendance is limited to those people who are concerned about their own use of a substance) because I found them extremely helpful for the insight they provided into the way a person in the throes of addiction thinks. It helped me to understand the process of addiction from the perspective of the client, to hear the perspective of the recovering person on the process of recovery, and also to understand the vernacular and the particular brand of humor that are part of the culture of recovery. I heard Father Joseph Martin, a Catholic priest who was himself a recovering alcoholic and a beloved teacher in recovery circles, say, "If you want to know about alcoholics, go where they are! Go to the source." He was not suggesting that we go to bars, but to AA meetings, where we could listen to stories of recovery. I went, I listened, and I benefited from listening.

Because of this previous experience, I applied the same thinking to my work with transgender people. I went to the source. And I learned in ways that were different from what I could learn from colleagues or textbooks, however valuable. I saw a perspective different than I could have seen within the confines of my office. I heard the personal stories of heartache, and of the triumph of the human spirit. Sadly, I learned about the injustices experienced by many transgender people and the harm some practitioners in my own field had done to people who had sought them out for help. I also learned what people had found to be helpful. Transgender people may offer a different and sometimes more candid outlook when talking with someone other than their own therapist. A community gathering may bring a therapist into contact with individuals who are different from the ones she might see in her office. One can meet people from different parts of the country, different walks of life, some who are not interested in therapy, and some who are doing just fine without it. I think in large part, due to my proactive approach to my own education, transgender people soon became the primary focus of my practice, fluctuating over time between 80% and 95% of my client base for nearly 15 years now.

3

The Birth of the Research Project at Hand

The People Who Were Studied

While I am not limiting the present discussion of sexual orientation among MTF transgender people to only those who were part of my research study, the foundation of my information comes from a group of 97 MTF transgender people who were specifically studied. These people, who are the source of the statistics presented in Appendix D, were my clients between January 1, 1992, and December 31, 2000. Those years span the time from when I saw my first transgender client, through the time when their percentage in my practice grew to what could legitimately be called an area of specialty. The statistics used for this research were drawn from the private clinical mental health files of these individuals. Each of the participants was seen for a minimum of three sessions, and each one gave permission for information from his or her records to be used in this way. Although this research study was not planned at the beginning of that time period, I did anticipate the possibility that, at some future time, a colleague might want to do research related to this population, and I recognized that these clinical statistics might be useful to him or her. For this reason, I routinely asked clients if they would be comfortable with having statistics drawn from their files for research purposes as long as their identities were protected. Almost without exception, they were willing and even eager to give permission.

This population on the whole is very aware of the lack of research related to transgender and is very supportive of it, as they themselves want better answers to help them understand their condition. Those who "donated" their information to this endeavor said they were happy to make this contribution, especially when they felt confident that their identities would not be revealed. Great care was taken to ensure a high level of privacy protection. Later in this chapter, I will say more about how this was done.

I was deeply touched when several people asked if there were any postmortem studies being conducted of the brains of transgender people, as they would be willing to donate their brains for such a study, although with no sense of urgency to make this contribution in the immediate future. Some naively thought it might be as easy as the driver's license organ donor program and were disappointed that there did not seem to be researchers eagerly waiting for such donations.

The people who constituted this sample would be considered a self-selected group of subjects because they each sought out a therapist who specialized in transgender issues. All but a few resided geographically within a four-hour drive of my office in Ann Arbor, Michigan. With the exception of a small number of people who were living on Social Security disability with Medicare insurance, which helped to pay for therapy sessions when they had a primary diagnosis other than gender identity disorder, they were all functioning well enough to have either health insurance with mental health coverage as a benefit of their employment or the ability to pay privately for therapy sessions. (For transgender clients who are covered under Medicare because of some other diagnosis, while GID is an excluded diagnosis, it is an unavoidable and integral part of whatever else may be going on in their lives and with their emotions, and GID can usually be addressed within that context.) A sample of people taken in a different clinical setting, or in a different geographical location, or a sample taken outside of a clinical setting might yield quite different results. That is why the results of this study should be viewed as only one small window into the sexual orientations of transgender people.

Only male-to-female transgender people were included in this study and are the focus of this discussion. The intent was not to ignore the presence of the female-to-male transgender population, nor to discount its importance, but simply to recognize that it was beyond the scope of this study, and that FTMs are deserving of their own separate study, especially since they typically have a different path than do MTFs. In addition, at the time when this study was begun, I had significantly greater numbers of files of MTF clients from which to draw data.

In spite of their concerns about their gender identities, the vast majority of the people in this study were functioning reasonably well in all other domains of their lives. The initial case files that provided the data used in this research dated from the time when I was just beginning to work with transgender clients. It took a little time (but only a little) for word of mouth to make me known to other potential transgender clients. My first few clients were all associated with a specific support group, but these individuals had contact with other transgender people who were not part of this particular group. Gradually my client base came from a wider range of sources. Gradually, too, the Internet became more widely available, and as information about my practice became available on the Internet, this also contributed to how clients found their way to me. These "grapevine" factors contributed to the characteristics of the subject sample for this research.

The case records of the people who participated in this study represent a range of outcomes, including people who quickly shied away from addressing their transgender issues after a few therapy sessions in which they got a glimpse of the enormity of the challenge that would be facing them if they continued. Others came in briefly, simply seeking information. This was especially true early on, before the Internet was so widely available. Many of these people disappeared for a period of time, but came back again once they were better prepared to address their transgender issues psychologically, socially, or financially, or when they became discouraged with their attempts to avoid the issue or to deal with it on their own or in some other way.

Some individuals initially chose only to become more at ease with occasional crossdressing. This continued to work well for some of them as a long-term goal. Others concluded that they needed to go beyond occasional crossdressing in their gender expression. Some individuals opted for or were only able to manage partial gender role transition during the time they were seen. Still others elected to pursue complete gender role transition. For some, this included genital reconstruction surgery. Some cases were still open, while others were closed at the time the study ended, but either way, that does not tell us what any of these people would do about their transgender at some future time.

The people who were studied here sought therapy for a variety of reasons. Some wanted to gain a better understanding of their transgender feelings, including what made them feel and behave this way. Others came in order to comply with the HBIGDA/WPATH protocols. Some came with the hope that I could "cure" or rid them of their transgender feelings. During the course of therapy, some continued to function for a part of their lives as male, whereas others fully transitioned to live as female, utilizing every means available to create congruency among their social gender role, their bodies, and their minds, the place where their internal sense of self as a gendered person resided.

At the time of our initial contact, these people were at various points in their process of transgender self-discovery. Some were novices who had almost no knowledge of transgender, while others were already well informed. Some were closeted, while others had already begun living full-time as female. The majority were somewhere between these extremes. Included were individuals who were married and some who were single, those who were virgins and those who were sexually experienced with multiple partners of one or both sexes. Included were young adults, and those who were well beyond the middle years in life.

The complete spectrum of transgender would extend from all of the intermediate forms mentioned above to the most extreme form of transgender—living full-time across natal gender lines with all the changes that hormones could provide and with surgical reconstruction of the genitals to make them match the new gender role. All of the manifestations of transgender mentioned exist in most other parts of the world, but they are not all represented in this study.

Becoming More Objective About Transgender Clients

From the time when I first began working with the transgender population, I have attempted to use a uniform process of interviewing, especially for initial assessment, thanks to the example of Alfred Kinsey. This format (see Appendix A for the intake evaluation checklist) has evolved as I gained insight about the questions that needed to be asked in order to have a well-rounded picture of the individual and her social context. Further refinements have been made since the study was completed, but the checklist in Appendix A is in the form that was used at the time of the study. However, changes made before or since did not lead me to change the basic content so much as I learned to fine-tune the wording and the sequencing of the questions and organize them for increased efficiency.

Since I consider this checklist a composite of formats that have been devised and employed by many therapists and theorists who came before me, I take no specific credit for it. As a format for a mental health evaluation, it is really not so very different from any other comprehensive mental health assessment format that might be used with a client who was part of some other population. This one differs only regarding the inclusion of questions related specifically to sexual history, gender awareness, and related behavior. Sexuality is fundamental to the human condition, and these are questions that really should be asked routinely in assessing all clients. Yet, regardless of discipline, very few schools that are training mental health professionals offer courses in human sexuality. None that I am aware of require a basic course in human sexuality as a requirement for graduation. Most therapists consider sex a sensitive topic and may not, themselves, be comfortable asking their clients about it, regardless of whether this discomfort is in the person of the therapist or is born of concern about the risk of making the client uncomfortable. Deplorable as this circumstance is, in my opinion, sex is an often-neglected topic in therapy. This means that an important piece of information is routinely overlooked by therapists and may contribute to therapy being less effective for all people than it could be.

As any client will do, the people in this study often volunteered information that made it unnecessary to ask some of the questions on the checklist, so the checklist was intended for use as a tool for the therapist, to make sure important information was not overlooked. As also might be expected, it was used in accordance with the needs of the individual client. For example, if someone entered therapy in crisis or on the brink of crisis, this situation was dealt with before a more extensive evaluation was undertaken. The answers to some questions made it unnecessary to pursue a particular topic further, whereas certain other answers were indicative of the need for further exploration. However, the checklist was intended to help in obtaining an overview of the circumstances of the person's life and was useful as an aid in identifying possible areas for further exploration and in developing therapy goals.

On occasion when gathering data, some case files lacked certain information. Although this was rare, when a question could not be answered the space for that piece of data was left blank. As was already noted, the data presented here are based entirely on individual self-report and subjective perception.

Preserving Privacy

At the beginning of therapy, each person whose data became part of the research study signed a consent for treatment form that included permission to use statistics from the case records of that person, on the condition that his or her anonymity would be preserved. While a specific effort was made to have each client feel free to refuse, no one did so. While I had assistance in the development of the raw data, all of the data were first collected from client files only by me, unassisted by anyone else. In this way, the confidentiality of the client files was in no way violated or compromised.

Each case was assigned a file reference number, and this number was used to track a corresponding data sheet. The key was available only to me, as was the case file of each subject. The data were sorted into categories. If there was a piece of datum that was unique enough to risk identifying a person, that item was placed in a broader category that was general enough to obscure the source of the individual item. After all of the data had been collected and analyzed, and there was clearly no further need to verify information, the key was destroyed.

As an example of the way in which information that might identify an individual person was obscured, if there had been a person who taught computer science, another who was a computer repair person, another who was in charge of corporate computer technology, and another who was a well-known inventor of some specific technology, all of these would have been subsumed under a general heading such as "computer specialist" so no one would stand out.

This would be a good time to say one more thing about individual privacy. Some personal stories have been used in this text to illustrate certain situations and to give a human face to the people being discussed. However, none of these stories are based on a single individual unless they are stories taken from my own personal life. Instead, they are composites that borrow from many individuals to illustrate something that is a commonly occurring pattern or situation. Some of these illustrate patterns observed in many clients, but they also incorporate stories told to me by individuals who were not my clients. On numerous occasions I have sat at a luncheon or dinner table at a convention where I happened to be seated next to an individual I had never met before, and had that person tell me his or her entire life story over the meal, as if compelled to tell it to anyone who would listen. Because, as a therapist, I seem to find the life stories of others endlessly fascinating and never seem to tire of hearing them, I have never minded when this has happened. While the story of every person is unique, there are certain similarities that are bound to recur because they are common to the human condition. In addition, there are other significant parallels that recur consistently in the stories of transgender people.

Telling one's story can be very healing for the individual, and very helpful to others with similar histories. Many transgender people have written their stories, either in book form or on the Internet. It is very common to hear a transgender person talk about reading the story of someone else and saying, "She told my story!" In this way, the parallels are easily recognized, and many people find this affirming. The struggles with self-loathing, the binge-purge cycles related to crossdressing, the attempts to conform or even to overcompensate with a hypermasculine façade, the attempts to conform to social expectations and conventions, the anxiety-filled first excursions out in public crossdressed, the compelling urge to tell someone, the fear of rejection or ridicule—these are themes that recur over and over again.

Because of this, it is inevitable that someone will read one of the vignettes I have used to illustrate some point and will wonder if (or even be convinced that) I am talking specifically about him or her. In such a case, that person would be mistaken. The vignettes I have used were taken from several sources, but not from the life of any one individual who was my client. I have used stories from my own personal life. In some cases I have borrowed from the stories of transgender people who I have known outside of my practice and who have given me permission to use all or parts of their stories. And I have created composite stories that drew bits and pieces from a variety of sources to illustrate a typical point, pattern, or situation that transgender people often face, but under no circumstance has a situation regarding any individual person whom I have known as a client been used. What is that cliché disclaimer? Any similarity to specific persons, living or dead, is purely coincidental!

Exclusions

When developing the sample to be used for the present research, of all the transgender clients who were seen by me during the designated time period, the only excluded files were those of FTM people or those who were seen for fewer than four sessions. The former were not part of the population to be studied, and the latter files contained insufficient data to be useful.

Once more drawing the attention of the reader to the diversity that exists within the transgender population, it is important to emphasize that the people in this sample reflect only one small segment of the larger MTF transgender population. In the general population of transgender people, there would be individuals who have not yet identified the meaning of their transgender feelings, others who continue to suppress these feelings, and those who have not sought out a gender therapist for whatever reason. That would include crossdressers who may remain entirely closeted or who have not yet made a decision to seek therapy. It would also include those who have not felt the need to consult a therapist. Needless to say, all of the people in this study are individuals who did seek therapy for some reason. Some were interested in therapy in the more conventional sense of the word. Others were more interested in obtaining information or referrals to medical providers, or in having the benefit of my experience to guide them in making decisions and moving forward with transition. Some sought help in preserving important relationships, such as with a spouse or child.

The broadest spectrum of transgender would include individuals for whom crossdressing is exclusively and consistently over time a fetishistic activity, although that would probably be part of the individual's arousal template rather than her gender identity, as was pointed out earlier, and would certainly not be reflective of all crossdressers. Many transgender individuals do experience a transitional time when their crossdressing is highly eroticized, as was true of some of the people in this study. If they were evaluated only at that specific point in time, gender identity could easily be mislabeled as transvestic fetishism. And even beyond that, it must be noted, *gender identity disorder* is probably a questionable term, for who can say that the disorder is in the gender identity and not in the physiology of the individual? Who can say if it is even a disorder at all, but perhaps only a normally occurring variation? As bears repeating, when something is different, it is not necessarily a sign that something is wrong. It may only be a sign that people tend to be uncomfortable with the unfamiliar.

In examining who would or would not have been included in this sample, we can assume that some transgender people remain closeted or do not seek therapy for a variety of reasons other than those already mentioned. There would be individuals who could not afford therapy. These people would not surface in a self-selected subject sample in a mental health clinical setting even though they would still fit as being transgender under the broad definition of the term. There are other transgender people who, for reasons related to family or religious constraints, would not openly face their transgender or who feel that transition is unattainable and would thus consider therapy pointless. There are those who have a cynical attitude toward therapy and who would avoid it at all costs. Some in the latter group might seek out alternative means of dealing with their transgender, such as the use of black market hormones and surgeons who operate outside the HBIGDA/WPATH protocols. Yet other individuals may have sought a religious "cure" rather than therapy (Besen, 2003). The people who are represented in this study would all be people who could see some value in therapy and something to be gained for themselves through it.

Especially in more highly urbanized geographic areas, there are marginalized populations of transgender sex workers and drag queens, some of whom are satisfied with their lives as they are and would not be inclined to seek any kind of therapy, and thus would not be part of our sample. There are others who are homeless street people, including those who have been referred to in the vernacular as throwaway youth, who would also not be represented in this study. In addition, there are the more successful MTF transgender individuals who live full-time as female without benefit of mental health therapy and may not choose to surgically alter their bodies. Neither would the people who are represented in this study fit any of those descriptions.

Willingness to Talk About Sexual Orientation

In the few years before I embarked on this research project, it seemed that transgender people in general were gradually beginning to feel more free to examine and speak openly and honestly about their perceptions of their sexual orientation—both among their peers and with the professionals who were providing various kinds of medical and mental health care to them. I observed that a significant number of my own clients were reporting a shift in sexual orientation that accompanied their shift in gender role. It appeared that the social climate was right for a study that would focus on this phenomenon, that it might be possible to obtain a clear picture of these numbers, or at least clearer than had previously been possible. I began to see my practice as a window, an opportunity to examine a group of transgender people and their reported thoughts, feelings, and behaviors related to sexual orientation during the course of therapy.

Meaningful Diagnosis and Changing Sexual Orientation

The vignette in the previous chapter, telling about the woman who transitioned without the help of a therapist and who then sought that help at a later time, is one that could be told by nearly any therapist who has worked with transgender clients for any significant length of time. Like most of the vignettes about "clients" that can be found in this book, it is composed of bits and pieces from many different people rather than representing a single individual. Some of these pieces were from people who had been my clients and some were from transgender people whom I have known but were not my clients.

The young woman in that story, like many of the people who are represented in this study, and like many transgender people in general, simply did not need therapy in the traditional sense of the word in order to transition successfully. Such individuals may benefit from talking with a therapist who is experienced with transgender, to help them think through how to manage complicated situations. They may need help locating other kinds of service providers, and they usually do need the referral letters required to obtain access to resources for hormones or surgeries. They also may be able to benefit from therapy in the same way as many nontransgender people often do, to help them deal with some kind of complicated life situation that they may have encountered. Having a personal problem that is vexing, confusing, or upsetting is not the same thing as having a diagnosis. Many people who seek the help of a therapist do not qualify for a diagnosis. Sometimes the problem a nontransgender client brings to a therapist is very analogous to those of the transgender client. Suppose this was a natal female who had met a man she was seriously interested in, but had not yet told some highly personal information, such as that she once had an abortion, or had genital herpes, or had a biracial grandmother. But also like the woman in the vignette, transwomen sometimes have complicated situations to deal with that are specific to their transgender histories. The dating situation is an example that shows both aspects.

Prior to transition, many transwomen do not anticipate having an interest in dating men after they transition. They may assume that no one will be interested and that the opportunity will simply not arise. Later, they may be quite surprised to find someone showing an interest in them. They may be both thrilled and panic stricken by this turn of events. They may suddenly be confronted with questions about if, when, and how to tell this man (if, indeed, it is a man) about their transgender history. Some simply reject advances to avoid facing this dilemma. Some wonder if the man already knows or suspects, and they are unsure whether to be pleased that it didn't matter to him or offended that they may simply be viewed by him as a sexual novelty. If he doesn't appear to already know about her transgender status, she may worry that he will find out from someone else before she can tell him herself. Will he reject her, feel as if she has embarrassed him, or become violent when he finds out? This situation may bring her to therapy, but does not, in and of itself, meet the criteria for any diagnosis of which I am aware.

The Cyber Revolution

This may be a good time to note that during the time of this study and since, the rise in the use of home computers and the Internet has skyrocketed. As a result of this and other technologies and social changes that have been occurring during the same time period, it is not the same world now that it was only a few years ago. The rapid spread of the use of cell phones is another example. This is reflected in the people who are represented in this study. The ones who were seen early in the study were often at a much different point in their process of self-awareness than those who were seen later. They were more closeted and more in need of basic information than is usually the case today. Over the course of the last decade and a half, there has been a dramatic change in the level of knowledge and sophistication among transgender people as they enter therapy. It has become rare for anyone to have as little access to information as was formerly the norm. The Internet has made it easy to obtain information readily and in the privacy of one's own home.

Saying the Word *Sex*

A high priority of my work with each client was to obtain truthful responses to the greatest degree possible. In any clinical setting, the truthfulness of the answers of a client, transgender or not, is based on a combination of the therapist's ability to create an environment that generates trust, the basic ability of the client to risk trusting, the perception of the client that disclosure is in his or her own self-interest, and the ability of both the client and the therapist to be objective in their perceptions of self and of the other person.

Some people have a wall of psychological defenses that prevents them from knowing themselves and which also clouds or distorts their perceptions of others. But whether the defenses of the individual are represented by a wall or just a low curb, all people have (and should have) defenses. In their best form, they are part of the protection that helps our egos function well. So, defenses are factors that were no less at work here, but recognizing their presence helps in assessing the validity of the responses.

With these things in mind, I encouraged each individual to think freely about his or her sexuality. I provided each one with information about the wide range of sexual behaviors to help them feel that it was safe and acceptable to speak freely, that I would not be shocked or uncomfortable, and they would not be judged or penalized for their responses.

I organized the data I collected into various categories, such as religion or marital status, which seemed likely to have influenced how a person thought and made decisions about his or her gender. I wanted to be able to compare each of these categories with what people reported about specific aspects of gender identity and sexual orientation. As will become apparent, these categories did, indeed, have some bearing on how individual subjects thought about their gender identity and sexual orientation. For example, confusion about gender identity could make it difficult for a person to define "the opposite sex." Vocabulary limitations played a part—not simply the limitations in the vocabulary of a specific person, but limitations in the English language itself. For example, we have no neutral second-person pronoun that is not pejorative when used in reference to a human being (no one wants to be an "it"), nor do we have a word to characterize a person who does not fully identify as either male or female, or who may be going through the in-between space of transition, which I sometimes refer to as being on "the bridge," although some other cultures do have words for such people (Feinberg, 1996).

Because of taboos that have existed about discussing things related to sex, our language lacks adequate terminology for describing some aspects of sexuality. Among the people who were part of this study, lack of self-acceptance related to gender identity was frequently based on the same reasons as lack of self-acceptance related to sexual orientation. It is a form of learned social homophobia and transphobia (which might be more accurately called transgender phobia), the inevitable result of growing up and being socialized in a cultural milieu that stigmatizes sexual minorities of all kinds. This is exacerbated by the individual's awareness of the existence of these same phobias in those who are significant in their lives. When a person seemed hesitant to talk about a sensitive subject, it was always necessary to ask enough questions to be able to distinguish between how the client felt about the topic herself and how the person had been sensitized to anticipate the reactions of others to this topic.

4

Findings About Sexual Orientation in MTF Transgender People

The Comparisons

What can we learn about the sexual orientations of the 97 MTF transgender people who were studied? As mentioned previously, several aspects or life circumstances of the participants were selected for comparison with sexual orientation, to look at the possible correlations between them. These categories were selected because they appeared to be the ones most likely to have potential bearing on sexual orientation. (Details about the basis for these selections and the findings can be found in Appendix D.)

Each of these factors was influenced by the others in one way or another, and were also influenced by some additional common determinates. These included the initial availability and means of obtaining information about transgender and the available options for taking action, the level of stigma the person had to overcome before being able to face her transgender issues, the degree to which she had invested in a male gender role before becoming ready to address her transgender, the possible losses and other sequelae to her exploring her transgender identity, how far she might ultimately decide to go with gender role transition, and her fund of coping skills to face the potential challenges associated with coming to terms with her transgender identity.

The Role of Age

The age of each person at the start of therapy was important because a more mature and experienced person entering therapy would be more likely to have a broad base of life experience from which to view her own sexuality, a perspective composed not only of her own experience, but of what the person had observed or known about others, and what the person had learned in various other ways.

The people who were studied ranged in age from 20–68 when they first entered therapy with me, when these measurements began (Appendix D, Table 3A). The ages of the vast majority were clustered in the middle ground of roughly ages 34–46 years old. There were many reasons why this was the case. Foremost among them was the availability of information about transgender and the age when the person first had access to or discovered the word *transgender* or some other related words. Was it early in the person's life, before they were deeply committed to an adult role? Was the information accurate, or was it pejorative? In addition, the presence or absence of a sympathetic adult with whom the person dared to talk about her feelings played an important role in the age at which the person decided to face her transgender issues.

In fact, the availability of information seemed to be the determining factor in the age at which the person entered therapy. As previously mentioned, the Internet revolution began to take place during the time of the study, and the people who came to therapy the latest, closer to the year 2000, when the study ended, tended to be younger, as is an ongoing trend for transgender people entering therapy. Even today, it is the more isolated people, the ones who lack information and have had the least contact with other transgender people, whether face-to-face or via Internet chat rooms, who tend to come to therapy later. This access to or lack of information was also reflected in the presenting concerns of people, as the least informed were more likely to confuse gender identity with sexual orientation, and thus were often unclear about the problem at hand. In some cases, they preferred to think that they might simply be gay, seeing this as less complicated to deal with than being transgender, but were then often confused by their history of attraction to women, thinking, "If I like to wear dresses, maybe it means I'm gay, but how can I be gay if I'm not attracted to men?"

Needless to say, the older a person was when she began to address her transgender, the more likely she was to have made multiple commitments to the adult male role, such as marriage, children, career, and social support system. Sometimes this commitment included involvement in a religious organization.

Religion

When religious influence was strong during childhood, especially if it involved a doctrine that emphasized guilt, a sense of shame, or sinfulness associated with sexuality and transgender, these feelings often persisted into adulthood, even if the individual no longer professed a significant religious belief system. This was true for the people in this study, but also appears to be true of transgender people across the board. For this reason, it is valuable for a therapist to ask about both past and present personal religious history.

Once more, I wish to emphasize the importance for the reader to keep in mind that the people being studied here were self-selected by the choice to enter therapy, among other factors. It is likely that many transgender people, because of the intensity of religious conflict about both gender identity and sexual orientation, never enter therapy. On that basis, it could be argued that this sample is skewed in the direction of being less intensely religious than the transgender population as a whole. Yet, conversely, there are other segments of the transgender population that are more socially ostracized and financially disenfranchised than the people represented in this study. It is possible that transgender individuals who are on the fringes of society could be more or less religious than this sample, and if they had been involved in this study, the outcomes might be different. We simply do not know the extent to which this particular sample is representative of the religious beliefs and practices of the larger population of transgender people.

Among the particular group of people who were part of this study, the importance of religion varied considerably. This was true at both initial contact and at the latest point in the study. The importance of religion had more than one basis. For example, it might be very important to the transgender person, or not very important at all. However, if religion was important to someone the transgender person cared deeply about, it might still have a high level of importance because of the implications for potential acceptance or rejection of the transgender person once she made her transgender status known to that other person.

This highlights one of the reasons that gathering information about family and friends is an important part of the helping process. Knowing about potential religious conflict in the client's ecosystem of family, friends, and other associates can help a therapist do a better job of anticipating trouble spots. This includes attitudes and beliefs about both gender identity and sexual orientation. In so doing, problems may be avoided, mitigated, or at least prepared for in what I sometimes refer to as a fire drill or a rehearsal with the transgender person for coping with immediate and later fallout from a negative coming out experience. We hope for the best but prepare for the worst.

The majority of people in this study identified themselves as Protestant, but there were also Catholics, Jews, and others, including those who had no religious beliefs. For the transgender people who valued their religious beliefs, they were usually able to find a way to reconcile their gender identities, and eventually their sexual orientations, with their religious beliefs. In general, it was my observation that significant others found this more difficult to do, perhaps because they were more reluctant than the transgender person to change their views and even their place of worship, as was sometimes necessary for the transgender person to do. Significant others have less motivation for change, and in fact may hold tight to their religious views as leverage in an attempt to resist the changes the transgender person is making.

The distribution of people among religious categories seemed fairly reflective of the population of the United States as a whole, although we would expect to find regional differences (see Appendix D). Perhaps most striking was the fact that over the course of time in therapy, the people who were part of this study reported no significant change in religious belief or in the importance of religion in their lives. While religious beliefs remained quite stable, the emotional pain of trying to reconcile religious belief with the search for personal congruity cannot be measured and was extremely painful for some. When this struggle was intense, it usually included dealing with the question of whether "God made me this way" and whether "I am a sinner for being this way." It also included emotional pain related to the struggles that others had with these questions and how this affected the way they reacted toward the transgender person.

Because of some of the stories I heard, I often marveled that the people involved did not become entirely disillusioned with religion. There were times when they were told they were no longer welcome to worship with the people who they had come to regard as extended family. They were sometimes told they were going to hell. They were sometimes called names and shamed mercilessly. This, of course, was not always the case, but it was more likely to happen in a place of worship than most other public domains. There were times when a church even attempted to come between members of a married couple or between parent and child. However, for every church that was rejecting, there was always another that was welcoming, supportive of couples and families, perhaps even saving a person from contemplation of suicide.

While there was little change in the religious beliefs of the individuals who were studied during the time of observation, a number of them did report having become disillusioned with organized religion prior to entering therapy. Because of this disillusionment, many of them made a clear distinction between participation in organized religion and their own personal spiritual or religious belief systems. Although it was not highly apparent among this particular group, I have otherwise observed a tendency among transgender people to adopt nontraditional religious practices such as Native American religions, Wicca, and Buddhism.

For the most part, the basis for the resolution of the disparity between religious dogma and transgender identity was the commonly shared belief among transgender people that "I was born or made this way," and therefore God must have had a hand in it. Although I did not formally measure it, I know anecdotally that subjects often changed the church in which they worshipped, finding one that was more accepting of transgender people or, once transitioned, simply presenting herself as female at a new church without disclosing her transgender status.

It is impossible to assign separate weights to the effects of social pressure and religious pressure in the daily lives of transgender people because religious influences are so closely intertwined with the mores of our culture as a whole. Even atheists are shaped by the religious values of the society in which they live. As the MTF transgender people being discussed here resolved feelings of religious conflict and became increasingly comfortable with their female gender identities, my observations suggested that there was an increased attraction and willingness to consider the possibility of engaging with a male sex partner. This observation was present before the study began and was confirmed when the outcomes were measured.

I have also observed that religious beliefs were a far more prohibitive factor in the degree of acceptance by family members, especially spouses, than they were for transgender individuals themselves. This has led me to speculate about the possibility that, earlier in the transgender person's life, during the time when the person was attempting to suppress transgender feelings, there may have been a tendency to choose a partner or wife who would provide external reinforcement to the transgender person's attempt to avoid facing her transgender feelings. Falling in love with a woman or choosing a wife who would be unlikely to accept transgender because of a religious belief system that was staunchly opposed to transgender expression, and especially when there was no appreciation for the distinction between transgender identity and sexual attraction, might well be used by the transgender person as a part of an attempt to avoid facing the transgender issues themselves. During the time when she was still trying to suppress her transgender feelings, the person may inadvertently have created a situation in which eventually coming to terms with her transgender feelings would be more difficult if not disastrous. Such a relationship would have a higher than average risk of not surviving transition (Samons, 2001).

It is also true that while the transgender person has a vested interest in finding a resolution to the conflict between religious beliefs and transgender feelings, the wife or other family member may have an equally vested interest in using religious beliefs as a means of resisting and attempting to dissuade the transgender loved one from going forward with exploration of these feelings. Thus, there is no way to clarify the extent to which the role of religious belief is actual or incidental, whether it is a true religious belief or a tool to reinforce a position of resistance that goes well beyond the religious belief system of the individual in question.

The religious beliefs of loved ones can have a profound impact on the dynamics of coming out. Both in and beyond this sample of transgender people, I have observed a wide range of family responses to the transgender issue, even among some Christian groups that are typically considered fundamentalist in their doctrine. In one instance, a minister who would otherwise not have condoned divorce actively sought to force a divorce between an MTF transgender person and her spouse because of his belief that exposing their child to the transgender parent would be detrimental to the child. He did this by threatening to report the spouse to Child Protective Services and have the child removed from parental custody unless the spouse took the child and left the marriage.

At the other extreme was a family of very devout Southern Baptists (often perceived as fundamentalist in the extreme) who were able to see the incongruity and distress experienced by their transgender family member in the male social role and rallied around her in support of her transition and GRS. They saw her transition as analogous to correcting a birth defect and perceived no religious conflict in taking this stance. And, as is so often the case, once they accepted her as female, her emerging attraction to men seemed to follow as natural. Interestingly, this illustrates how it is possible for a religious belief system to be accepting of transgender while still rejecting homosexuality.

When it comes to the relationship between a transgender child and his or her parents, transgender male-to-female adults often report a profound degree of fear and self-loathing related to the religious belief system of the family or community, which originated in childhood and continued into adulthood. In an attempt to eliminate feminine behavior and eradicate a child's transgender feelings, many parents took strong measures, even became emotionally or physically abusive toward their child. This can begin with the first innocent words or actions of the child that suggest a tendency to identify with things associated with being female and is frequently associated with homophobia in the parent.

Religious beliefs may be used as a means of disallowing this femme expression. With such treatment, the child may feel unworthy and unloved, unacceptable in the eyes of family, society, and God (Burke, 1996; Rottnek, 1999). In an attempt to conceal their true feelings, to avoid disapproval, punishment, and a general sense of sinfulness, and to conform to expectations, many MTF children become withdrawn. Others learn to present an exaggerated macho image. Yet others rebel. Any of these reactions will contribute to the masking of inner conflict. At a later time, if the transgender person decides to disclose to others her transgender identity, these earlier responses may make it harder for her to establish credibility in the eyes of others when her feminine feelings seem so contrary to their previously established perceptions. This is a pattern that I observed many times among the people in this study.

Marital Status and Living Situation

Lonely people of any age, gender, or sexual orientation can become involved in brief but intense relationships. Brief or not, these relationships may include strong feelings of attachment. Transgender people would be no less susceptible than others to involvement in such relationships. Requiring some line of demarcation to serve as a guide when looking at serious primary relationships, I arbitrarily chose a minimum duration of one year as a consistent way of examining relationships that were more than brief or superficial. I made an exception for marriages that were less than a year in duration, as any marriage represents a considerable level of commitment.

At the start of therapy, the vast majority of the people in this study were either living alone or with a spouse (as opposed to living with a roommate or some other type of family member). The remaining others were scattered in small numbers among the other possibilities: living with a female partner, living with parents, living with children, living with nonrelated roommates or with another relative. A sister was most often the other relative with whom the transgender person resided. None of the people in this study were at any time living with a male partner. This is significant when it comes to examining sexual orientation.

Roughly half of the people in this research group were living alone at both the start point and the end point of the study. However, a significant number of them did live with a spouse. A few others lived with a person other than a spouse. The number of people who were living alone increased, and the number living with a spouse decreased over the time studied. In the past, the majority of the research participants had been in one or more marriages or long-term relationships with female partners. These relationships had ended for a variety of reasons, some directly related to the person's gender issues, and some for other reasons.

However apparently unrelated these other reasons might have been, there was usually a connection to transgender in one form or another. For example, the transgender person who felt inadequate or unworthy might have tended to be excessively tolerant of difficult behavior and to be more easily drawn into a marriage that was seriously flawed from the beginning. If the transgender person had abusive parents, she might be inclined to recreate the environment of her childhood in her marriage. But when she became emotionally healthier, with improved self-esteem and greater self-acceptance, this type of relationship might no longer be tolerable for her. In other words, just because a marriage or relationship ended, we cannot assume that it was ended by the other party or that the change was not a positive one for the transgender person.

The Implications of Marriage

Perhaps the reader has heard the old saying, "If you marry in haste, you will repent in leisure." It reminds us that there have always been people who entered into ill-advised marriages. One might assume that a man being married to a woman is reflective of heterosexual orientation. Although this did indeed seem to be the case with the people in this study, it is not necessarily so in the general population. As is sometimes the case with homosexual individuals, the MTF transgender individual might choose a female sex partner and might even marry her for any number of reasons besides sexual orientation, including family pressure, religious influences, or institutionalized social homophobia (Epstein, 2006). The person may have never allowed himself/herself to consider the possibility of attraction to males. There may have been an attempt to conform to social norms, to avoid the risk of having homosexual or transgender feelings exposed, thereby avoiding the risk of disapproval or rejection by society, by family, and at work. It is possible that some people had a preference for the traditional family lifestyle and did not believe this could be achieved with a male partner, especially while the transgender person was still functioning in the male gender role.

Family pressure can lead a transgender person into marriage, just as it can with some other people. How many people marry because of pregnancy? How many have second thoughts but still go ahead with a marriage because they think it is too late to back out? How many parents encourage marriage, at times prematurely, in an effort to get a somewhat wild young person to settle down? Certainly, transgender people are not the only ones who marry for what might be considered the wrong reasons. One must also keep in mind the potential for bisexuality, which Kinsey (Kinsey, Pomeroy, & Martin, 1948) and others (Devor, 1989; Diamond, 2000; Epstein, 2006; Hutchins & Kaahumanu, 1991; Klein, 1993) have suggested exists in varying degrees in a large percentage of humans, and perhaps to some degree in every one of us.

Having said all of this, I want to emphasize that the vast majority of the partner attachments of the people in this study appeared to be based on genuine feelings of love and sexual attraction. I mention other possible reasons solely in the name of objective inquiry, to make it plain that they were not overlooked. When people who were part of this study identified themselves as being attracted to females, their responses appeared to be honest and truthful.

The greatest change in living situation I observed at the most recent point in therapy was a decrease in the number of people who were living with a spouse (down from 33 to 28). Observation suggests that the longer a transgender person continues to pursue her transgender journey, the less likely she is to be living with a spouse or female lover in a relationship that began while she was still functioning in the male role. This is not necessarily due to the preference of the transgender person, but is usually due to the increasing likelihood of rejection by the female partner, whose sexual orientation is to males rather than to females. Typically, the more they come to see their transgender spouses as female, the less likely they are to find them attractive.

Unless they are bitter, the couple may still have a great deal of affection for each other and be able to live together amicably for a period of time. Although not as part of this study, I have seen several couples stay together for a time, as it served some purpose. This might include staying together until the transgender person has recovered from surgery, or until a house is sold, or until a child has graduated from college because it was cost-effective for them both.

The transgender partner may fervently believe that she wants to preserve the marriage. She may be very persuasive with her spouse in her attempts to make this happen. However, this could be a pre-emptive response to the normal grief about the marriage ending. By that I mean that should the spouse decide to stay with the trans-gender person, it is possible that the transwoman could find herself attracted to men. She could find that she wants to end the marriage, after all. In human terms, think of the guilt that would be created if she began to realize she had made a terrible mistake, that she should have let this woman go when she first wanted to leave, because she was no longer attracted to her and had come to realize that she was now attracted to men. Think of how emotionally yanked around the wife would feel. This is why it is so important for a therapist to dis-cuss this possibility early on, no matter how uncomfortable it may be for the client, who may still be trying to preserve the marriage and who may be convinced that talking about this possibility with her spouse would destroy any chance of her staying.

In this study, the greater numbers of individuals were in the early stages of transition. Only a small number had actually undergone GRS, and for most of those who had, the surgery was recent. It is impossible to do more than make an educated guess as to the likeli-hood of additional breakups with female partners.

None of the participants were living with male partners either at the start or the end of the observation period, but the trend was clearly in the direction of increased attraction to a male partner, sometimes being described as a shift from exclusive attraction to females to now being attracted to both females and males, but this may still be part of an ongoing process that was as yet incomplete. Unless we could follow people for a longer time, we cannot know how many of them might move from exclusive attraction to females to exclusive attraction to males. Once more, this may be evidence of a highly selective subject pool and the limited duration of the study. All outcomes must be considered in that context. We must also remember that people of any sexual orientation do not always have partners. Their not having a partner tells us nothing about their interest in having a partner.

Can Falling in Love Be the Cure?

Regardless of when MTF transgender people first became aware of indications of a female gender identity, as they grow into adulthood many transgender people fall in love and convince themselves that the strength of this emotion will enable them to extinguish their transgender feelings, or they rely on the belief that somehow everything will just work out. Some transgender people are able to integrate a measure of feminine expression into their lives and be content with that, not finding it necessary to live exclusively as either male or female. Crossdressers often do exactly that. For some, the intensity of transgender feelings appears to wax and wane, so they are better at suppressing it at some times than at others. This encourages them in thinking they can live with it. Others would consider this insufficient or frustrating, because it would only serve to make them want more. Some have easy access to transgender peer support and other resources, whereas others do not, and may not feel able to relocate closer to these resources.

Avoiding Transgender Identity in Self

Would being insane be preferable to being transgender? As far-fetched as this might seem, for some transgender people this is the case. Their self-loathing runs so deep that some would go to nearly any length to avoid facing and resolving their transgender feelings. As is reflected in the number of people in this study who married prior to facing their transgender feelings, many transgender people make repeated concerted efforts to conform to societal expectations. This is confirmed by my observations of the transgender population in general. Some simply believe that biology is destiny and feel hopeless. Others have some knowledge about transgender and accept it in others, but resist accepting it in themselves. The attempts to conform observable in the histories of the research participants were often driven by the belief that their feelings were an indication of a shameful flaw in their personality. Some even feared that it was an indication of mental instability. Many were driven by fear of rejection by members of their family of origin, rejection by a spouse or someone they hoped would become their spouse, fear of never finding a life partner, of never having children, of losing friends, of not having access to a desired career, of being doomed to live a solitary life, or even of being unable to provide for themselves financially.

Age at First Memory Related to Being Transgender

With regard to the people in this study, the age range for being able to identify a first memory associated with transgender was 3–14 years old. The median was 5 years. When awareness of being transgender was described as "from earliest memory" and the person was unable to specify an age, it was counted as age 3, making this age group better described as "3 or under." An astonishing 90% of the people studied reported awareness of their transgender identity well before reaching puberty. The awareness of the few remaining others came trickling in at a rate of one or two per year until age 14, by which time they all had indicated awareness of being transgender.

However, both before and since engaging in this study, I have known of other transgender people, including several clients, for whom awareness came at a later point in life. The transgender identities of these people appeared to be no less valid for seeming to emerge later, and I have no way to explain why this happens, except to say that more careful study may show that these people had preexisting feelings that were simply not recognized or were more strongly repressed. The contrast between the earliest awareness of transgender and the age of the person when she first sought therapy illustrates how long it took the average participant to reach a point that might be defined as critical mass, when the person gave up the struggle to avoid the issue and decided to face and address it.

I anticipate that the difference between the age at first awareness of transgender issues and the age when a person becomes ready to address them will decrease as time goes on, as the general population becomes more aware and accepting of diversity and transgender people feel freer to be open with themselves and others about their identities. This is already being reflected in the increasing number of young adults who are being open about their transgender and seeking help at an earlier age, and by the positive media attention to a few transgender children.

To my amusement, it is still considered rare for a child to express transgender feelings. But I would have to point to the people in this study, most of whom were once children and most of whom knew on some level that they were transgender from a very early age. If we know that most transgender adults knew they were transgender when they were very young children, then it follows that the number of transgender children is equal to the number of adults who knew when they were children. They are just hidden from the eyes of the public.

The Approach to Therapy

As we can see from the participants in this study, when first coming to therapy, the MTF transgender client may be wracked with fear, anxiety, and ambivalence about her transgender proclivities. The individual may have made several false starts in addressing her transgender issues, including previous therapies with providers who were not experienced with transgender issues and were unable to be very helpful. These attempts were interspersed with attempts to avoid the issue, to find another remedy for it, or to find a "quick fix" treatment. Cost is also a common factor that influences timing for pursuit of the issue.

In more traditional practice of therapy, a person comes to a therapist with a problem or complaint. The therapist does an assessment and makes recommendations, goals are set and means of achieving them are identified, and the client is seen weekly, or at least biweekly, until the problem is resolved. Therapy ends, sometimes after a brief period of tapering off to see if the client will continue to do well. Then the client goes on about life.

Assuming the transgender person is starting from a place of being totally closeted, it is usually not quite that simple with a transgender client. Sometimes the person comes in for one or two sessions and then might not be seen again for several months. This may be due to the person feeling overwhelmed by the magnitude of what lies ahead. They may have come only to find out more about what would be involved in addressing their transgender, but the person may not yet feel ready to act on this information or be fully committed to facing their transgender. The person may need to think about the potential losses and do some anticipatory grieving. In fact, the entire preparation process may be fairly analogous to the grief process in that the person may go through stages of denial, of bargaining, of feeling as if life has dealt them a bad hand, and may only return to therapy when they are satisfied that all their attempts to rid themselves of their transgender feelings have failed.

So, sooner or later, the person does usually return to therapy, and then the initial frequency of sessions will be determined by fairly traditional factors. If the person is in crisis, they will be seen more frequently. If not, and if there does not seem to be some comorbid diagnosis complicating the picture, the person may be seen weekly while an in-depth assessment of the person's circumstances and coping patterns is completed, and goals are agreed upon. This assessment not only includes a history, but allows the therapist to gain an understanding of the person's interpersonal networks in all important life domains, as this will become the basis for a coming-out plan, if coming out is one of the person's goals. Because the therapist may also need to provide information about the various procedures and options, to equip the person to make good decisions, the assessment will need to include what the client already knows about transgender. The therapist also needs to know how the person feels about it, as this will be reflected in the therapy goals.

Once goals have been established, it is often the case that the person will move forward in increments. There may be plateaus between these increments, during which the person assimilates and consolidates the gains and changes she has made before being ready to take a new step. For this reason, during those times, the client may need to be seen less frequently and will return to a period of more traditional frequency when preparing for the next step.

Some steps involve considerable cost in terms of dollars. Facial hair removal is an example of this. It may be hard for the person to juggle the cost of the step with the cost of therapy. Unless the step involves some risk or the person is on the brink of a crisis, the frequency of sessions can be titrated to meet the individual needs of the person. This is the essence of any good therapy, but the application can be quite different with the transgender client.

Measuring the Length of Time in Therapy

All of the above helps to explain why therapy was measured both by the number of 50-minute sessions and by the total number of months in therapy. The number of sessions does not tell us how long the person was seen, and the length of time in therapy does not tell us how often the person was seen. Both are required to complete the picture. The mean number of sessions was 25. The mean number of months was 24. This included periods of time when contact with the person was interrupted, perhaps because of one of the reasons indicated above.

As described, the frequency of sessions may be inconsistent when working with this population, not because the individual person is inconsistent, but because the frequency of sessions needs to be tailored to the needs of the individual client over time. Transgender people do tend to work in therapy for intense periods and then have periods during which they are assimilating and becoming accustomed to an increment of change. After this adjustment period, they often become ready to consider the possibility of taking additional steps on their transgender journey. An experienced therapist will vary the frequency of sessions during the course of the therapy process to meet the needs of the client at specific points in time.

In addition, most people who come to a therapist do so because they consider themselves in need of therapy. This is not so true with transgender people, who may come to therapy for a variety of other reasons, including information and referrals. These clients may not be in need of therapy in the traditional sense of the word, but may benefit by the information and guidance of a therapist who has experience with the particular challenges they are facing. And when they do engage in therapy, they may still need to work in increments, rather than going straight forward.

Length of Time in Therapy

Many of the subjects initially came to therapy for only a few 50-minute sessions and would then disappear from therapy for a time. They would sometimes report at a later time that when they had attended a few sessions and obtained a clearer understanding of what their transgender identity meant in their lives, they had become fearful or overwhelmed by the magnitude of the implications, or just needed time to assimilate what they had learned. After a period of time for coming to terms with their feelings, they would often return and resume therapy with a more clearly defined sense of direction.

Another reason subjects would sometimes come for initial brief periods of time was because they were only seeking information about the transgender condition, about the possibility of making their transgender feelings go away, or about the requirements for transitioning. However, in this process, they would learn that therapy does not make these feelings go away and would also learn more about the requirements of the transition process and the probable impact transition could have on their lives. After obtaining this information, they would ponder the implications before deciding what, if anything, to do with this new information. For some subjects who returned after a brief contact, the time-out was a matter of getting their finances in order, once they had a better idea of the costs involved in various procedures or processes. Many of these people returned to therapy after preparing themselves to become fully engaged.

When a client returned to therapy after an initial hiatus, for research purposes the time in therapy was counted from the date of first contact, although significant time might have elapsed without the subject being actively involved in therapy. I decided to count the time in this way because the initial contacts contributed to a process that continued even when the person was not being seen in therapy.

Not all transgender clients are in need of ongoing psychotherapy on a regular and frequent basis. Most will benefit from some degree of assistance over an extended period of time, but needs vary from individual to individual and vary over time with the same individual. The client may come for an initial period of evaluation and to identify goals. From that point on, the frequency of sessions will depend on whether the client has any other issues that might not be related to transgender but which could complicate a transition. Frequency would also depend on the amount, rate, and type of changes the individual was experiencing at different points in time; the obstacles encountered; the client's emotional state and level of coping skills; and even on how the important people in the life of the client are doing.

The personality of the client needs to be taken into account, as some are verbal processors who need more face-to-face contact to talk things out, while others need more private time to ponder. The potential for conflict within a client's geno-ecosystem, including the family, social circle, and workplace, may influence frequency of sessions. Some clients are very good at knowing when they need to make a therapy appointment and at being pro-active about doing so. Others need to be seen at regular intervals of some frequency, simply to monitor their well-being. Once a therapeutic foundation has been established, the frequency of sessions can be titrated to fit the prevailing situation and individual needs.

Because therapy is expensive and rarely covered by insurance for transgender people, it is best for the therapist and client to make wise use of this resource. The cost of therapy can be analogous to adding a car payment to the person's budget, perhaps impossible for the young and less affluent, and difficult to afford for anyone who is not wealthy. This points up the need for therapists and other service providers to offer a sliding fee for those clients who need it most, and especially to reach out to young people who may not be able to obtain help any other way.

The Uniqueness of the Transgender Path

The journey of each individual is unique. Not every transgender plan includes taking hormones or going for surgery of any kind. Some clients need more help than others with interpersonal, social, and emotional coping skills. Some require more emotional support than others. Some are more introspective and can benefit from processing insights more than others. For all of these reasons and others, therapy must be geared to fit the needs and requirements of the individual client.

New Shoes

To illustrate the change process for a client, I often use the analogy of new shoes. Imagine that you have a favorite pair of shoes. You've had them for quite a while and they are comfortable. You wish they would last forever. But, alas, nothing lasts forever, so finally you are forced to go shopping. You go to several shoe stores and you look at a lot of shoes. You try on several pairs. Finally, you choose a pair, you pay for them, the clerk takes your money, gives you a receipt along with the shoes in a bag, you take them home and now they belong to you.

So, you go home and you put these new shoes on your feet, but your feet don't know about the receipt. They say, "These aren't my shoes! I want my shoes!" It's not enough that you made a choice and paid the clerk. But hopefully you have made a good choice and now you have to walk around in these new shoes for a while to make them your own.

New behaviors are like this. They are unfamiliar and sometimes uncomfortable at first. You have to walk around in them for a while to make them your own. Think about all the first times you did something new in your life and you will recognize the truth of this. It applies to new behaviors we have chosen and others we have not chosen. We get caution signals when we are making mistakes, but we also get them from the unfamiliar, and we have to try to distinguish between them.

There is stress associated with new behaviors, but despite this fact, we all do new things at frequent intervals. When was the last time you went to a new restaurant where you hadn't been before? When did you meet someone new? How did it feel? Gerontologists recommend doing new things, or doing old things in new ways, to help keep the aging brain rejuvenated. Specialists in infancy and early childhood development recommend exposing babies to new things, recognizing that these things help to feed the developing brain and build neurological pathways. They may even raise the IQ level of the child. New ideas and experiences help to keep all our brains active, and yet we often fear them.

It is common for a transgender person who is bound for GRS to spend two to three years, or even more, in the transition process. During this time, they experience and gradually adjust to many new experiences and ways of doing things and of viewing the world. Thinking about new shoes can help.

With the mean number of months being 24, only a few of the people in this study reached the point of having genital reconstruction surgery within the time period studied, if that was indeed their goal. Also at the time of this study there were only a small number of people who had been followed for any length of time postsurgery. Thus, while I did observe a certain amount of change in sexual orientation and practices, and always in the direction of increased attraction to a male sex partner, we cannot know how much additional change would have occurred had the study lasted longer. Some of the change observed was in thought and feeling rather than in action, fantasy, and awareness of certain sexual feelings and desires that were new or of different intensity than previously experienced, but always they were in the direction of increasing attraction to male sex partners as the participant's own self-image as female became more fully consolidated.

Then there is the question of how lasting the observed changes might turn out to be in a longer study, and whether those individuals who did report change might change even more, as well as how much change might eventually occur for those who did not exhibit any changes during the course of this study. My clinical observations subsequent to the end of this study seem to confirm that change would continue to occur over time, specifically in the direction of increased attraction to male sex partners.

The length of time each person was in therapy was a factor that could potentially influence how the person perceived and felt about her own sexual attractions. Therapy should provide a neutral environment that does not lead or persuade a client in any particular direction, but includes educating the client about the range, frequency, norms, risks, and rewards associated with certain kinds of sexual feelings and behaviors. This information alone, presented entirely neutrally, could influence how the person feels about her own sexual attractions.

Experience With Transgender Expression

Specific questions were developed (see Appendix B, questions 16 and 17) to assess, for each participant, the amount of experience she had with transgender expression, her preferences about the kind of female image she wanted to present, and the degree of objectivity she had regarding self-presentation as a transgender female at the start and at the most recent point of contact. For each person, the responses were used as benchmarks on a cross-gender continuum.

While arbitrary and far from flawless, these were the best indicators I could devise.

At the beginning of the continuum were indicators such as "never experimented with makeup or dress" and "experimented only in private." Next came "has gone out in public as female 3–10 times." In the middle of the continuum were "out to most of friends and family," "goes freely in public as female," followed by "spends most of the time outside of work in female role." At the farthest end of the continuum were indicators such as "lives full-time as female" and "has had genital reconstruction surgery." Each person was assigned a place on the continuum at both the start and most recent time of contact, based on the characteristics described in the combined 49 questions, so that changes in the transgender expression of each could be looked at over time. This was important because of the light it shed specifically on changes in perception of sexual orientation. For instance, was there an identifiable cross-gender change or behavior that correlated with becoming sexually attracted to a male partner? Correlations that were ruled out were sometimes as telling as those ruled in.

Most dramatic in my eyes was the finding related to use of feminizing hormones. There were 38 people who never took any feminizing hormones during the entire time they were in therapy, and of these 38 people, 7 reported change in sexual orientation at the most recent point of contact, a significant number. There were 35 people who were not taking hormones at the start of therapy but began taking them during the course of therapy and continued to do so at the most recent time of contact. Of these 35 individuals, 5 reported change in sexual orientation at the most recent point of contact, also a significant number. Another 14 people were already taking hormones when they entered therapy and continued to do so at the most recent time of contact. Of these 14 subjects, 3 reported change in sexual orientation between first and the most recent point of contact. Once more, this was a significant number. However, since the change was consistent among those who did and those who did not take hormones, it does not appear that hormones caused the change in sexual orientation observed here. I will note that all of these changes were consistently and exclusively in the direction of increased attraction for male partners. Soon I will be saying more about what I do consider to be the reason for this change, since it certainly did not appear to be directly related to use of feminizing hormones.

Primary Sexual Fantasy

At no time did any of the people in this study fantasize about themselves as male with a male sex partner. While my clinical experience tells me that there are a few MTF transgender people who start out perceiving themselves as gay men and then reevaluate their gender identity, I believe they are in the minority and experience a somewhat different process. It appears to me that these individuals usually remain attracted to males as they shift their gender identification to female, but this creates its own dilemmas. Whereas they originally would have been attracted to gay men, as females their attraction and only available male sex partners would probably be to heterosexual men, which involves a major social as well as sexual change. This would be true both because, as heterosexual females, they would not tend to be attracted to gay men, but also because, as they no longer could be considered men, and especially if they no longer had male body parts, gay men would not be attracted to them either.

In the present study, all the participants experienced an increase in identification as female but began with a predominant attraction to female sex partners. Over the time period studied, there was a consistent increase in the number of individuals who fantasized about self as female with a male partner. This was the only observed direction of change. There did appear to be intermediate stages in the process that included self as female with a female partner, and even self as female with a transgender partner.

It should be remembered that choice of sex partner, even in fantasy, is in part a function of the other party. While many subjects could imagine themselves as heterosexual females, they were often fearful of male sex partners because of the risk of rejection or even potential violence toward themselves. This was reflected even in fantasy. Growing confidence in self in the female gender role appeared to increase the ability to consider the possibility of a male sex partner, and to do so in fantasy seemed to be a possible rehearsal for reality, although, in general, this is not always the case with fantasy. Most of us are familiar with a kind of erotic fantasy that the individual has no real desire to act upon.

Bisexuality is an elusive concept when looking at people who are in the midst of a process of examining and reevaluating their gender identities and sexual orientations. For this reason, no specific effort was made to include bisexuality as an identified category. I wanted the participants to be as free as possible to mentally move around in that middle ground with no attempt to categorize themselves in any specific way.

The outcomes imply that even those who may have been bisexual had a dominant preference for either a male or a female sex partner, and experienced an increasing preference for a male partner as they consolidated a female gender identity. The same was true for those who reported fantasies about self as male with a female partner (two at start and zero at the end). Of those who reported having no sexual fantasies, there were 13 at the start and 14 at the most recent point in therapy. It should be remembered that no attempt was made to categorize these individuals based on length of time in therapy, but I believe the ones who reported no sexual fantasies were usually those who had been in therapy for the least amount of time and whose sense of self as a sexual being was most repressed. This too would be an interesting topic for further research.

Since participants often reported unwillingness to act on their fantasies until their bodies were "right for this" (i.e., sufficiently feminized, with "sufficiently" being a highly subjective concept), the infrequency of acting on these fantasies is to be expected in a pool of cohorts where large numbers of participants had not (yet) had GRS, and many had not even used feminizing hormones.

The overall change in primary sexual fantasies in the direction of increased sexual attraction to male-bodied partners was significant. This change was not limited to only those individuals who planned to or already had GRS. This suggests that these changes were related more to self-acceptance as a transgender person or as a female person than they were to changing one's body to become more feminine. Again, it should be remembered that there is no evidence to indicate whether these changes were temporary or permanent, or how much additional change might happen over a longer period of time.

Gender Identity

It was interesting to observe the ways in which these individuals struggled to define their gender identity. Some clearly thought of themselves as female, but did not feel entitled to call themselves such, while others demanded recognition of their female identity. Some feared that claiming a female identity might be viewed as disrespectful by natal females, and some feared not being taken seriously. Many of them strongly claimed a female gender identity, usually from birth or earliest memory, but recognized that their bodies had been masculinized by male hormones early in life, sometimes in ways that were irreversible.

Many acknowledged that their initial socialization had been to the male gender role, some vestiges of which remained unavoidably and permanently integrated into their personalities, while others felt that they had never identified with the male gender role, but rather had always been feminine in expression, had never adopted male behaviors or engaged in activities typically associated with male children, and had always fit in better in the company of girls. Often, for the latter, the onset of puberty was doubly upsetting because not only were their bodies betraying their childhood fantasy of growing up to be women, but the social interactions of adolescence meant that they were now excluded from the company of girls and had no where to fit in socially.

Although these influences were present at both the start and end of the study, the overall trend was toward more fully claiming a female identity. This did not appear to be so much a change in self-concept as it was in self-confidence about their ability to make a credible presentation in the female role, and the feeling of the right of the individual to define self with regard to gender.

Among those participants who planned to have or already did have GRS at the time of most recent contact, there was a significant change in how they defined their gender identity. As with some other findings in this study, it should be remembered that there is no evidence to indicate whether these changes were temporary or permanent.

Self-Defined Sexual Orientation

Inevitably we find ourselves asking the question that every transgender person must eventually ask, "Exactly who is the opposite sex?" And then, along with it, there is that other plaguing question of autogynephilia. Although there was one person at the beginning and one at the end of the study who identified as autogynephilic, these were not the same individuals, and no one who was in the therapy process for a lengthy period of time remained self-identified as or appeared to be autogynephilic. Many individuals went through a period in which they might have been considered as such if they were only observed during that limited time period. This suggests that it is an artifact of the transition process, at least in these cases.

Some labeled themselves as autogynephilic because they lacked information about sexuality and tended to pathologize what could better be defined as normal human sexual responses. Some had visited websites where "symptoms" of autogynephilia were listed. However, examination of these websites made it plain that the criteria were so loosely defined as to include a large portion of the general population of the United States, if not the world, at least at some point in the life of the individual. As has been stated previously, this is not meant to say that there is no such thing as autogynephilia, but only that it is probably more rare than has been indicated by its proponents, and that self-diagnosis is a risky thing, especially among vulnerable populations.

No one, at either the start or the end point of the study, preferred a masturbation fantasy to partnered sex with either a male or a female partner. Among those who preferred a sexual partner who was male, there were 18 at the start and 27 at the most recent point of contact. None of these people identified as gay males, but instead they consistently identified themselves as heterosexual females in their sexual attractions or relationships with male partners. For each of them, the growing ability to see self as female increased the willingness to consider a male sex partner.

Those who preferred a female partner numbered 59 at the start and 48 at the most recent point of contact. This decrease was the obverse of the increased attraction to male sex partners. It too was associated with a growing sense of self as female and the associated attraction for someone of the opposite sex. Many of these people, early in therapy, were strongly confident that their exclusive attraction to female partners would never change. As time went on and they became more comfortable in the female role, they were often surprised, confused, and sometimes amused by their own reactions to the attentions of men. Since this was something that we had already discussed as a possibility, it did not represent a topic that was being addressed for the first time. The early acknowledgment of this possibility by the therapist probably makes it easier for a transgender person to reopen the discussion when she observes this change in her self.

Puberty Revisited

In discussing this situation with a client, I would often make an analogy to a young natal female just entering puberty and trying to make sense of her emerging sexuality. Prior to this time, a girl child might not have given much thought to her femininity or have viewed herself as a sexual being. Then, gradually she might become aware of changes happening to her body. She might notice that she is beginning to look more like a woman. She might notice that she is kind of pretty. Next, she might discover that boys become attentive or brighten up in her presence. She would know this feels good, but initially would not fully understand it.

Gradually, she would become aware that this newly discovered attractiveness of hers carried with it a certain amount of power over boys. She could get them to do things for her, or to do things she wanted them to do. It would be like a new toy for this woman child, and she would need to discover how it worked. At first she would not distinguish between the euphoria of a boy being attracted to her, and thus affirming her own attractiveness, and herself being attracted to that particular boy. At first she might be attracted to any boy who is attracted to her, only knowing that it feels good, but not being clear about the reason. She might not know at first if she is attracted to the boy or to the feeling she gets from the boy being attracted to her.

To a degree, this is similar to the MTF person as she experiences her newly found femininity. Even a crossdresser who is clearly and unequivocally attracted to females will report getting a big charge out of it if a man asks her to dance while out at a club. It is the affirmation of her femininity that is implied by a man treating her like a woman by asking her to dance that is euphoric, even though she may have no desire for sexual intimacy with a man. MTF people can benefit from the analogy to the process of a natal girl child becoming a woman as they try to sort out their own reactions to experiences with their new gender role.

For the participants in this study, along with the process of self-discovery came the associated process of socialization to the female role, especially in relation to males. What is "proper" female behavior toward men? How and when do you flirt? How do you date? In fact, do you date? The point where the person was at in transition always affected the answers to these questions, especially whether the person had undergone GRS.

While they were not included in this study, I am aware of a significant number of transgender people who have had transient intermediate attractions to other MTF transgender people during the process of transition. Although there are individuals, both transgender and not transgender (sometimes called tranny chasers), who are turned on by someone who has the appearance of a female but the genitals of a male, and who find having sex with people who are sometimes termed she-males (natal males who appear as females and may have both a penis and breast development) sexually attractive and exciting, it is more likely that some transgender people use this as an intermediate step, as they become more willing to experiment sexually and as they attempt to gain the self-confidence to experiment with a male partner, especially in view of the fact that a male sex partner can be a risk to the personal safety of the transgender person. A sex partner who is also transgender would not pose the same kind of threat.

And then there is the matter of refusal skills. I sometimes define this aspect of socialization to the female role by saying that females are taught to be the gatekeepers of sex (because they are the ones who can become pregnant, and perhaps because males often become sexually aroused more quickly) and males the gatecrashers. A client once defined this as males being the gas and females being the brakes. At any rate, being the one who says no or who delays sexual intimacy was new behavior for many MTF people, making them feel uncomfortable and unsure of themselves at first. This, too, is analogous to the early socialization of adolescent natal females. Young girls and transwoman sometimes want so much to be wanted by a boy or a man that they are afraid of losing him if they refuse him sex. Or she may simply not know how to say no gently and would be concerned about hurting his feelings if she makes him feel rejected. The analogy between the young adolescent girl and the new transwoman holds.

Most of us only get one shot at losing our virginity. A post-op transgender person finds herself in the unique position of being a virgin all over again (assuming she was not a virgin as a male). Where she may once have been concerned about passing, she may now be concerned about her vulva passing. She may simply be self-conscious, or if she has not told the man she is seeing about her transgender history, she may be afraid of his reaction if she is discovered. While I do not recommend a transgender person having sex with someone who does not know about her transgender history, human beings have been known to engage in many ill-advised sex behaviors. A sex partner who is also transgender may feel like a safe choice of a person to begin experimenting with sex, whether after GRS or simply in the female role.

The Outliers

There was only one person in the study who preferred a transgender female partner at the start and one at the time of most recent contact, and as I have mentioned before, my observations both within and beyond this study suggest that this was not so much a primary sexual orientation as it was either an artifact of the transition process, a basically bisexual person, or a lonely person who was willing to accept the only option available. As mentioned, certainly there are people who are specifically attracted to a transgender sex partner. Sometimes referred to as tranny chasers, these individuals are turned on by someone who has the appearance of a female but the genitals of a male. This did not appear to be part of the attraction template of any of the people in this study. When such a person is attracted to a transgender person, he would probably lose interest in her if she had GRS, and so she would not remain a suitable partner for such a person.

When Is a Change Really a Change?

These figures indicate a trend toward increasing preference for a male sex partner correlated with an increasing identification of self as female. Because of the lack of long-term follow-up in this study, we cannot predict how far this trend would go in the future, but the direction is clear. From those within the transgender community, I have heard estimates that place the ratio somewhere in the range of 70% of MTFs attracted to males versus 30% attracted to females. This is only speculation. In a world of the future, where it might become possible for transgender people to transition earlier and experience adolescent socialization in the gender with which they identify, we might see an even greater predominance of attraction to the opposite gender (that is, MTFs attracted to males), perhaps coming closer to the ratio of heterosexuality to homosexuality in the general population.

The Perceived Power of Hormones

Because it seemed so likely that the use of feminizing hormones might be thought by some people to explain or at least contribute to changes in sexual orientation, these changes were examined in the context of hormone use. I could easily believe that hormones could be the determining factor at some critical point in fetal development, but they were clearly not the determining factor for the people in this study. If you decide to examine the figures in Appendix D, please remember that individual people were not tracked for change during the course of the study, but only the accumulation at each end of the study. There were those who never took hormones during the study period, those who did so for the entire time, and those who began taking hormones during the study period. For each group, there was a decrease in preference for female sex partners and an increase in attraction to male sex partners. Thus, we would have to rule out hormones as the causative factor for change in sexual orientation. The one influence that was shared by all was the fact that they were all in therapy, and through this process they all became more comfortable and accepting of themselves as transgender women. This increased self-acceptance of their transgender female identities was the most obvious critical influence upon their sexual orientations. This was true even for those who did not wish to completely give up their male identities, an option that was consistently pointed out as a viable and acceptable possibility.

Considerations Other Than Therapy

It was not possible to isolate and examine separately the impact of the amount of time spent in therapy on individual changes in sexual orientation. We must remember that, while the level of self-acceptance was a common focus of therapy and, where indicated, improving this level was a goal, there were other simultaneous influences on self-acceptance. Thus, self-acceptance was not always or entirely attributable to therapist intervention, but could also be attributed to influences such as peers within the transgender community and finding acceptance from family members, friends, and co-workers. Therefore, changes in sexual orientation in relation to time spent in therapy were not a completely reliable indicator, and therefore therapy cannot be viewed as the single, or even the most significant, agent of change. It did, however, appear to be an element of the change process, and beyond its primary influence was likely to have been at least a secondary factor, in that therapy often contributed to a person making contact with other transgender people and taking the risk to come out to some significant people in the person's interpersonal realm.

It should also be noted that although it was beyond the scope of this study to examine the safety of the sex practices among the participants, it was observed that very few of these people acknowledged ever having had a sexually transmitted infection (STI) of any kind, and most of the people who were sexually active with a partner professed to routinely use some sort of protection from STIs, most frequently condoms, unless they were in a long-term relationship where both partners were committed to being sexually monogamous with each other. It seems likely that some of these people were simply saying what they thought was expected of them. However, it can be hoped that the information they were routinely given about the benefits of using safe sex practices and the risks of not doing so would have some influence on future behavior. This topic would be an important focus for further research.

Genital Reconstruction Surgery

The majority of the 97 participants had at least given some thought to the possibility of genital surgery. The fact that only a small number (16) of them had actually gone forward with it by the end of the study can be explained in part by the fact that most of them were too early in their process of transgender self-discovery to have reached the point of having genital surgery. Consider the magnitude of such a decision. Many people entered therapy literally having told no one as yet about their transgender feelings. For anyone to have gone from there to having had genital reconstruction surgery in so short a period of time would be a reason for concern. A person who has had genital surgery would typically have taken hormones and lived full-time as female for at least a year prior to surgery. That some individuals had GRS during the course of the study was usually because they had entered therapy already part way through the transition process.

When considering the monetary cost of the surgery alone, preparation time can be considerably longer than one year. For most people, this year of living full-time in the desired gender role would be preceded by a period of self-discovery, both internal and external. By that I mean that the person would have gone through considerable emotional and intellectual self-examination in combination with outward social and behavioral exploration. The latter would include coming out to others and experimenting with the female social role in increments short of full-time living before going so far as to live full-time as female.

It is usually possible for a MTF transgender person to experiment with the female social role in comparatively small steps, but some steps, by their very nature, are big. Coming out at work and beginning to work en femme is a huge step for most transgender people to take, and often the last step to living fully in the female social role. But coming out to anyone is a big step because there is no way to reliably predict how that person will react, but one can be certain the person will never forget what he or she has been told. That alone makes coming out to another person a big step. Other steps, not as huge but potentially more costly in terms of dollars and also time-consuming, might involve permanent removal of facial and body hair.

So it was that only 16 of the participants had gone forward with GRS by the end of the study. An equal number had decided against GRS by the end of the study (but still might reconsider it at some future point in time). As I have pointed out, the decision against genital surgery is not a reliable indication of whether the person is truly transsexual (whatever that actually means). I can think of several transgender people who meet all the diagnostic criteria but who still decided against GRS for one reason or another. Sometimes it was about money or health. Most often it was because of the personal losses that would be incurred, such as a marriage or a career.

When it comes to GRS, it is reasonable to assume that in a more neutral or accepting social environment, where the criticism, ridicule, stigmatization, and ostracization of transgender people in their various forms of expression would not be a limiting factor, some MTF transgender people who do not presently elect GRS might elect to have it. It is equally possible that some who presently choose to have GRS do so only to conform to the either-or expectations of society, and in a more accepting environment might choose to live openly as a transgender person without having GRS.

When it came to GRS, early in their process some people reported that they did not want or were uncertain about having genital surgery simply because they believed they would never be able to blend into society as female, and would forever be viewed and treated by others as weird. This fear about being able to fit smoothly into society in the female role was realistic in some cases, and in other cases was driven by anxiety and fear, but was not realistic, as these were individuals who, perhaps with the help of hormones and facial hair removal, or perhaps minor facial surgery, would be able to blend into society as female with ease. Part of the therapy process was for the person to address fears, obtain better information about feminizing procedures, overcome internalized transphobia, and do some reality testing of life as female through increasing levels of experimentation. All of these would contribute to building self-confidence for living life as female.

During this process, it is always critical that therapists remain neutral and give broad permission for the transgender person to stop or even pull back from a level of experimentation. Many transgender people reach plateaus in their process and might remain at that point for quite a while as they assimilate the changes they have made so far. Some individuals find that they have achieved a level of comfort with their gender role that will suffice for them to live happily. For others, after a while they may feel ready to move forward again. The transgender person should be validated for giving careful consideration and should be reminded that she is making decisions that will affect the rest of her life. She should be told that expressing uncertainty will not be held against her if she wants to move forward with transition at a future time. In fact, I usually tell clients that I am even more likely to leave the decisions fully in their hands when I am reassured that they have taken responsibility for making thoughtful decisions. We should always remember there are a number of medical, psychological, financial, and social reasons why a person might want but be unable to have GRS. These will be discussed in the following chapter.

In summary, of all the factors that one might expect to influence a change in sexual orientation, it seems that self-acceptance as a transgender person—as an anatomical male who has an innate female identity, or at least a strong element of female identity—is the single most important consideration. And although we cannot rule out other factors, attributing this female identity in some way to in utero development is one possible explanation. This explanation, which is an unproven theory, seems to be the most viable at this time, and is least likely to do harm to the individual who is struggling to accept a gender identity that the person appears powerless to change. Understanding and accepting one's own gender identity seems to be a prerequisite to clarifying objects of sexual attraction.

5

Approaches to Therapy With Transgender Clients

There are a number of theories that one might attempt to apply when working with transgender clients. Always, the bottom line should be the approach that is best indicated for the individual client, not the preferred approach of the therapist. When working with transgender clients who have no other mental health issues, choice of approach boils down to the question of causality and whether this lies in subtle social influences or is biologically based. Most current theorists hedge their bets by saying the cause may be a combination of both biological and psychosocial influences. The fact is that no one really knows beyond a doubt, so we can only use an educated guess and go forward within the edict of "Do no harm."

However, based on my own extensive clinical experience with both transgender clients and clients who were clearly comfortable with their gender of birth, people who found their genitals congruent with their internal sense of self, it seems that a biological explanation fits most closely with our current knowledge and clinical observations. It is also the one that fits best with what we hear most often from transgender people when they talk about their own experience of self. It is the working theory that is least likely to do harm. It serves no purpose for parents to blame themselves or for others to blame them, thinking there must have been something wrong with the way they parented, when, in fact, the parents of transgender people appear to be no better or worse than any other parents.

Furthermore, when considering the effect of poor parenting practices, most children prove to be remarkably resilient, and most of us manage to survive relatively in tact despite the fact that none of us have perfect parents. In fact, when it comes to poor parenting practices, this is more likely to interfere with self-esteem, and therefore with self-acceptance as a transgender person, than it is to be a causative factor in a child being transgender in the first place.

Neither does it serve any constructive purpose for transgender people to view themselves as mistakes or as flawed in some way, as would be implied by therapist efforts to discover what went wrong or attempts to "cure" their transgender, when, in fact, their transgender status may be a normal part of human variation, just as similar variations exist in other species (Roughgarden, 2004). Just as we recognize that variations of other kinds, such as left-handedness or green eye color, to be normal in humans even when they are outside of the norm—we now recognize that these things can be normal even though they are outside of the norm, although we did not always do so.

Is There Really No One or Nothing to Blame?

This might be a good time to digress for a minute by addressing a question that I am sometimes asked. Is it possible that playing dress-up caused or contributed to the person becoming transgender? No one knows with certainty the answer to this question. I think it is fairly common for males of all ages to play at dress-up on occasion, unrelated to transgender. A boy might dress as a girl for Halloween, but that does not appear to be an indication that he is transgender or to be a cause of his becoming so. If the boy is not already transgender, it will not hold that much attraction for him. The transgender boy child who dresses as a girl for Halloween may want to do it every Halloween, although he may not say so because he is too afraid of discovery. Many adult males do the same thing, just for laughs or maybe for a sexual turn-on. It would be hard to find a male comedian who did not crossdress as part of his act at some time. Yet, as far as we know, this crossdressing does not permeate the rest of his life or become a recurring part of his sex life.

For several years, earlier in my career, I worked with adjudicated adolescents (and their families), a population for which it was the norm to have been poorly parented and often abused in some way. I heard many stories of male children being punished by being made to wear a dress. It was done to humiliate the child, and it was emotionally harmful, but it did not make the child become transgender. I also heard stories about older sisters who dressed up their little brothers just for fun. But the boys quickly got bored with this game. For some, they found it aversive. Some resented it and were not cooperative or willing participants. Others thought it was fun and funny, but quickly tired of it.

It appears to be different for transgender children, who, as adults, also sometimes report playing dress-up with a sister when they were children. But we may be asking a chicken-or-egg question. The transgender child may have first discovered the enjoyment of dressing when a sister or other young girl dressed him up, but I have heard many stories from transgender adults who reported that this immediately became their favorite childhood game, and they then became the instigators and persisted in seeking out this activity long after the sister (or other play partner) became weary of it.

Now, transgender clients sometimes tell me about a parent attempting to extinguish childhood feminine behavior by making them wear a dress to humiliate them. In such a case, the feminine behavior preceded the forced dressing. Yes, the child would feel humiliation by being exposed and ridiculed in this way, but would still secretly like the dressing.

So, in my observation, many young boys are exposed to crossdressing in a variety of ways and for a variety of reasons, some more malevolent than others, but transgender children appear to respond differently to this experience than do those who are not. I do not think this causes transgender. It just makes the transgender child more secretive. Only a few of the subjects in my sample experienced early involuntarily imposed dressing en femme, no more than I have encountered among people who were not transgender.

Crossdressing Among Non-Crossdressers

To carry this theme into male adulthood, I can use an example from my own life. For several years, when we were younger, my husband belonged to a fraternal organization that I will not name. This group held an annual event that was traditional for many years, and may still be part of the organization's activities. It consisted of putting on an annual skit—the same skit every year.

There is a minor American poet by the name of Robert Service. He wrote many story poems of the Yukon during the gold rush years, and one poem in particular is called "The Shooting of Dan McGrew."

The skit involved the reading and acting out of this poem. The scene was a saloon in the Yukon, with a bartender, a piano player, a narrator (who reads the poem as the players act it out, mostly in mime), lots of miners and prospectors, a group of chorus girls (including some improvised music and dancing), and, as you may suspect, one particular femme fatale, "the lady known as Lou." You can do an Internet search for the title of the poem and read it yourself if you wish.

Anyway, as you can probably guess, all the parts were played by the men of the organization, and they particularly vied for the female roles, and especially for the role of the female lead of Lou, sort of the "Miss Kitty" of the Malamute Saloon. When it came to costuming and the creation of false boobs, the guys were especially ingenious. I recall one occasion when strainers with handles were used, the handles pointing downward under the clothing, where they could be grabbed and jiggled dramatically, which got a lot of laughs. It was all done with great fun and good humor. They certainly enjoyed it, and apparently so did everyone else, as the performance was always well attended in spite of the fact that it was the same play every year!

These were not transgender guys (I assume), but it does illustrate my point regarding this common tendency in males to enjoy cross-dressing on occasion, sometimes beginning in childhood but persisting into adulthood. While I think it is normal and understandable for anyone to wonder what it would be like to be the opposite sex, in our present social climate men tend to be self-conscious (an understatement) about exploring any feminine feelings they may have, and they either do it in private or need a socially acceptable excuse for doing it openly. Because of the way this group of men used this poem, it could easily be viewed as playfulness and comedy, an example of a safe and covert way for men to experiment with femininity. You, the reader, may know of other examples.

So, using psychoanalysis, or employing some other method of therapy designed to understand the causes of someone being transgender, has not proven to be very effective or helpful to the transgender person. The same is true when it comes to attempting to "cure" it. Instead, therapy approaches that help the individual with self-acceptance, which builds self-esteem, and teaching effective use of coping skills to deal with being transgender in a world that is poorly prepared for diversity, seem to be the most helpful and do the most for improving quality of life for transgender clients.

Assessing for Coexisting Conditions

Thus, it is important for a therapist to assess for depression and anxiety disorders in transgender clients, as well as for associated feelings that may not rise to a diagnostic level but which still require attention as part of a treatment plan. Building self-esteem and self-acceptance are additional important parts of working with transgender clients.

Transgender people do not have automatic immunity from other mental health conditions, and some other diagnoses, such as the schizophrenias, bipolar depression, and borderline personality disorder, are characterized by confusion about identity and sexual orientation. An assessment such as one would do with any other client is an important part of making an accurate determination about the best treatment approach to use when a new client has questions about his or her gender identity. While most mental health conditions do not appear to be closely associated with transgender, it behooves a therapist to rule out the presence of some of these other conditions, because, if present, it would need to be determined if the transgender feelings were symptomatic of that condition or a valid coexisting concern. If the latter, it would then need to be determined if it was possible to treat both together, which would be optimal, or if it would be necessary to treat one before the other. Where the other condition is secondary to transgender, it is often true that addressing the transgender identity results in spontaneous resolution of the other problem. Reactive depression is an example of this.

Treating Co-Occurring Diagnoses

Since transgender people may have any of the same psychological or emotional problems that anyone else could have, when present, these should be treated the same as one would do with any other client. Assuming that gender confusion is not a symptom of one of these other conditions, the transgender feelings should always be taken into account while treating the other condition, and their importance should not be made secondary to this treatment.

I want to be clear that addressing the transgender feelings should not have to wait until some other condition has remitted. For example, if the problem is depression, treatment should be paced so as not to overwhelm the client, but being made to wait can deepen the depression. More than once a client has said to me, "I have waited my entire life to do something about my transgender! No wonder I'm depressed. Don't ask me to wait even longer."

If the other condition is substance abuse, it is a little more complicated, but both should still be addressed together. Therapists currently recognize that women with substance abuse problems sometimes need a group for women only, and may specifically need a woman therapist. There are treatment programs specifically for gay people. Nothing like that exists for transgender people, so it becomes necessary to take extra care to ensure that the treatment offered is at least safe for the transgender person, and that treatment planning includes support for self-acceptance and hope for the transgender person to move forward with transgender as well as substance recovery goals.

If the transgender person is not coping very well with life, we must not be quick to pathologize. All of us have our emotional and psychological strengths and weaknesses, and this is equally true of transgender people. Included among these are our varying abilities to employ coping skills in the face of stress, and to problem solve effectively in a variety of situations.

It is fairly common to see a transgender person with an anxiety disorder vacillating for extended periods of time, trying to decide what to do about gender issues. Having gender identity conflicts may contribute to the development of an anxiety disorder, but when the anxiety invades other domains of the person's life, it is no longer simply about gender and needs to be treated like anyone else's anxiety disorder. It may then become possible for the person to face and sort out concerns and make decisions about gender identity. Thus, regardless of which came first, they are intertwined and need to be sorted out while both are being treated.

There certainly are some psychological problems that result in gender confusion. Borderline personality and the schizophrenias are examples of this. When these are present or suspected, therapy should proceed much more slowly. The transgender feelings may only be symptoms of the other diagnosis. They may also be co-occurring. In the latter case, they are valid issues, but the person may be ill-equipped to deal with the outcomes of being more openly transgender. In either case, it is usually possible to agree with the client about some means of exploring femme expression that do not burn any bridges for the client while working out the validity of the gender concerns. One must weigh the possibilities of how the person can achieve the best quality of life.

What Price Would a Person Be Willing to Pay for Gender Congruity?

Transgender people often risk significant losses if they face and act on their transgender identities. When they are married and have established families, they could lose their wives, and even their children. They may also risk the loss of parents, siblings, friends, jobs, and possibly even their religious affiliation, especially if they were to transition and have GRS. The risk of these losses is enough to prevent some individuals from going forward, although others do so despite all risks. A number of factors appear to influence these decisions. They relate to such things as the intensity of the transgender feelings, the magnitude of the dependency needs, and other personality components of the individual person. These include how much the individual is a risk-taker, the ability to sustain rejection or tolerate isolation, the importance of her religious belief system, the availability of alternate sources of emotional support, and the financial circumstances of the individual. For example, if there were minor children to support and real risk of job loss, this would be a consideration of major magnitude, as compared to the circumstance of someone who has no financial dependents and has savings and secure employment.

Also needed, and therefore important to assess, are skills for improving interpersonal relationships, such as empathy, active listening, and effective problem solving. In this way transgender people are no different from anyone else in their frequent need to enhance these skills, especially in the face of demanding challenges of life. It has been my observation that these interpersonal skills are the single most determining factor in how well others accept a transgender person. If the person was well liked before coming out, people are more inclined to value their relationship with the transgender person enough to work on adjusting to this new information and to the changes in gender role the transgender person may make. This also applies when the person is transitioning on the job.

The Stress of Daily Life

Many people have life challenges to face and struggle through and learn how to live with. Many people have high demands on their coping skills. Where transgender people sometimes differ is in being the object of social stigmatization, the nearest analogy perhaps being to African American people, who also have to deal with such stigmatization to one degree or another. This is a social and intergenerational issue. If parents suspect that their child is transgender, their fears about their child suffering from social stigmatization are compounded by their own fear of social stigmatization for themselves. This can influence how they parent the child, who may be viewed as a problem child. We can learn from African American parents in this regard, as they have always needed to help their children develop the coping skills to weather the social stigma of their race, with the ability to navigate through childhood and become healthy adults.

Unlike transgender people, African Americans do not have a choice of hiding their ethnic origins. They never have to "come out" as being of African descent, unless, of course, they are light skinned enough to "pass," a term that is then common to both groups. But specifically for transgender people, the stress of hiding their true selves from the world can limit their ability to develop intimate relationships and can, in itself, create stress and limit the development of intimacy skills. An MTF transgender adult may avoid engaging in a primary intimate relationship if she is concealing such an important part of herself from the other person. Intimacy is based on allowing another person in—to allow that person to get close and know who you are. The transgender person who holds back will be keeping the other person at arm's length. The other person may not know why, but will certainly feel it and will be likely to limit his or her own level of intimacy in the relationship, even if he or she is not consciously aware of doing so. Without having opportunities to practice interpersonal skills, the transgender person may be limited in this area of personal development.

For others who choose or feel compelled to be more open about their transgender feelings, the risk of ridicule, rejection, or even of violence is an ever-present concern to which a therapist should be sensitive, and possibly even proactive in counseling the client about safety. This is true in both childhood and adulthood. The transgender child will be discussed in more detail later, but for now it can be said that there is risk of being harmed or abused by parents and other family members, as well as risk that comes from other sources, such as being teased and bullied by other children. I have heard numerous reports from transgender adults about being bullied as children, but when they went to their parents for help, the parents told them they were bringing it on themselves by acting too "girlie" or "sissy," and instead of getting support, they were blamed for being the way they were. Why is it that we understand that it is not OK to tease someone if they are different because of a physical disability, but we do not understand that it is not OK if the person is different in some other way?

For the adult who is openly transgender, when others do not accept or do not know how to relate to her, she can avoid being in a situation that makes her feel uncomfortable, or she can be aggressive with words or actions to protect herself. The transgender child is often not at liberty to leave the situation, such as school, and may be ill-equipped to protect himself. Being openly transgender not only has these potential social risks, but as the child gets older, transgender-related behavior would eventually be likely to limit his opportunities to date and cultivate primary relationships.

The Need to Belong

Perhaps most harmful and insidious is the damage done to self-esteem when one is made to feel unacceptable to others. Like the ants and the bees, we humans are a social species, and we need a certain amount of acceptance from others of our own kind. To withstand a lack of this acceptance, the transgender person needs to be stronger than the average person. Under that strong exterior is often a great deal of pain, grief, and sometimes anger. These are normal feelings and not necessarily a sign of psychopathology or emotional disturbance.

The upshot of the various ways that transgender people are impacted by a hostile social environment is that they appear to be at higher than average risk for low self-esteem, anxiety, and depression, and possibly a higher than average risk for suicide. These are reactive conditions and need not be viewed as indications of weakness on the part of the transgender person, but rather as normal human vulnerability in a person who has been made to feel like a pariah.

Therapy can be very helpful in addressing and alleviating these uncomfortable feelings, and in helping build better interpersonal skills to alleviate social isolation. For some individuals, social contact with other transgender people is often very helpful too.

Current Risk for Suicide

Sometimes a new client will tell the therapist that suicide is or is not an issue even before being asked. If this doesn't happen, it is always wise to ask about the risk for suicide. When asking, the therapist should be direct with the question and explicit with the choice of words. If the therapist skirts the issue or appears reluctant to use words like *suicide*, the client may interpret this as reluctance to deal with the issue, and may follow the perceived lead of the therapist and, in a sense, shield the therapist from information that the client feels the therapist is not prepared to deal with. If the therapist determines that the risk of suicide is present, it should be safe to assume that any well-trained therapist would know how to deal with this situation, and therefore unnecessary to elaborate on here.

It then becomes necessary to state the obvious. Do not hold the transgender client hostage to a suicide prevention plan. The suicidal feelings may be a direct result of feeling hopeless about the transgender condition, yet therapists who are inexperienced with transgender issues have been known to say that no progress with transgender can be made until the risk of suicide is past. This makes no sense whatsoever, and in fact is likely to exacerbate the situation. A therapist cannot effectively treat suicidality by withholding hope! Neither can the person be helped by adding frustration and delay, when the repeated experience of frustration and delay has been part of the problem for which a remedy is being sought.

Current Risk for Life Crisis

The transgender client may have already taken precipitous action that is not based on careful consideration. She may be unaware of potential pitfalls. The decision to seek therapy may be part of her having reached a larger decision, and making a therapy appointment may not be the only thing she has suddenly done or is about to do regarding her transgender. She may have hit a wall, in a manner of speaking, and feel totally unable to fight against her transgender feelings any longer. She may have adopted a "damn the torpedoes" attitude and already taken steps that are not well thought out, or may be at high risk of doing so. Asking, "What steps have you taken and when did you take these steps?" is a good place to begin. The next question should be: "What are you thinking of doing or planning to do next?"

The response to the first question may mean that you need to do a "fire drill" to prepare the client for the possible sequelae of the action already taken. As for the second question, it may be wise to ask, "Are you willing to hold off on taking any additional steps until we can talk about them?" Telling the client that you may be able to help with planning in order to maximize the odds for a successful outcome may make it easier for the client to slow down and think through the steps she is contemplating.

In the current study, one of the things that was taken into consideration was the length of time each person spent in therapy. Careful thought was given to how this should be measured. With the transgender client, this is not as straightforward a question as it might appear to be at first glance.

Determining the Current Status of the Client

Any therapist should begin where the client is. This is true at the beginning of every session as well as the beginning of therapy. How can a therapist begin where the client is unless one knows exactly where the client is? Even in today's world a therapist may encounter a wide range of experience among transgender clients. A new client could be someone who has never even tried crossdressing, but has ruminated about it for years. She could be someone who has considerable experience with crossdressing in the privacy of home, but who has never gone out in public dressed. She could be someone who has never told another person about her transgender feelings, or perhaps only one other person. She might be someone who has gone out freely in the club scene but nowhere else, or someone who has already lived openly as transgender except at work for months or years. The person may or may not already be taking hormones, could or could not already be living full-time in the gender role with which she identifies. Determining the status of the client with regard to her transgender is an imperative step to take before moving forward.

Knowledge and Experience

The average transgender person now has far more knowledge about transgender matters than was the case before the wide availability of the Internet and the more frequent media coverage of gender identity issues, as has become increasingly common in the last 15–20 years, and especially in the last 5 years. However, it would be a mistake to make assumptions based on this. A therapist can still get a new client who has been too fearful to even watch a PBS documentary for fear that showing an interest in this topic will draw attention to himself and arouse suspicion in family members about the reason for the interest. Even if the person has access to the Internet, she may still be afraid to search for information about transgender. Perhaps other family members use the same computer, or perhaps the person is not sophisticated in ways to maintain personal privacy when using the Internet, and so is unwilling to risk discovery.

One of the responsibilities of a therapist who works with transgender clients is to provide information. This means that the therapist must educate herself or himself and must also assess what information the client already has and may need. The therapist must also be at least a little knowledgeable about a wide range of topics that relate to transgender in one way or another, whether specific to therapy or related to the various other disciplines from which services may be required.

Included is knowledge of the larger world of transgender. There is tremendous variation among transgender people, just as there is among people in general. This particular client may not be like the last one, or even the last dozen. She may be reluctant to talk about things that she fears the therapist will view as kinky. Not knowing there are others like herself, the client may even think of herself as kinky when, in fact, she is nothing more than a garden-variety transgender person. The client's own perception of what is kinky may be naive or skewed, but the therapist needs to put every client at ease in order for that person to risk being open about his or her situation and feelings. Part of an assessment is asking questions about a variety of experiences associated with transgender feelings and expression.

The therapist also needs to know a little bit about a lot of other things that are ancillary to a transgender journey. This includes some basic knowledge about hair loss and its remedies, from Rogaine to hair transplants and wigs, but also the effect of hormones on hair on various parts of the body. It includes having some basic knowledge of methods of facial hair removal, and the effects of hormones on the growth of facial and body hair. It includes having some knowledge about other typical responses to hormone therapy and typical time-frames in which these responses occur. The therapist needs to have connections for responsible and knowledgeable medical referrals, especially for hormones. This holds true for estrogens, antiandrogens, and androgens.

In addition, the therapist must be familiar with the surgeons who are best known and most experienced with the various surgeries associated with transition. For the MTF, this is fairly simple, since the surgeries desired or required are fewer. They include genital reconstruction surgery and, on occasion, orchiectomy or breast enhancement. The client may have questions about the success of surgery on the vocal cords, and there may be an interest in facial feminization surgery (FFS), or a trachea shave.

For the FTM, it can be much more complicated, including top surgery as usually foremost, but also hysterectomy, then possibly a vaginectomy (removal of the vagina), scrotal implants, and either a metoidioplasty (essentially freeing up the clitoris from its hood to allow it to lengthen freely, as it will do somewhat with hormone stimulation) or a phalloplasty, along with urethral lengthening—all proving the point that subtraction is easier than addition. Like MTFs, FTM people may also be interested in some form of facial surgery, more often the reshaping of a nose.

One of the best ways for a therapist to learn some of the essentials is to attend a conference that is sponsored by some part of the transgender community. There are several, and by attending, the novice transgender therapist will have the opportunity to examine her or his own response to being immersed in the culture of transgender. This self-awareness is an essential part of being an effective transgender therapist. There will be the opportunity to interact with a wide variety of transgender people in ways that would be impossible in a clinical setting. There will also be the opportunity to meet and interact and learn from other professional people who are there to learn from each other and to share their experience by offering workshops on various topics. In my opinion, no therapist has the right to work with this population unless they are willing to invest time, effort, and money in their own professional growth in this area.

There are several annual conventions that are sponsored by some part of the transgender community. Noteworthy among them are Southern Comfort, with the largest attendance, held annually in Atlanta, Georgia. In Chicago is an annual convention called Be-All, representing Be All That You Can Be, and in existence long before this became a slogan for the U.S. Army! The International Foundation for Gender Education (IFGE), which publishes the community journal *Transgender Tapestry*, also sponsors an annual convention, simply known as the IFGE Convention, often held in Philadelphia, but equally often moving around the country and sometimes even into Canada. In Provincetown, Massachusetts, it is Fantasia Fair, sometimes also known simply as Fanfair, the longest running annual transgender convention. There are several others as well, but these are among the best known. Opportunities to attend one of these events are so widely available as to make it inexcusable for transgender therapists not to avail themselves of one of them. Details are readily available on the Internet.

These are the practical aspects of the therapist's job. The true therapy comes in helping the client sort out where she is on the gender spectrum, coming to terms with her identity, deciding how she will live with this knowledge, and how she will deal with it among family, friends, and people at her work. There is the weighing of the costs versus the benefits with every step the client may be contemplating. There is often a huge chunk of emotional and reality work involved. It includes helping the client to know her own personality well enough to determine how many risks to take, how well she can tolerate rejection and being alone. It also includes helping the fearful client assess the reality of her fears, so that she does not create disaster in her life, but neither does she allow her fears of the unknown to needlessly hamper her progress.

The therapist needs to know enough about the transgender spectrum himself or herself to be helpful to the client, and must also be familiar with typical patterns of reaction, to know when it is helpful to slow a client down and when this is simply being obstructionist. The therapist must also be able to distinguish between a timely well-placed word of encouragement and leading the client, using the former as indicated.

Steps Already Taken

Recognizing the importance of beginning where the client is, which has already been emphasized herein, deserves to be emphasized again. It is endlessly surprising that a therapist who practices this principle routinely with nontransgender clients will suddenly lose sight of it when confronted with a transgender client. Transgender people have learned to be resourceful at finding what they need without benefit of a therapist. To some therapists and transgender people alike, this seems like highly risky or even manipulative behavior. To others, it is a creative solution to the problem of how difficult it can be to find knowledgeable professional help. To yet others, it is simply taking responsibility for managing one's own life when professional help seems like a patronizing and unnecessary requirement. This is especially true when the client may actually know more about transgender care than any of the therapists he or she has found.

It is also true that a therapist who is very respectful of the client's right to self-determination and ownership of his or her own life when it comes to other types of clients, may suddenly lose sight of this when confronted with a transgender client. The therapist may start being directive, giving advice and making recommendations, trying to be in control of the client's life, and may even view the client as "noncompliant" if the client refuses to follow the therapist's admonitions. I believe that this response is largely due to insecurity on the part of a therapist who is inexperienced with transgender clients. His or her own lack of self-confidence may lead him or her to want the client to slow down until the therapist can become comfortable with what the client is doing. This calls for careful self-examination on the part of a therapist so that his or her own feelings do not cloud the client's therapy. Some call this a matter of transference and countertransference. I prefer to call it a question of boundaries.

The Thorny Issue of Hormones via the Internet

So, what should a therapist do if a new client reports that she is already taking hormones, perhaps obtained via the Internet or perhaps from a primary care physician who may lack knowledge of transgender care but was easy to persuade to prescribe? Factors to be considered include how long the client has been taking these hormones, and how she feels about what she is doing. Many times a client will say that the primary motivation for coming to therapy is because she is worried about what she is doing but is unwilling to stop. She wants help from the therapist to get herself under knowledgeable medical supervision.

The immediate answer to the question of what to do is "nothing." An assessment should always precede any action on the part of a therapist unless there is an overriding crisis. This should be followed by the formulation of goals and a treatment plan that are all mutually agreed upon, not imposed on the client by the therapist. If there is some reason to believe that the hormones the client is taking pose an immediate threat to the health or balance of the client's life, then this should be discussed with the client. If the client and therapist are so at odds that it appears they cannot work together, then this is a good time to discuss that too. When a therapist is respectful of the client's right to set the course of her own life, including the right to make mistakes as long as they are not life threatening, it is usually possible for the two to reach an agreement. If not, then the client should feel free to find another therapist.

Sometimes a therapist will think that the client has deliberately obtained hormones prior to starting therapy as a manipulative way to circumvent getting a letter of recommendation for hormones from the therapist. Be that as it may, it is not the role of the therapist to give medical advice, much less to make requirements about medications. If the client is being manipulative, and if this is an established behavior pattern that interferes with interpersonal relationships, then it will show up in other ways and can be dealt with in therapy when a pattern that is causing a problem for the client becomes evident. The most immediate concern is the well-being of the client, not to establish who has the power, even if that includes getting the client under medical supervision as soon as possible.

Dealing With the Gatekeeper Role

There are therapists who require a lengthy period of time in therapy before they will agree to refer a client for hormones. If there are no other diagnoses present, it does not take that long for an experienced therapist to determine if the person is a good candidate for hormones. To withhold them because of a rule that was not made for this specific client is sometimes like holding the client hostage. The therapist may lack confidence in his or her own ability to make an expeditious determination. Sad but true, a therapist may be self-serving because a client is, after all, a source of income, and if all the client really wants is a hormone letter, he or she may disappear from therapy once the letter is obtained. As mentioned above, the therapist may be overly concerned about being manipulated by the client. It is true that a client who wants a fast track to hormones can get them via the Internet, and then use the fact that they are already taking them to obtain a speedy referral from a therapist. But manipulation is often the act of seeking a way around an obstacle. It is unnecessary for a therapist to put himself or herself in the role of being an obstacle. This will allow the client to feel free to return to the therapist if she feels the need for help at a future time.

There are well-meaning but inexperienced therapists who might be so touched by the apparent pain and sense of urgency of a transgender client that they would be too quick to try to alleviate the pain, leading them to circumvent the needed assessment. Again, this is a boundary issue, for the therapist to avoid taking on the discomfort of the client, so that the need to alleviate his or her own discomfort makes him or her feel compelled to premature action. Conversely, a common concern of therapists who are inexperienced at working with transgender clients is the uncomfortable position of being a gatekeeper to services, since the client needs a letter of referral from a therapist to begin hormones through legitimate providers. The same is doubly true for the client seeking GRS. However, the therapist can join with the client in seeking the best possible outcome for the client. When there are no co-occurring diagnoses and transgender is the only concern, then it should be fairly easy to establish a collaborative relationship wherein the highest quality of life for the client is the fundamental goal of both client and therapist. If the only contraindication for taking a particular step is that the person's life is not well prepared for it, discussing it with the client should result in a reasonable resolution. Perhaps, upon graduation, in addition to a diploma every new therapist should receive a plaque for the wall of his or her office, reading "Do no harm."

6

Transgender Children and Transgender Parents

We will now focus some attention on children. This will include the child who is or appears to possibly be transgender, and also the child who has a transgender parent or some other person who is close. Most people have no idea how to talk with a child about such things. They are fearful of saying the wrong thing and possibly harming the child. They may even think it is best not to talk with the child at all about things like this. I believe that we underestimate the ability of children to understand, although they may do so in a simplified way. I also think we tend to overestimate the risk to a child when it comes to talking about certain things. We project onto the child our own discomfort with a topic and assume that the child will be equally uncomfortable, when, in fact, it is our discomfort that is more likely to make the child uncomfortable.

Just as with everything else about transgender, with a child who may be transgender there are accompanying implications regarding sexual orientation. Adults often wonder if a transgender child is gay well before they consider the possibility that the child could be transgender, even if the child is plainly telling them so. When telling a child about a transgender parent, the child who feels free to voice his or her questions will sooner or later ask about what this means in terms of sexual orientation, although probably not using these words. The child will wonder about the distinction between transgender and homosexuality, but will also wonder what it will mean if the transgender parent falls in love with a new partner. Will this mean a new stepmother or a new stepfather? Adults, especially parents, will need to be prepared for these questions.

The Transgender Child

Everyone was once a child. Yet, there is so much we do not under-stand about the mind of a child. What do we bring with us into the world, and what do we absorb from the world around us, once we are here? Relying on the sense of self that is most often reported by transgender adults in recalling their childhoods, the majority of them report seeming to have had an innate sense of their gender identity from earliest memory, or at least from a very young age.

Sometimes a transgender child will try to tell a parent about his feelings. The child may not have the vocabulary to articulate very clearly how he feels. The male-to-female child will probably say either that he is or wants to be a girl. Typically the parent will not take the child seriously, dismissing it as childish fancy and assuming that the child will outgrow these feelings. Or the parent may feel threatened and embarrassed, especially by having a male child who identifies or behaves like a female. In my experience, particularly a father may take it as a personal rejection, as if the child was saying he did not want to be like him, when it really has nothing to do with the father, but only with the child's sense of self. The parent may make it clear that this is not an acceptable topic for discussion, much less to act upon, and may even punish the child for expressing his transgender feelings. Children like these are at risk for abuse if their parents lack coping skills, if they interpret the child's behavior as a negative reflec-tion on themselves as parents, or if they are ashamed or threatened by the child's protestations. Transgender children are also at risk for becoming the target of bullies in their peer group and may experi-ence the disapproval of teachers and the parents of their playmates.

When children are very young, we are not yet good at project-ing outcomes. We desperately need more research in this area, but it does appear that some children may outgrow these feelings, and that some children who grow up to be gay men also experience some confusion about having feminine feelings. The most reliable indica-tors seem to be based on the intensity and persistence of the child's feelings about gender identity. It appears that the best we can do for the child, for now, is to protect and support the child's self-esteem, saying it is OK for the child to be who he or she is, and that it is OK to be different. Sometimes it is even wonderful to be different. Geniuses and other gifted people are different. If a child is different in such a way, we teach him to be glad about who he is and how to handle the feelings and social consequences of being different. The same is, or should be, true of gender differences. Sometimes parents bring their child to a therapist for help with this issue. Because it is hard to find a therapist who knows about transgender identity, especially one who will work with young children or the parents of a young child, there is risk that the therapist may have no prior experience in this area. But good intentions are not enough when it comes to transgender. If a therapist lacks adequate knowledge in this area, it is appropriate to make a referral to a specialist. That may even include making the effort to search out resources for the parents, who may not have the same level of skill as the therapist for finding a good resource.

If the child indeed seems to be transsexual, seeing an endocrinologist before the onset of puberty may be indicated as part of the required care. The changes of puberty can be delayed without making irreversible changes. An endocrinologist will know how to slow down or halt this process completely, but temporarily. Many of the changes of puberty are irreversible, but those that are reversible might later need to be reversed. Those that are not reversible can have a lasting negative effect on the quality of life of the child in adulthood. By delaying these pubertal changes, we give the child time to mature mentally and emotionally, so that he or she can participate in decisions about physiological changes that will affect his or her entire future. The cost of such a course of action means only that the child's physical body will mature more slowly. This can have a social effect on the child as well, but still may be less harmful in the long run than the alternate course of action. Thus, helping the transgender child is a two-pronged approach, social and medical, that includes supporting the child's self-esteem and creating as neutral an environment as possible to allow the child to work out his or her own gender identity, and possible medical intervention.

When it comes to poor parenting skills and abuse, I recall one transgender person in particular who, at age 7, was caught dressing in his sister's clothes. His mother made him sit on the front porch in these clothes all afternoon, in full view of all the neighbor children, apparently thinking that he would be so humiliated that he would never want to engage in this behavior again. He was indeed humiliated, but it did not make him stop wanting to be a girl. It just made him loathe himself for wanting it, and it made him much more cautious about getting caught. Of course, he was teased by neighbor kids about this, but by acting very tough he was finally able to live it down. He barred his closet door with steel bars, figuratively speaking, by adopting a very masculine facade.

I also recall the story of another child who seemed to get caught dressing in his sister's clothes repeatedly. Every time he did, his father beat him mercilessly, but he just kept doing it anyway. His mother showed no concern about the beatings, seeming to think the father was doing the right thing and that the behavior had to be extinguished at any cost. These parents seemed to think only that this was "bad behavior" that required punishment, and appeared to have little sensitivity or insight into the feelings of their child. This sad little child seemed to lack the ability to feign being someone he was not, but the foundation was laid for a low-key but lifelong depression (dysthymia).

Oddly enough, I also recall several personal reports by nontransgender adult men, in which they were punished as children by being made to wear a dress. It was done as punishment for some misdeed that was seemingly unrelated to transgender. As adults, they were typically very defensive about their masculinity, but it certainly did not make them become transgender, dispelling a common myth that parents have somehow caused their child to be transgender by planting a seed for it in this way.

Then, of course, there is the common myth about parents who really wanted a girl and the male child becoming transgender in an effort, whether conscious or not, to please the parents. Again, I have found no basis for this in my practice with both transgender and nontransgender clients.

In bygone days, very young children of both genders were often dressed in dresses, I assume for ease in changing diapers. Boys gradually graduated to short pants, and then to long pants, almost as a rite of passage. As far as I can tell, this did not result in the creation of more MTF transgender people in those times either.

When Parents Want a Therapist to Fix Their Child

Sometimes parents bring their transgender child to a therapist, but all too often to a therapist who has no knowledge of transgender and may counsel the parents to discourage transgender behavior in an effort to extinguish it, while gently guiding or even pushing the child to engage in what he or she considers to be more gender-appropriate activities. The child may conform, or he may eventually be rejected by one or both of his parents because of his persistence in his transgender expression. Or, when old enough, he may run away from home to obtain the freedom to be himself.

In large urban areas, children have more opportunities to learn about transgender and may have exposure to the groups of nonconformist teens who can be found as part of the population of homeless street kids in larger cities. Thus, children who live in these areas may have the opportunity to become more sophisticated about diversity at an earlier age, but may also find something to run toward, as opposed to running from an uncomfortable home situation.

Of a slightly different generation, I have known of a couple of transgender people (who, to my knowledge, did not know each other) who spent several of their adolescent years traveling hand-to-mouth with followers of the Grateful Dead. In some subcultures it is possible to mooch off others enough to survive as long as you spread it around and do not mooch too consistently from one single person. In each case, the person eventually found a protector/predator who "took care" of the person until she was able to completely break free to self-sufficient independence. Such is the life of some transgender people. Remarkably blessed with resilience, these individuals, after transitioning, went on to live productive adult lives as the women they felt to be reflective of their true inner personas.

In addition to street youth, with social changes and changes in insurance coverage having led to the closing of so many mental hospitals, with long-term inpatient mental health treatment becoming a rarity, some stories I have heard in the past are not likely to occur again in the foreseeable future, but do still bear noting. Although I never encountered this routinely, I have had at least three clients who were hospitalized in mental health units as children because of their transgender feelings, and have heard a couple of similar reports from transpeople who were not my clients. In each case, the child figured out that the only way to get out of the mental hospital was to pretend the transgender feelings were gone. Of course, this meant continuing to pretend for the benefit of their parents, so there would not be a repeat hospitalization. Another well-built closet!

Having said all of that, I want to mention once more that not all children who express cross-gender feelings grow up to be transgender adults. Some of them grow up to be gay. Some of them grow up to be very ordinary gendered heterosexual adults who are at home with their natal gender and sexuality. The most important thing for a parent to do is to nurture self-esteem and allow the child to blossom into who he or she will become. Children fantasize about a lot of things that they do not ultimately identify with or act upon. One of my husband's nieces, beginning at around age 9, spent nearly two years insisting upon being called Renée. No, that was not her given name, but apparently it sounded more exotic to her than her "ordinary" name. Left alone, even indulged, she eventually gave it up and now appears to be entirely happy with the name her parents gave her.

One of my own sons, influenced by a particular television program, spent several years dreaming of becoming a Texas Ranger, a far cry from his more mature life goals. Had we made fun of these childish dreams, the only result would have been lowered self-esteem. There is no need for adults to be threatened by their children's fantasies, but there is a need for adults to show respect for their children, even as they engage in childish behavior. This is even more true if the behavior proves to be a reflection of the child's true inner self. The longer and more persistently a child is adamant about feeling discomfort with his or her assigned gender, the more likely that the child is truly transgender in the ultimate sense of the word.

A Child Is Not a Free Agent

Children cannot seek therapy independent of their parents. They need parents to give permission, to pay, and to transport them to appointments. Many parents would not want to take their children to a gender identity specialist to address gender-related issues. They would be afraid that if you are a hammer, everything will look like a nail, that their child will be encouraged in behavior that the parents prefer would go away. They cling to the hope that the child's transgender feelings will prove to be a passing whim if they are not validated. For a parent to avoid taking a child to a gender therapist because that person specializes in the problem at hand makes about as much sense as going to an allergist for chest pains out of fear that a cardiologist will be too quick to diagnose a heart problem. However, that is exactly what happens to many transgender children. I have observed it myself when working with young clients and their parents. And what happens if one parent supports the child and the other does not? It is usually the no veto that carries the day.

I do not mean to sound as if I am lacking in sympathy for the parents of a child who persistently expresses transgender feelings. Having such a child has a profound effect on the parents that may last for their entire lives. But I also know that if parents do have a child who is genuinely transgender and they refuse to face it, for whatever reason, that too has a profoundly harmful effect on everyone concerned. So, as painful or frightening as it may be for the parents, it is better for them and their child if they face it squarely. Any ethical therapist is going to exercise great caution when working with a child, being keenly aware of his or her responsibility and dedicated to the concept of "Do no harm." It may be of some consolation to such parents to think about the trust their child must have in them to tell them about having these feelings. It is a gift of love, although it may not seem like it at first glance. Most parents would not want to betray the trust their child places in them.

The Colombo Approach to Therapy

Do you remember the Colombo detective series, with Peter Faulk in his rumpled old trench coat? Do you remember his disingenuous approach to a suspect, in which he would scratch his head and, as if baffled and thinking out loud, say, "There's something here I don't quite understand." This is an approach to therapy I sometimes use when confronted with a contradiction and wanting to draw the client's attention to it. I also think of it as analogous to what goes on inside of a transgender child when trying to figure out gender issues in the face of a family and a world that takes for granted a definition of gender based on genitals at birth.

At some point, the transgender child begins to notice that something does not feel exactly right, but usually lacks insight about what that is. At first, more often than not, the child will assume he is wrong and others are right about his gender, and will try hard to comply with what others take for granted and expect him to be. Unless something happens to open a door for discussion, it may not occur to the child that this could be discussed with a parent, especially with a parent who appears to have already reached a conclusion, or a parent who has been overheard to make disparaging comments about some forms of diversity.

Meanwhile, the child may be scratching his head, figuratively speaking, and saying to himself, "There's something here I don't quite understand." Then one day, on TV, in a magazine or newspaper, in a book or a movie, or by accident on the Internet, he may run across something that fascinates him. He may not even be sure why it does, but he will want to pursue the topic further. Whether as a bolt of lightning or as a gradual dawning, he may come to realize what "it" is. But he may still hide his discovery for a long time.

Is Anatomy Destiny?

Usually the first question asked when a child is born, often even before asking about the health of mother and child, is whether the baby is a boy or girl. This knowledge can affect how parents feel about themselves and how they relate to their child, even as an infant. Women have been known to feel as if they have failed if they do not produce a baby of the sex desired by their husbands. Parents who produce several children of the same sex tend to long for a child of the other sex, and this may influence the entire family dynamics.

I have had more than one client whose mothers had difficulty sustaining pregnancies, but when they did succeed, produced only female babies. These families lived through the trauma of multiple (and sometimes dramatic) miscarriages in repeated attempts to produce a male child. Meanwhile, the girl children increasingly felt as if they were inadequate disappointments along the way to getting a son. In some cases, when a son was finally born, the family then revolved around this child. (Imagine what it would have been like for this child if he had been transgender!) It can certainly happen the other way around, as well.

Fathers have been known to feel that their own masculinity was or was not confirmed by the sex of the baby they produced. Even though it is now known that the sex of a baby is determined by the sperm, we have looked at the woman as the responsible party. Kings have been known to reject (or worse) a wife in favor of another woman who could (supposedly) give them a male heir. Exclusive of transgender, the gender of a child has meaning for the parents, so it is little wonder that having a transgender child is of such importance to parents.

If a child begins to express transgender feelings, and if the parents define transgender as something "wrong" with their child (as opposed to something different), often they will each examine their own parenting and that of the other parent, looking for a cause. As mentioned before, no parent is perfect, so if parents look hard enough, they will certainly find something to which they can attribute "the cause." If they find the fault in self, their self-esteem will suffer. If they find the fault in the other parent, it can put tremendous strain on the marriage and may even lead to divorce.

Even if the parents are able to recognize that they did not cause their child to be transgender, they may not agree as to what should be done about it. They may be very concerned about what other people will think, and sometimes for good reason. Parents who decide to support their minor child in transgender expression may be at risk of being reported to Child Protective Services by someone else who is convinced that the fault is in the parenting. An uninformed or biased Child Protective Services worker may even agree. Obviously, this could have far-reaching consequences.

Magical Thinking Is Like Wishing on a Star

The very young child, with a child's magical thinking (Fraiberg, 1959), will not always be able to distinguish between reality and fantasy. Most of us are familiar with the superstition: If you step on a crack, you'll break your mother's back. Most young children believe in Santa Claus and the boogeyman. Superstitions illustrate how magical thinking sometimes persists even into adulthood. Many adults readily admit to at least one superstition. Do you believe in some form of the paranormal? Have you ever stared at the telephone and willed it to ring? Do you believe that "things" run in threes? The many variations of Murphy's law indicate our half-hearted disavowal of a kind of cynical superstitious belief system. A MTF transgender child may harbor the secret fantasy that even though he is a boy now, he will grow up to be a woman.

Poignantly, many adult clients have told me about having such a childhood fantasy, or of falling asleep every night praying to wake up as the gender with which the child identifies. As the child reaches puberty, he will come to realize that this fantasy, long harbored with both fear and anticipation, is simply not going to happen. With the onset of puberty, there may be a sense of betrayal as the body becomes more masculinized; these undesired physical changes may become a further basis for self-loathing, but may still be combined with a confusing newfound sexual pleasure, and with relief that the "secret" is still hidden (Rottnek, 1999; Burke, 1996).

I recall the story of one transgender person in particular who "suffered" in childhood from a condition called gynecomastia, in which there is excessive breast development in a natal male. In some cases it is symptomatic of some other underlying condition. For this person, that was apparently not the case. However, at the age of 10, he required some other surgery, and without telling the child, the parents arranged for him to have surgical breast reduction while already anesthetized for the other surgery. Whether it was a projection of the parents' own discomfort with the condition or a naive assumption that the child was unhappy about the size of his breasts and would welcome this surgery, we may never know. I was inclined to believe the former, based on the fact that the child was not told in advance. I suspected that the parents were afraid the child would object. The child awoke from surgery to be grief-stricken about the loss of his breasts, feeling betrayed by his parents for doing this to his body without consulting him, but unable to express any of this because it would have required that he openly acknowledge his transgender feelings.

Just Who Is the Opposite Sex?

It has been my observation that one can expect some degree of confusion about sexual orientation to exist if, as a child, a person was confused or conflicted about gender identity. While there are certainly many exceptions, for many people it seems as if the final developmental stage of sorting out sexual orientation, which usually occurs before and during adolescence, cannot be completed until the question of gender identity is first resolved. Many MTF transgender people have reported to me that when they were attracted to a female, they were unable to tell if it was because of sexual desire for her or due to the desire to be like her—to look like her, move like her, to be free to dress like her, to enjoy having and doing the female things she was allowed to enjoy and do, and to fit into the female social circle. Whereas other males may experience erotic pleasure when they look at attractive women, the MTF transgender person will often report looking on with envy and longing, even when they were very young children.

I find this response to be reminiscent of the way a young girl will sometimes look at an attractive older girl and think about the possibly of becoming as attractive and self-assured herself one day. Of course, erotic enjoyment may also be present, but when it coexists with envy and longing to be alike, it can be doubly confusing. The struggle with gender identity, and the concomitant uncertainty about sexual orientation, varies in degree and form among transgender individuals, but it appears to be universal. It can be viewed as parallel to emerging sexuality in adolescents, even though it has been delayed until a different point in life (Berkovitz, 1972; Grinder, 1969).

Although each individual's struggle is unique, reports by my clients and others suggest this struggle with confusion between gender identity and sexual orientation influences the timing of when a person will eventually seek help. Intrapsychic factors such as internalized transphobia or a passive or conformist personality type will also play a role. So will the nature and degree of external forces, such as family attitudes toward diversity, the person's career aspirations, and even the culture of the community in which the person happens to live (for instance, a small, rural southern village as opposed to Berkeley, California). However, I would like to point out that these contrasting environments do not prevent or cause a person to be transgender; they simply influence how the individual will deal with it when it is present.

Being Different Can Be Good

Not long ago, I turned on the television and happened upon a movie featuring Danny DeVito. And then I began to think about the topic of being different in that context. Who could not love Danny DeVito? He's delightful just as he is. I can't imagine anyone wanting to change him, and if they did, he just wouldn't be the Danny DeVito we know and love. If you could make him of "normal" stature, it would ruin everything. Yet, when he was a child, I imagine his parents were concerned about how he would make it in the world, being different. Somehow, he found a way to be happy with his difference and even to capitalize on it. I think his parents must have played a part in that. Danny DeVito is an example of how a person can be different, probably at times a point of concern, and still be able to celebrate the difference. We could do that with our children who are different in other ways too!

More realistically (unfortunately), when parents learn or suspect that their child is transgender, even when it is an adult child, they can be expected to struggle with the reality of it before reaching acceptance. Some parents are never able to do this, and may even abandon their relationship with their child to avoid facing it. The parents who do try to face it will go through a grief process for the loss of the image they formerly had of their child. For parents or other family members it is a process that involves stages that are analogous both to the general grief process and to the coming-out process of the transgender person, that is, coming to terms with the gender identity of their child within themselves, and then in increments to coming to terms with the reactions of others as they become increasingly open about having a transgender child and begin encountering varying degrees of acceptance or lack thereof.

More than anything else, grief is integral to the process of accepting the transgender status of a child (or of any friend or loved one, for that matter). There is grief for the loss of the child they once had, or thought they had. There is grief for the dream of the future that is now irrevocably altered. There is grief about the loss of the once familiar face and voice, the former relationship. Even though there may ultimately be wonderful rewards associated with the new relationship that will be achieved, wherein they may be closer than ever before once they are no longer separated by this huge secret. These rewards cannot be found and enjoyed until the old relationship is "lost." This includes struggling with denial, with anger, with attempts to delay, avoid, or mitigate the outcome, and coping with the fear that the process itself will not put an irreparable wedge in the relationship with the transgender son or daughter before the rewards become apparent. Many parents do not give up hope that the transgender feelings will go away until the (adult) child has had genital reconstruction surgery, as they often see this as the burning of the last bridge and crossing the point of no return. At this time, resignation can finally change into acceptance.

Also integral to the entire process that parents experience when coming to terms with having a transgender child and developing a new relationship with that son or daughter is the breaking of old patterns and establishing new ones. Just the use of the new name (instead of the name that was once so carefully chosen for the new-born baby) and the associated new pronouns can be a tremendous change in pattern. The kinds of gifts they buy each other, the cards they choose to send, the kinds of things they do together, the ways they touch each other—all of these things change.

Sometimes, within the privacy of the family and with the mutual agreement of family members, I suggest having a conversation in which the transgender person uses the wrong pronouns when referring to another family member. This helps the transgender person appreciate just how difficult it is for family members to break old patterns of pronoun usage, because the transgender person usually finds that it is more difficult than she realized to use unaccustomed pronouns. It also helps the family member who hears or is the object of the altered pronoun usage in the conversation to appreciate how much it grates on the ears and the heart of the transgender person when the pronouns used feel wrong to her. This little game often helps everyone involved become more sensitive to the feelings of each other and facilitates the process of change.

There is another exercise that I picked up somewhere along the way and sometimes use with a client during a session, to help her be patient with family members who are struggling with change. I give the person a pencil and paper and the following sentence:

The city of San Francisco is in the United States of America.

I then ask her to write it without any capital letters, and to not dot an *i* or cross a *t* or put a period at the end of the sentence, so it would look like this:

the cily of san francisco is in the uniled slales of america

If she makes a mistake, she must start over from the beginning. This exercise can be a difficult and frustrating experience, but it can help her appreciate how difficult even simple changes can be when a pattern is deeply engrained.

Choosing a New Name

When it comes to names, I always think of a particular transgender person who loved her mother very much and told me a story about changing her name. All her life she had felt that her mother was never entirely pleased with her. Even as an adult, she still sought her mother's approval and love. Privately, I wondered if her mother ever really wanted to have children because this was a pattern I had seen many times before I began working with transgender people, when I was working with abused and neglected teenagers. The more rejecting the parent, the greater the approval-seeking behavior, and the more it was fraught with anxiety and heightened intensity. You could almost see the very young child within, desperately clinging to the parent as if survival depended on it, as it once did.

However, the resolve of the above-mentioned transgender person to go forward with her transition was unwavering. At that time, her mother lived halfway across the country from her. She tried to discuss her transgender with her mother both by phone and by mail, but was getting nowhere. Her mother just kept avoiding the subject or not responding, and finally avoided her phone calls altogether.

So, she planned a trip to visit her mother in person. When she got there, she sat down with her mother face-to-face and told her she was changing her name to fit her new gender role. She had the "Request for Legal Name Change" form with her, all filled out except for the new name. She said to her mother, "Mom, you named me once. I am offering you the opportunity to name me again." She was willing to place this decision in the hands of her mother, and to live with the choice her mother made, but her mother turned away, saying, "Do whatever you want."

I don't know if this mother had any idea what a beautiful gift was being offered to her, but she turned her back on it. What else could the transgender person do but walk away? Just as a parent may grieve for the loss of a child they never really had, so can a child grieve for the loss of a parent they never really had. I find this one of the more poignant transgender stories I have ever heard.

However, a heartwarming story in close competition is the story of the parents who went to talk with their neighbors who were the parents of the local bully, a child several years older than their child. When they sat down to talk, the other parents told their son to go on outside and play, but the parents of the transgender child interceded and asked that he be allowed to stay. They explained how they had discovered they had made a mistake, that their child was not a boy, as they had believed up until now, but was really a girl, and that they were planning to let her start living that way. They told about their struggle in making this decision and how they were very concerned about doing the right thing for their child. They talked about their fears, including the fear that other children would not understand and would be mean to their child. At this point, the "bully" child spoke up and said, "You just leave that to me. I'll make sure no one picks on your child!" Negative energy was transposed, and a once harmful tendency was given a constructive outlet. The transgender of one child changed the life of another child for the better.

The Role of Geographic Location

Historically, people who wanted to get lost in a crowd because of their differences have migrated to large urban areas. My practice is in an affluent mid-size, mid-western college town. The poor, marginalized urban transgender street youths will not usually be found here. They will be found in Detroit (about an hour's drive east) or Chicago (about a 3½-hour drive southwest), but not here. And, if they were to be found here, they would not be able to get to my office (no bus service and too far from town to walk). Even if they could get here, they would not be able to afford the cost of a session. The location of my office and the cost of my services would make seeing me prohibitive for transgender street teens. This illustrates how the geographic location will influence the kinds of clients a therapist will see. In turn, it influences the therapist's approach because the needs of the client are different, and the kinds of ancillary services that are available in the community are also likely to be different.

This is a situation that is beginning to change. In relation to my own practice, it is becoming increasingly common to find, on the University of Michigan campus, a small but vocal group of very bright queer-identified students. For some of these young people, their determination to be different is based in a residual of adolescent rebellion, but for others, it represents a genuine claiming of their independent identity. Differentiating between these two can be a challenge for a gender therapist. I believe that, as different as they are, young people like these will eventually make the world a more hospitable place for their urban street sisters and brothers. They will reshape the way we all look at both gender and sexual orientation.

Children and Transgender Adults

When someone close to a child is gay or transgender, adults may worry about the effect on the child if the child finds out or is told about it. Understandably, the first question often is, "Should the child be told?" I believe that, in the best of all worlds, we should talk openly about these things with children. Still, it may not always be necessary to tell a child, such as when a parent is an occasional cross-dresser. This is especially true if the other parent is not in agreement about being open with the child or children. It is of critical importance to the well-being of the child that the adults come to terms with the transgender issues themselves, if at all possible, before telling the child.

The age of the child will determine the ability of the child to understand and will also influence the ways the parents approach the topic. Of secondary consideration will be the social milieu of the child. In general, the younger the child, the more easily the child will take the information about a transgender person in stride. Very young children will simply be accustomed from earliest memory. The way a child should be told should be in keeping with the developmental stage of the child and couched in terms that are familiar to the child. For example, a very young child who has enjoyed dressing up, even for Halloween, can be told that even grown-ups sometimes enjoy dressing up. This may seem to trivialize the transgender in the eyes of the adult, but it is in keeping with the experience of the child and the ability of the child to understand. As the child grows, with each new stage of development new questions will come up, and these can be answered as they occur. In this way, the child will adjust in increments that are in keeping with the child's own rate of development.

The expectations the adults have of the child should be realistic. You cannot make a 6-year-old behave, think, or feel like a 10-year-old. To expect it would be unfair and would result in failure to obtain the desired outcome. If a child cannot yet keep a secret about what we are giving Mommy for her birthday, then the child cannot be expected to keep it a secret that Daddy likes to dress up like Mommy. If the child is young, but of school age, the parents will need to anticipate that the child may go to school and say to a teacher, "My daddy has a dress just like that." The sweet innocence of children can be hard for adults to handle. In light of this possibility, the parents will need to discuss telling the teacher in advance, helping her to understand and prepare herself to answer any questions that may come from other children in the class. There will also be the question of talking to the parents of the child's playmates. Yes, there is the risk that some people will not be accepting, but in general, the more open people are about the transgender, the better the overall acceptance. People tend to fear what they do not understand, so helping them understand is worth the effort.

If the parent or some other person close to a child will be transitioning to live in a different gender role, there is no way to avoid telling the child unless the transgender person is excluded from the child's life. Even then, some explanation will be needed. When the transgender person is one of the child's parents, the person cannot be excluded without harming the child, so facing the situation is usually best for the child and everyone concerned. But it must be emphasized that the adults will first need to work through their own feelings and attitudes, and at least get them under control, or their negative feelings will contaminate what they say and do with the child, and with anyone else they are telling, limiting their ability to help the child deal with the situation. It is usually true that the child will get through this situation just fine if the adults are coping with it in a constructive manner.

For this reason, when a therapist is working with a transgender client who is a parent, it may mean taking time to work with the nontransgender parent, if possible, as this person will be critical in determining how well the child will do. With the child, the topic should be treated as matter-of-factly as possible, acknowledging feelings and allowing the child to find his or her own solutions. What to call the transgender parent in public is an example of this. I have seen many different ways of handling this often thorny question. Keep in mind that things are happening over which the child has no control. When it is possible to give the child control over some part of it, such as thinking of a nickname for Daddy, this small measure of control will help the child feel some ownership of the process.

If possible, the child may benefit from having a therapist of his or her own to talk with, but now we are talking about therapy for each individual member of a family. This is something not everyone can afford. If resources are limited, it is my opinion that working with the parents is the first priority, helping them do better at working with the child themselves.

Children of Divorce

Divorce is traumatic for children. The work of Judith Wallerstein and others is forcing our society to face this unpleasant truth (Waller-stein, Lewis, & Blakeslee, 2000). Often, for the children of a trans-gender parent, there are issues of divorce in addition to those of the transgender itself. If the adults involved handle the transgender issue with maturity and mutual respect and consideration for everyone involved, the children will usually adjust well to having a transgen-der parent. Of course it is a challenge, but contention and animosity between parents is even more painful and damaging for children.

It is a challenge for a child to have a celebrity parent, but we do not think these children should be protected from this challenge. In spite of all the negative publicity about the private lives of Bill and Hillary Clinton during the years of his presidency, I never heard any-one suggest that Chelsea Clinton should be removed from parental custody. I'm sure it is hard for a child to have a movie star as a parent, or a rock star. It's even hard to be the child of a minister. It is hard for a child to have a parent go away to war, but we take it for granted that this must happen at times. We do not even take away custody of children from parents who are convicted criminals, unless they have specifically been convicted of abusing their children.

Many warm and humorous stories have been written about peo-ple being raised by loving but eccentric parents or parent figures, of which *Auntie Mame* (Dennis, 1955) and the two fathers in the film *The Birdcage* (Nichols, 1996) are examples. Through these charm-ing stories, we realize that the most important thing for the child is to feel loved and safe. When a child has that security, he or she will likely be resilient despite the vagaries of the parent figure. Why would we even consider taking a child away from a devoted and con-scientious transgender parent?

Becoming an Expert

When adults make the child an expert, it builds self-confidence, and in turn, the child will be able to respond in informed and construc-tive ways if questioned by others. If the others are critical, and if the child feels confident in knowing, the child will be insulated by recognizing that it is the ignorance of the other person, and not a flaw in the family member or the child that is causing the problem. There is a short video that I have found to be very helpful. It is called *No Dumb Questions* (Regan, 2001, http://www.nodumbquestions. com/). This is a tool that can be used by a therapist or simply by family members who are dealing with similar situations.

So instead of hiding reality from a child, we should teach the child to cope, which all parents should do anyway. One important way that adults can help a child cope with having a transgender parent (or other person in his or her life) is by making the child feel like an expert. The video *No Dumb Questions* is an ideal model for this approach. Answer all the child's questions as truthfully as possible, using age-appropriate and correct terms. Do not talk down to the child. When you don't know the answer to a question, say so, and either search for the answer (good role modeling for the child) or, if you find that no one appears to know the answer to a particular question, tell the child that.

If the child is met by an inappropriate or cruel remark, the informed child will know it is coming from the ignorance of the other person. It may still hurt, but knowledge with be a buffer. Talk with the child in advance about the fact that there are such people. Discuss some of the things these people might say, and discuss ways the child can respond to such remarks. Tell the child in advance what he or she should do if an incident does occur. Tell the child who he or she should tell and what will probably happen if he or she does tell. Tell the child to tell you if an incident occurs, even if the child is pleased with the way he or she handled it, so you will be able to affirm the child. If the child tells you of an incident, do not intervene directly unless it is a dangerous or very persistent occurrence. Instead, discuss it with the child and try to help the child find ways to deal with the situation personally. Brainstorm with the child for possible solutions, using the child's own ideas as much as possible.

If adults use this approach, the child is much more likely to tell the parent if things like this occur. Often, when children don't tell, it is either because they are afraid they did the wrong thing and will be scolded, or they are afraid the adult will intervene in a way that will make matters worse in some way. They might simply fear they would be embarrassed, or they may fear that adult intervention will exacerbate the situation. While this may or may not be true, premature intervention on the part of an adult disempowers the child, and the child feels this, even if unable to articulate it. When an adult intervenes in a situation that belongs to the child, the message is that the child is incapable of handling it himself or herself. Sometimes children really do feel able to handle the situation, and want to do it themselves. They will only tell the adult if they trust the adult to respect this.

The child needs to feel like an expert in terms of having information about transgender, but also about approaches to problem solving. Just as an experiment, I did an Internet search for "problem-solving techniques." You would be amazed at what a wealth of information is available from so simple a search. In today's world, no parent with Internet access needs to feel at a loss in teaching these skills to his or her children.

For children, the world is full of amazing and inexplicable things. Parental behavior is often among these. Being open and providing as much information as possible in keeping with the ability of the child to understand, encouraging discussion to allow for expression of feelings and to correct misunderstandings, is essential. It is perfectly all right for the adults to tell the child that they too do not understand some things about transgender, but simply know they must find ways to be loving and supportive with each other.

The issues related to children will change with time, but will continue to present themselves in new ways. What about the teenager's friends and neighbors who drop in unexpectedly? How will the prospective in-laws be told? Who will walk the daughter down the aisle at her wedding? Then the initial cycle of questions will return to be recycled with the advent of grandchildren. Like coming out in general, it is a never-ending process. It is helpful to remember to treat the issue as a matter of personal privacy, but never as a shameful secret. Personal privacy has many levels, and the question of when and with whom we share personal information is determined by circumstance and the relationships involved. For the therapist who is working with transgender clients and their family members, it is important to keep all of these things in mind.

When it comes to working with transgender adults who are parents, even if they are not planning to tell the children about the transgender, at least not at the present time, if the circumstances lend themselves to it, I tell them to begin while their children are very young, teaching the children to respect everyone, even when they are not like themselves. Teach them that content of character is more important than outward appearance. Teach them to be sensitive to the feelings of others, to appreciate gender and sexual diversity as well as racial, national, ethnic, and religious diversity. These things can be taught compatibly with teaching children about personal safety. Tell them that, while most people fall in love with people of the opposite sex, there are some people who fall in love with people of the same sex, and that most people are sure of their gender from the very beginning, but some people are born with bodies that make their gender uncertain (intersex). Some have ordinary-looking bodies, yet are still not sure about their gender, or feel as if their bodies do not fit with their sense of their own gender.

These things can be talked about with even very young children. When children are of school age, you can tell them it is likely that someone in their class is or will grow up to be different in one of these ways, or that someone in their class has a loved one who is different in this way, perhaps a favorite aunt or uncle. Tell them that if they speak badly about these things, they cannot be sure who they might hurt, and that the other person will not trust them to talk about these things, but will only avoid being their friend. Ask them if this is the way they would like it to be.

Developing an accepting attitude toward diversity will be good for children whether or not they have a gay or transgender person in their lives. If, at some later time, they are told or find out that they have a transgender parent, they will be better prepared, their attitude will be more positive, and they will do better with knowing. If both parents can work together, asking, "How can we best help our child understand and cope with this?" it will be the best gift they can give their child and will be an exercise in employing good parenting skills for each of them, regardless of what happens to their marriage. No child should be put in the position of having to take sides or choose between warring parents.

Keeping that in mind, a therapist should not be quick to attribute every problem the child is having to transgender. If the parents are not getting along, or if they have gotten or are getting a divorce, the child may be more troubled about the conflict between the parents and the divorce, or its prospect, than about the transgender itself. The child may blame the transgender because that happens to be what the parents are arguing about, but the underlying and real concern is the divorce. Under these circumstances, the therapist should always take divorce issues into account when working with a child or with the parents of such a child.

7

Wives and Partners

When referring to wives and partners, I am including anyone who is in a serious primary relationship with another person, in this case a natal female in a relationship with a natal male who identifies as MTF transgender on some level. For the sake of brevity, it will be easier to simply refer to wives and husbands.

For research purposes, to distinguish between a passing infatuation and a serious commitment, I looked at only married couples (man and woman) and unmarried couples who had been together for at least a year. However, I will now speak more broadly to include other people, singles and couples I have known both in and outside of my clinical practice, people who were not part of the research study. Since I have no experience of gay male couples where one of them transitioned to female, and since the MTF couple is beyond the scope of the present work, my focus will be on those MTF couples whose initial appearance is of a heterosexual couple. I will begin with a review of how the typical transgender husband has contributed to getting himself and his wife or partner in this situation in the first place. Understanding this is vital to understanding the perspective of the wife as well.

"I Don't Know Where I'm Going, but Please Come With Me"

Usually, the transgender person begins coming out to family members while he himself is still in the process of exploring his transgender. Although it is best not to wait and spring the transgender issue on family members late in the process, still, it can complicate matters for everyone involved when they are told about the transgender feelings early on because the transgender person may not yet be certain about his own course of action with regard to gender role, and family members may feel that they are aiming at a moving target as they try to understand and adjust. They may view the tentativeness of the person who is still in process as an indication that this is a passing phase that may spend itself with time. Why should they be quick to accept and invest in a new gender role when there still appears to be reason to hope that the transgender person will reconsider and not go through with a full transition? In fact, the transgender person may not yet be sure if that is what he wants to do, or should do, or can do.

In order to understand how it is that an adult natal male who is transgender may have made such a considerable investment in the male role in life, and how difficult it is for him to even begin to discuss these feelings with his family members, it is necessary to retrace how he arrived at this dilemma. Otherwise, it can be all too easy to either discount the validity of his feelings or become exasperated with him for not being more honest about them all along.

Consider again how we, all of us, decide if a child is a girl or boy. Naturally, we use the most obvious indicator. And in the vast majority of cases, the genitals at birth are a reliable indicator of gender. Most of us, including parents, take this for granted. In the absence of obvious physical anomalies, the people in an infant's world make the assumption that the gender identity of the child will coincide with his or her genitals. Even before a baby is born people often ask, "Do you know if you are having a boy or a girl?" Typically, after the birth, the first question people ask is, again, "Is it a boy or a girl?" Gender plays a very large role in forming our perceptions of other people, including infants.

And this matter of gender and genitals is also taken for granted by the transgender child, even if it does not feel right, because what else is a child to think? When the child has a gender identity that is different from that which is taken as a given by all the people in his world, when this has been the way his body was from his earliest awareness, it takes time and increasing maturity for the child to recognize the nature of the problem, then to obtain information, and finally to reach some level of understanding and self-acceptance. This would be a challenge for anyone!

I am not suggesting that we abandon the use of genitals at birth as an indicator of gender, but only that we recognize it as a tentative conclusion. What I would like to see is a society that is more at ease with diversity; that does not think being different means that something is wrong; that is comfortable with giving even very young children information and with talking about sexuality and gender diversity without fear of destroying the innocence of the child, without fear of encouraging him, or even causing him to be different. Imagine a parent teaching a child about the diversity of the world, and including things about sexuality just as naturally as he or she would if talking about the many animals or climates of the world, and asking a young child, "What would you do if you thought that you or someone you know was different in one of those ways?"

What an opportunity for an open and frank discussion with a child, for teaching sensitivity and stimulating thought! In such a world, a child would feel free to tell a parent about worries and fears, and the parent would possibly have the opportunity to save the child from many years of anxiety and pain, and to help him with the gigantic task of charting a course for his life. Isn't that what most parents profess to want? However, parents can only help a child reach a level of comfort with self that they possess themselves. If a parent is riddled with self-doubt and fears and biases, he cannot help his child grow beyond his own level of growth. Beyond that point, the child is on his or her own.

Much has already been said here about the transgender child, and also about the transgender adult who, prior to facing his own transgender, has built a life in the male role and invested highly, perhaps because of ignorance of other options, and perhaps in an attempt to avoid even considering the frightening possibility of being transgender. And so, for these and perhaps other reasons, the transgender husband has not been honest with his wife about his transgender. She feels understandably angry and deceived when she discovers this, but this is a story with two sides and one where no one is necessarily evil, but only human, with each party muddling through the best each knows how to do.

A Transgender Person May Wonder If It Is Too Late

Sometimes, when the child—or the adult he becomes—realizes his gender role is not working for him, he may live in despair for many years before discovering that help is available. Even then, he may feel he cannot avail himself of this help because he has made too large an investment in the male social role, made too many commitments, or would hurt too many people if he even questioned his gender role, much less experimented with it or outright changed it. He may feel so ashamed of his transgender feelings that he expects others to feel the same way, thinks they would find him repulsive if they knew his secret. He may fear being abandoned by everyone he loves if he does not keep his secret to himself. Thus, it is extraordinarily difficult for a person to become ready to deal with a transgender identity. This is especially likely to be true when the person does not live in a location where he might encounter diversity in human expression, perhaps on a daily basis, while he is still too young to have made extensive commitments to the role of an adult male (assuming he is a MTF person).

Emotional Energy as a Limited Resource

I have a theory about another factor that I believe plays a part for individuals who do not come out about having transgender feelings until they are in the middle years of life. This theory relates to emotional energy. When people are young, they are full of all kinds of energy. Unless the gender-related feelings of the transgender person are particularly intense, it may only take a small part of their total fund of emotional energy to suppress them. But never being able to be fully one's self is a hard way to live. Always having to suppress a part of one's self uses up a constant flow of energy, like having a short in your electric meter might do.

With time, this fund becomes depleted from overuse, while at the same time this energy is not as easy to regenerate as it was when the person was younger. Eventually, for some transgender people, this fund of emotional energy becomes so depleted by the effort to keep the transgender feelings suppressed that the person can no longer successfully maintain it. The feelings come surging to the surface, demanding the attention of the person and often compelling him to act on them. Of course, the level of intensity of the feelings would also play a part, as would the nature and level of opposing forces in the world of the transgender person. This would be another possible area of study for some energetic person, a retrospective study of those transgender people who do not become aware of or act on their transgender feelings until later in life.

Bargaining and Avoidance

The use of avoidance techniques is common to all human beings, but transgender people have several unique ways of trying to avoid facing transgender feelings that are routinely reported and are specific to their situation (Samons, 2001). One of these is to enlist in military service (Brown, 1987). This may be done both as overcompensation for feminine feelings and as an attempt to "make a man" of himself, to make the transgender feelings go away. This is but one example of a flight into hypermasculinity. It serves to hide the individual's feminine feelings from the other people in his life, which makes sense when he still hopes to rid himself of these feelings. Typically, this flight into hypermasculinity serves only to delay addressing the issue. In the long run, it makes addressing the transgender feelings with family, friends, and co-workers more difficult because these later claims to transgender will seem even more incongruent to others when they have perceived the person as being masculine in the extreme.

Additional avoidance techniques include seeking employment in a field that is considered stereotypically masculine, or committing to a marriage or a religious belief system that would reject transgender. These techniques can be combined, as when the person chooses to pursue a relationship with someone who is involved in a religion that is very intolerant of diversity. When such a relationship results in marriage, it can be doubly restraining. These actions may be thought of as attempts to reinforce a flagging internal psychological structure of defenses and diminishing emotional energy by creating external structure as additional reinforcement (Samons, 2001). These commitments to other people or life situations and goals not conducive to addressing one's underlying transgender issues can help to suppress transgender feelings for a time, but they appear to reemerge eventually, turning the prior commitments into impediments to facing the issues.

This is not to imply that transgender people are lacking in psychological or emotional strength as compared to the average nontransgender person, but rather as a testament to the intensity of transgender feelings and how emotionally exhausting it can be to keep these feelings in check in the face of unrelenting pressures for social conformity. Neither is it meant to imply that the emotional attachments of the transgender person are mere coping strategies. Indeed, they often involve strong feelings of love and devotion. However, once the person has created this external structure, what was originally intended as a safe hiding place may become a trap from which it is difficult to break free, further delaying the decision to seek help. But eventually, like a claustrophobic person, the need to break free intensifies. If the efforts to avoid the issue were ultimately successful, we would not now find ourselves in need of addressing the corresponding dilemma of the woman who has married such a person.

Wives of Crossdressers

There are many women who are happily married to crossdressers. Some of them say that they would not trade these husbands for ones who do not crossdress, but who might be abusive, or drink too much, or be unfaithful, or have a pejorative attitude toward women. The crossdressing husband, while he may crossdress, may also be kind and generous. He may like to talk about feelings, may like to go shopping with his wife, might even like to cook or otherwise help around the house. He may be a great combination of husband and best friend.

Still, when most women first find out about their husband's cross-dressing, it comes as a shock. How much of a shock depends on how and at what point in their relationship they find out. When a therapist first sees such a wife, she has usually sought therapy in the midst of a crisis, so the first thing the therapist needs to do is help her calm down. The therapist must try to prevent her from taking precipitous action while she is in an agitated frame of mind and should not be making major decisions.

Some women simply dig in their heels and say they will not tolerate any form of femme expression in their husbands, upon threat of divorce. A woman like this would probably not agree to see a gender therapist, as she would be afraid that the therapist would be sympathetic to transgender behavior. Even agreeing to see such a therapist would, in her view, be a form of concession to the transgender. She may not even want to hear the word *transgender* or any associated words. She typically views transgender behavior as a choice, and she would then believe that taking a stand could make it go away. Since any recognition of this as a valid issue would be viewed as opening Pandora's box, such a woman would not likely agree to come to a therapist who knew about transgender. She might be willing to seek a therapist who she expected would agree with her, that the cross-dressing is wrong and must stop—end of discussion.

If it is the crossdressing husband who has come for help, the therapist should make every effort to include the wife whenever possible. But if the wife refuses to come with him to an appointment, the therapist can only try to reach the wife through him, by guiding him to use the most constructive and effective approaches when talking with her.

Some crossdressers will not want to include a wife in therapy, and the person certainly has the right to refuse, but the therapist should point out the possible implications and consequences for the marriage, and help the individual weigh the pros and cons of this decision. Although, in most cases, including the wife would be desirable, one must keep in mind that a therapist is not God, and that the client knows himself and his wife better than the therapist and might be a better judge of what is best in his individual situation. After all, it is the client, not the therapist, who must live with the consequences, good or bad, of the choices he makes.

The woman who is likely to be seen by a gender therapist is someone who has recently found out about her husband's crossdressing. She would probably be in shock, angry, and full of questions and fears. It is vitally important to ask how she found out. Did he simply decide to tell her? Did she accidentally discover something that led to questions and a confrontation between them? Sometimes a husband will be careless, with a sort of behavioral Freudian slip, because he wants to tell her but cannot bring himself to do so. Sometimes a wife will discover an item of femme clothing that she knows is not her own. She may think he is having an affair. In a sense this is true, but the other woman is his woman within. However, the analogy is good to keep in mind, as it may relate to how the wife feels about it.

In some cases a wife may have had lots of evidence that she chose to ignore, using some of the same defense mechanisms that her husband has used. Recognizing this can help each of them (if the therapist is able to work with them as a couple) understand the other better. In other cases, the wife will have known about the crossdressing even before the marriage, but she may have thought it went away. Being afraid to talk about it, with the idea of letting sleeping dogs lie, is really avoiding the subject due to fear of the truth—back to denial. Then, something may have happened to make avoiding the issue impossible.

In some cases, there has been open recognition of the crossdressing, but there may have been a recent escalation that has frightened the wife. Where once she may have viewed it as a fairly harmless pastime, she may have begun to worry about where it is leading: Will he want to transition to live as a woman all of the time?

In a marriage with a crossdresser, much negotiation needs to take place so that the feelings of both parties are considered. This often revolves around seemingly mundane questions such as: Will he shave his legs? Will he wear a nightgown to bed? Can he paint his toenails? Can he buy another pair of shoes? How much money should he spend on dresses? Will he be allowed to borrow her clothes? If, when, and where will he be able to go out in public dressed? All of this adds up to a single question: How far will this go?

The wife may have been tolerant of a certain amount of crossdressing, but the husband's transgender feelings may have increased, and the wife may have become frightened or angry about the change. She may feel that she has already been very lenient and is now being asked to accept more and more transgender expression. Her fears about how far this will go may have increased. What he is telling her about his transgender feelings may be what is frightening her. He may have begun to question whether he needs to transition.

The initial questions a wife will have are fairly predictable. She will need brief answers to these questions, followed by more in-depth discussion and more detailed information as she is ready to deal with it. When a person eats a dinner, it is best done one bite at a time. Shoving the entire meal down in one bite will cause choking! Part of the job of a therapist is to titrate the progress in a way that is manageable for the client. To do otherwise can precipitate a crisis. In the situation at hand, it could lead to the breakup of the marriage, when this may be unnecessary and harmful to all the parties involved. Even if the marriage will ultimately need to end, it should be done in a thoughtful manner that takes into account the needs of all parties (both spouses and any children). This cannot happen if it is done in the midst of a crisis.

The wife will want to know: Does this mean he is gay? And the therapist can tell her that it is not likely, that most crossdressers and transgender natal males are attracted to women, with only a few exceptions. While the person who transitions to live as female often does experience a shift in sexual attraction as the opposite sex is redefined, it would be premature to discuss this with a wife who has just begun to face the fact that her husband crossdresses. It is also true that some crossdressers are attracted to natal males while they are in femme mode. This is very different from being gay and is not the case with everyone who crossdresses, but the therapist cannot give guarantees that the woman's fears are groundless. This issue will need to be addressed in more depth, possibly with both members of the couple. A medical checkup may be in order, to make sure neither of them has a sexually transmitted infection. Included may be preparing the wife (or both of them) for what she will tell her doctor about the reason for the request. It is common for both crossdressers and their wives to neglect getting needed medical attention because of their fears of exposing the secret of the crossdressing.

The wife may wonder if her husband is disappointed in her sexually, and if this could explain his transgender behavior. Sometimes a woman hopes this is true because, if it is, there may be something she can do about it. It would mean that she has some control over it, that she might be able to make it go away. This may be part of the larger question of "Why is he doing this—what causes transgender?" Understanding that it is not her fault and neither has her husband chosen to be this way can reassure her and also be a source of additional fears. Knowing it is beyond her control can leave her feeling helpless. If he cannot fully control it, then where will it lead?

She will probably be worried about who else already knows or will find out about his transgender and what will happen if they do. This is a matter that requires some negotiation on the part of the couple regarding if, when, and how much to be open about the crossdressing, including with the children. Also a matter for negotiation is the question of how much money can be spent on "her" and where "her" things will be kept. The outcome will be influenced by whether he is going to transition, but it is important to keep in mind that he may not know the answer to this question right away. He should be discouraged from making promises that he may not be able to keep, even though right now he may think it is a promise he could keep.

When discussing this issue with a wife, I frequently use the analogy of all couples on their wedding day. They usually make vows to each other in good faith, in general believing that they will be together for life, but also knowing about the divorce rate, and knowing that many couples do divorce. They hope it will not happen to them, but know it is possible. No one has any guarantees that their marriage will survive. No one has any guarantees about marital fidelity. Wives of crossdressers are no different from other wives in this respect. It may be small consolation to the worried wife of a crossdresser, but it can help put her situation in perspective.

If the husband will not be transitioning, then many of the questions that require negotiation may remain matters of personal privacy, and those who need to know can be limited. When other people are told, how and what they are told will be important for the therapist to discuss with the couple. They may need help with improving their problem-solving and communication skills as they negotiate around who should be told, and the question of which one of them has a right or responsibility to tell or not tell whom. When the situation permits, I usually suggest that they begin only by saying that there have been some long-standing questions about gender and that the person has begun to explore what they mean, but does not yet have answers. This prevents others from jumping to conclusions that can become expectations that do not serve the person well.

When a woman first finds out about her husband's crossdressing, she may look at him and wonder if she ever really knew him. She may ask herself how she could have failed to recognize something as important as his wanting to dress as a woman. She may wonder what else he has not told her, and often there is more because he has had a lifetime of hiding and keeping his secret. He is probably fearful of losing her, so he has tested the waters by telling her just a little, to see how she will react. He may be afraid that if he told her everything at once, she would panic and leave him. He may not even be sure what "everything" is, as he may still be trying to work this out for himself. He may reason that telling her a little at a time will give her time to adjust in increments, and when he sees how well she handles one piece of information, he can decide whether to chance telling her more.

There is a certain amount of logic in this thinking, but the problem is that she can never relax and assume he has told her everything. When there are multiple shoes and you don't know how many, you will always be waiting for the next shoe to drop. It puts a major strain on the trust in the relationship. It is important to talk about her desire to know when he has told her everything when he may not even know what everything is himself. There will not be a single solution that fits all couples, or even a way to predict what will work best with any individual couple, but still it needs to be addressed.

Then, the wife may wonder, "What does this say about me to myself and to others? If I am attracted to him, does it mean I have lesbian tendencies? How would I feel about it if I did?" Or she may be so firmly convinced that she does not have lesbian tendencies that she will become entirely turned off by him, sexually. This reaction would be a possibility if she really has no capacity for being attracted to females, or even if she simply has unaddressed homophobia. And there is the ever-present question of what others will think if she stays with him. Will they think she is a lesbian? Will they think there is something kinky about her? And if he transitions and they stay together, that will surely make her appear to be a lesbian. Hopefully this is a woman who is not afraid to explore her own sexuality and who is not so concerned about what other people think as to allow that to determine how she will live her life.

Most often, this is a woman who defines herself as heterosexual and who entered a marriage with a male-bodied person to have a heterosexual relationship. She will probably not define herself as lesbian, but she may be able to see some bisexual tendencies in herself. If not, she may not be content to remain married to him, especially if he transitions. In that event, it becomes the task of the therapist to help them come to terms with going separate ways, and to do so with as much mutual respect as possible, especially if there are children involved. This includes even grown children because there will be events in their lives when they may want both parents to be present, and there may be grandchildren who would benefit by the mutual regard of their grandparents.

Understandably, this concern about the possibility of his wanting to transition is ever present. It is helpful to remind the couple of that. No one, transgender or not, has any guarantees about the future. Aside from divorce, no one of us can guarantee that our spouse will not die relatively young. We cannot predict so many things in life, and transgender is only one among these many things.

As a therapist, I am not above calling upon Dear Abby, who printed a letter several years ago that was apropos to this topic. She quoted a woman who had given birth to a child with Down syndrome, and who had subsequently become an activist for awareness of Down syndrome (Emily Pearl Kingsley, elected in 1976 to the board of directors of the National Down Syndrome Congress). In giving a speech, this woman told about being asked what it was like to have a baby and find out this baby had Down's. To paraphrase, she described it with the following analogy:

> Suppose you had dreamed all your life about going to Italy. You weren't sure if it would ever happen, but still you worked toward it, and dreamed about it; the fountains of Rome, Michelangelo's *David*, the Sistine

Chapel, the Coliseum, the quaint villages and streets and shops. And finally, after a long time of saving and dreaming, it finally happened. You had saved enough money and you made your final plans. You bought your ticket with mounting excitement. The day of departure arrived and you boarded the plane and off you went. After several hours, the plane began its decent and the flight attendant said, "Welcome to Holland."

"Welcome to Holland?" you gasped. "Wait a minute! There's been a terrible mistake. I'm in the wrong place." Calling the flight attendant, you explained that you had bought a ticket to Rome. But the flight attendant only shrugged and said, "Well, I don't know what happened, but you are in Holland."

So, there was nothing else for you to do but get off the plane, but you hated being there and kept thinking about what you were missing and how unfair it was that this had happened to you. But gradually, as time passed, you began to notice that while Holland was certainly not Rome, it had its own beauty. It had wonderful canals, and windmills, and tulips, and famous artists of its own. And, while it would never be Italy, it was not such an awful place, and it was possible to enjoy being there, while still looking back on occasion to think about how wonderful it might have been to see Italy.

Very few of us get through life without some major disappointments, and rarely does life turn out just as we had planned. This does not mean we cannot have a good life. Different is not necessarily bad. Different is only different. This can be as true for the wife of a transgender person as it is for someone else for some other reason. There needs to be time for grieving our losses, but healthy people eventually get beyond their grief and get on with their lives.

If the husband does feel the necessity to transition, there will be many more questions related to telling others, including their children, if they have any. Some couples do remain together, and happily so. However, their relationship certainly changes. It may or may not continue to be sexual. And this is not simply a question of her sexual orientation, but what about his (now hers)? What if the wife makes the hugely loving decision to stay, only to have her once husband discover that he too is now attracted to men? Now they are two heterosexual women married to each other. What a conundrum! (And since our laws were not written with this kind of situation in mind, legal decisions about these things seem to be made judge by judge and case by case. However, the transition itself does not automatically nullify the marriage.) This question of possible change in sexual attraction on the part of the transgender person should be addressed before it reaches this point.

When Other People Ask, "Are You Going to Get a Divorce?"

The marriages of some of the participants in my research study survived for the duration of the study, and some did so even without the support of family and friends. This was also true of clients and others I have known since the study ended. It was sometimes true even when the transgender partner transitioned to live full-time as a woman, and even when this person had genital reconstruction surgery. Typically, in those cases where the marriage did survive, the couple went to great effort to educate others about transgender issues and reassure them about their happiness together. Most of the time it seemed that when others understand that the individuals involved were being thoughtful and making carefully considered decisions, and that the choices they were making were truly voluntary, and that the wife was genuinely happy even though the relationship may have evolved into something different than when it began, they became more able to let go of their own concerns and allow the couple to find their own solutions.

This particular research study was not of sufficient duration to project the number of relationships that were yet to dissolve or to determine how many participants would form new relationships. Other therapists who specialize in transgender consistently report clinical observations that indicate the number of marriages to survive gender transition of a spouse is small. Nevertheless, some can be saved, and many more possibly could be saved if there were more social support for the couple.

A therapist who is not experienced with transgender issues may not fully appreciate just how complicated it can be to work with transgender individuals, much less with couples, but working with couples is a vital part of this work. Everyone must begin somewhere, so being inexperienced is not, in and of itself, a reason to avoid work with transgender clients. But it does mean accepting responsibility for educating one's self and, if possible, finding supervision with someone who does have this experience. For those who choose to do so, this would necessitate learning to work with couples as well as individuals. The broadening of clinical experience in this way will force the therapist to grow and become a better clinician. Skills will be developed and honed that will be useful with all clients, regardless of what their issues might be. Since I believe that the prevalence of transgender in one form or another has been grossly underestimated, I think it would benefit all therapists to have some basic understanding of gender identity.

8

Some Further Comments on Transgender and Findings of the Current Research

For the therapist who chooses to specialize in transgender issues, the learning processes is never ending because social change continues to happen within the world of transgender and in the larger society. Each of these realms impacts the other, resulting in changes on both sides. When I first began writing this book, the term *transgenderism* was considered acceptable. Now, the reader will note that this term has been eliminated from the pages of this book. This is because so many transgender people now consider this term, specifically the *ism*, to be pathologizing, so, out of respect, I have changed it.

The Uniqueness of the Transgender Path

The journey of each individual is unique. Not every transgender journey includes taking hormones or going for surgeries of any kind. Some clients need more help than others with interpersonal, social, and emotional coping skills. Some require more emotional support than others. Some are more introspective and can benefit from processing insights more than others. For all of these reasons and more, the help a therapist offers to transgender clients must be geared to fit the needs and requirements of the individual client. This helps explain why being able to contrast the number of sessions with the length of time in therapy, when examining the research presented here, offers a more accurate picture than would be obtained by counting either one alone.

Experience With Transgender Expression

The participants in this research entered therapy with different levels of knowledge and self-awareness. Their life circumstances varied, as did their goals for integrating degrees of feminine expression into their lives. Some were more concerned than others about the risk to existing relationships and the impact of their transgender feelings and behaviors on their significant others. Many were uncertain as to what they wanted and what they could or could not do about their transgender; clarifying this was frequently a primary goal of therapy. Others were entirely clear about what they wanted to do, right from the start of therapy. Some were closeted and fearful, having never before spoken about their "secret." Others were already living as female when I first had contact with them. Because of their widely varied characteristics, it sometimes seemed like trying to compare apples and oranges, even though they all had transgender issues.

Some of the research participants were fairly knowledgeable about transgender issues at the start of therapy, while others had almost no information at all. Some were so well read on the subject that they put me to shame and forced me to continue to grow in my own knowledge just to keep up! However, the majority had informally given themselves female names, and many of them reported going freely out in public while crossdressed.

Feminizing the Voice

Some MTF transgender people are able to feminize their voices quite well with practice. Some availed themselves of voice training. But taking feminizing hormones does not reverse the timbre of a voice that has been masculinized by androgens. For some MTF transgender people, this is one of the greatest obstacles to being able to blend in socially as women. While voice training can help, some opt for vocal surgery. This remains an unreliable and risky medical procedure. Sometimes it is very effective, but the outcome can range from almost no noticeable change to having a voice that sounds like Minnie Mouse when her tail is being stepped on. For this reason, I discourage clients from having this surgery, but make it clear that I will respect their right to decide otherwise. While I did not measure this procedure for this study, I can say that I have known several people who had this surgery, but I have only had two clients, to date, who did so. The results were varied, just as I described.

It must be kept in mind that an individual can do a considerable amount of walking around in public while dressed en femme without verbally interacting with others. Browsing around a mall is an example of this. Using the voice to interact with others can be avoided up to a point. Therefore, verbal interaction can be viewed as one increment of cross-gender experience and a way of gaining confidence in the ability to function en femme.

Do Clothes Make the Woman?

There is another question that makes it difficult to assess the degree of femme expression of the individual: how to define *being dressed as female*. If the person is wearing jeans, tennis shoes, and a sweatshirt, no makeup or jewelry, and a neutral hairstyle, would this be considered being dressed as female only if the sweatshirt has a flower on it? Would a bird on the sweatshirt qualify? Our society allows so much latitude in female dress that defining *being dressed as female* is a challenge for most of us unless it is far enough removed from the middle ground to be clearly feminine. It seems unfair and inaccurate to say that the transgender person would have to be wearing a skirt when half of the natal females we meet in public may not be doing so. Therefore, regarding this research, the arbitrary decision was made to leave it to the individual to self-define when she felt she was dressed as female, although this definition was reserved for outer clothing that was observable to others, since many transgender people wear feminine undergarments even when dressed outwardly as men.

Defining *Community*

The transgender community, geographically scattered as it may be, includes educational organizations, peer support groups and social clubs, and a variety of other organized social and political groups. It includes a vocabulary and a body of literature, the availability of conventions, and other gatherings scheduled at regular intervals throughout the country. It includes recognized community leaders, political activist groups, and support services and professional

organizations geared to address the needs of the transgender population. It also includes a wide variety of Internet resources. While
the term *community* usually refers to these things being established
in a specific geographic location, this is not necessarily the case,
and the existence of these many components certainly constitutes a
community.

Forty-six of the 97 participants in this research project had little
or no initial awareness of the existence of a transgender community.
Some of them were no more than vaguely aware of the existence of
other transgender people, while others had been actively involved
with other transgender people and with transgender community
organizations before entering therapy. Still others were living full-
time as women before entering therapy and knew about the transgender community, but had no desire to become involved with it.
They simply wanted to live their lives in the gender role that seemed
right for them. However, I used involvement with the transgender
community as one of many possible indices of an individual participant's level of transgender experience because it played such an
important part in the lives of so many of them.

Taking the Risk to Explore Gender Expression

At the start of therapy, 72 of the participants reported experiencing fear and shame about being transgender, which had a significant
effect on the individual being willing or having the courage to experiment with feminine expression. Some had never completely crossdressed; some had done so only in the privacy of their own homes.
For some, their fears were based in reality, but for many, their fears
were simply of the unknown, sometimes exaggerated and out of proportion to the risk involved in experimenting with gender expression. Others were experienced and entirely comfortable with their
femme presentation in public.

Some had feelings of fear and shame even at the most recent point
in therapy, but these were usually the participants who had been in
therapy for the shortest periods of time. Some came to therapy knowing (or believing they knew) that they wanted to fully transition to
eventually have GRS. Others were looking for help in evaluating the
social, interpersonal, emotional, and financial costs and benefits of
transition, or to achieve a modicum of self-acceptance with some

compromise between their transgender feelings and desires for feminine expression and the other parts of their lives that were incompatible with transition.

The Role of Hormones

Sixty-four of the participants reported never having experimented with female hormones before the start of therapy. Fifty-three of them were taking hormones on a regular basis at the most recent point in therapy. This figure is skewed by the number of early dropouts, an artifact that is also frequently reported by colleagues who work with this population. These are the people who come in briefly for information and then do not return, either because they decide to try a different approach to transition or because they retreat back into the closet. Some are daunted by the potential cost, both financial and otherwise, and need time to decide if it is really worth it to them. For some, we can only speculate as to what happened to them. Others may eventually return to therapy, more ready to address their concerns than they were initially. For many, their primary goal in entering therapy is to gain access to hormones. They want a letter and a referral to a physician who can prescribe them. Therapists should not be offended by this, but should go right ahead and assess the client. The person may really not need therapy, or perhaps only a little support and information to help make good decisions. If the therapist sees the need for therapy around some aspect of the person's personality or the person's life, this can be discussed with the client after it is recognized.

Generational Differences

Transgender people often report a history of leaving treatment with other therapists, and the reasons they give us lend insight into the process. When the transgender people participating in this research study reported leaving previous therapists, it was usually because either they did not feel comfortable with that therapist, they did not consider that therapist to be knowledgeable about transgender issues, or one of them moved to another geographic area. At other times, the person was looking for a quick fix and may have sought a therapist who was willing to put her on a faster track to transition. The person may have failed to recognize that therapists have a responsibility to be certain that the client has sufficient information to make well-informed decisions, and that her life is adequately prepared for the major steps involved in transition. In order for a therapist to do this, it is necessary for the therapist to get to know the client and become familiar with her life. The two of them must take the time to establish a collaborative relationship in which they will be working together to improve the quality of life of the transgender person. This need not be overly time-consuming if the client works with the therapist to move the process forward, but sometimes a transgender person will not understand or want to invest time (and pay for) for this process to occur. Because the transgender person feels so ready, she may fail to recognize that it is not realistic or fair to expect the therapist to make the desired referrals and write the associated letters of recommendation without first making this assessment. She may also fail to realize that there are potential benefits to herself in this process that are beyond just getting the letters and referrals she sees as her immediate goal. This includes the availability of professional help from someone who is already familiar with her situation should some unforeseen problem develop along the way.

With the participants in this research, as well as with any other transgender client, I made every effort to ask questions about the history of use of feminizing hormones in an open-minded and nonjudgmental manner, so as to obtain the most truthful answers possible. However, a certain percentage of subjects may have taken hormones before the time of initial contact with me, but may have been unwilling to acknowledge it. If hormones were obtained without prescription, the subject might be fearful of legal consequences for herself or for her source, thinking the therapist might report this to the authorities. She may have been unaware of or skeptical about the confidentiality of the therapy process (although information about privacy rights was always given to each client).

Disclosures That Are Withheld or That Come Belatedly

Many clients did disclose the various extralegal means they had used to obtain hormones. The hormones may have been prescribed for someone else, such as birth control pills prescribed for a wife or female friend, used with or without her knowledge or permission. The client may have purchased hormones from someone else, another private person who obtained them in some unknown way. Transgender people also have been resourceful in finding doctors who can be persuaded to prescribe hormones for them without the involvement of a therapist. In these cases, the doctor may be unethical or simply well intended but unaware of the WPATH *Standards of Care* (HBIGDA SOC), or may be a strong believer in patient self-determination. When a transgender person finds such a doctor, she will usually protect this resource, both for her own possible future needs and for the benefit of other transgender individuals. Out of loyalty to the doctor, appreciation for his or her help, and concern about getting the doctor in trouble, the person may be reluctant to report it to a therapist.

Probably the most commonly reported way of obtaining hormones outside of the WPATH *Standards of Care* is via the Internet. The laws with regard to dispensing hormones and other drugs that typically require a prescription in the United States vary from country to country, so it is possible to buy certain hormones from a pharmaceutical company in another country and have them mailed to you. Many transgender people report obtaining hormones via the Internet, and for some it becomes a reason for entering therapy.

Among my own clients, they say they realized it was risky for them to be self-prescribing without medical supervision, and they sought a therapist as a route to obtaining a referral for medical supervision. I have known therapists who viewed this as manipulative behavior and who required the individual to stop taking hormones as a condition of beginning therapy with them. They view it as an attempt to get a quick referral to an endocrinologist. I consider this a way to encourage a client to lie to the therapist and tell him or her what he or she wants to hear. After all, the transgender person has already obtained hormones and can continue to do so without this referral. I consider coming to a therapist and asking for help to obtain medical supervision a positive step that should be encouraged. Of course there are some individuals who will use this method as an end run around the SOCs, but still, the best interest of the client must come before everything else, and medical supervision is foremost. The therapist should still do an evaluation before giving the referral, and if some contraindication comes to light, this can be discussed with the client. The therapist is under no obligation to make the referral if it does not seem to be in the best interest of the client.

Meanwhile, through the Internet, hormones may be purchased from countries with fewer regulations on pharmaceuticals than is the case in the United States, and also at lower cost. This issue is being brought to public attention as senior citizens and others are finding it a less expensive way to obtain the prescriptions ordered for them by their own doctors. Our laws have not kept pace with our technology, so the use of the Internet to obtain prescription medicines is not well regulated. Some think it should not be. Some think it would be impossible to regulate even if we wanted to do so.

The Pattern of Hormone Use

Another benchmark used in this study pertains to whether feminizing hormones were used, and if so, when they were used. It must be kept in mind that hormones were not part of the past history of many of the participants, and many did not want to take hormones because they did not plan to fully transition to the female role. Others would have liked to take hormones, but were ineligible because of medical risk or unwillingness to risk the loss of a primary relationship. Fourteen participants entered therapy already taking hormones. Another 35 began taking hormones regularly under the WPATH *Standards of Care* during the therapy process, and were doing so at the most recent contact. The remaining 38 participants were not taking hormones at either the earliest or latest point of contact. Some of the 38 would have been among those who had entered therapy most recently, had been seen for a shorter period of time, and were continuing therapy when this study was completed. There is no way of knowing how many of them would have eventually engaged in hormonal therapy.

As indicated in Appendix D, of the 38 people who did not take feminizing hormones during the time period covered by this study, 7 reported change in sexual orientation at the most recent point of contact. This was a statistically significant number (Table D.11). Of the 35 people who were not taking hormones at the start of therapy but began taking them during the course of therapy, 5 reported change in sexual orientation at the most recent point of contact, also a significant number (Table D.11). Of the 14 people who were already taking hormones when they entered therapy and continued to do so at the most recent time of contact, 3 reported a change in sexual orientation. This was also a significant number (Table D.11).

However, since the change was consistent among those who did and those who did not take hormones, it must be emphasized that it does not appear that taking hormones caused the change in sexual orientation observed here, but was merely concurrent with that change.

Table D.9 illustrates this pattern and also shows that hormones do not appear to have a causative influence on change in self-reported sexual orientation. Rather, self-acceptance as a transgender person, increasing self-confidence, and a sense of ease in the social female gender role appears to play a more important part in a person's willingness to reexamine sexual orientation. This is an extremely important finding.

A Brave New World

The Internet is a growing force in transgender awareness. It is worth noting that the changing technology of communication and transmission of information is having a huge impact on the transgender population, just as it is having on the rest of the world. Transgender people now often have their first contact with other transgender people via the Internet. The impact of this experience has frequently been reported to me, both by clients and by others in the transgender community. A wealth of knowledge (and a fair amount of misinformation) can be obtained from the privacy of home, anonymously. Transgender people can readily discover resources that provide information about the transgender condition and about services geared to the needs of transgender people—information that might formerly have been hidden from them or might otherwise have taken months or years for them to discover. Clients report that if they were able to find information in local libraries, they were often afraid to check it out and take it home, as if it would somehow be on record that they were reading these things. And how would they hide the book from family members once they took it home? Examples of Internet resources can be found in Appendix E. Many Internet resources provide links to other related resources, so I have only listed a few, and in no way do I mean to slight the many other very good resources. I just want to give the reader a place to begin.

There is yet no way to know how increased access to information will affect transgender people in the future, but if access to information means people will seek professional help sooner, we could expect to begin seeing people entering therapy at an increasingly younger age. In fact, that is exactly what appears to be happening. It would then follow that the parents of transgender children would become more aware of the issue and would gradually become more open to educating themselves. When this happens, it will be easy for them to obtain information via the Internet. This is one of the most hopeful prospects for the future in offering early hormonal intervention for transgender people.

The Individuality of Self

The participants in this research project had differing styles of feminine expression and differing self-images, some of them seeing themselves as not exactly male or female, and feeling most comfortable with themselves when presenting androgynously. This study cannot inform us as to whether these behaviors and preferences were transient parts of the exploration of gender or more permanently incorporated forms of gender identity and expression. In addition, just as one might see a wide range of feminine appearance among natal females, the same was true of the participants in this study. Many natal females choose not to wear makeup, and some view certain styles of clothing and grooming as the trappings of a paternalistic society that keeps women subjugated to men and prevents them from developing their potential as individual human beings. Some are just indifferent to social pressure and the latest fashions, while others find great enjoyment in them. Women pursue personal fulfillment in a broad range of ways, from Dolly Parton to k. d. Lange, by presenting themselves androgynously or as flamboyantly feminine. Some seem to settle comfortably and inconspicuously into the middle ground of the traditional female role. The participants in this study aspired to a similarly wide range of femme presentations.

Feminine Heart—Masculine Voice

Transgender individuals are bound to some extent by physical characteristics caused by pubertal masculinization (or lack thereof) of their bodies that limit (or enhance) the potential for achieving a feminine appearance. A woman may be petite, with fine bone structure and delicate features, or she can be robust and buxom and still be feminine. However, in the natal male transgender woman, extreme height, large, angular bone structure, the body type of a linebacker, large meaty hands and feet, and a voice like gravel can all make blending in as a woman difficult or perhaps impossible—however feminine she might feel at heart, and despite all the feminization she can obtain from hormones or surgeries or personal grooming. Others seem to be phenotypic naturals for transitioning to female. Most fall somewhere in between.

Learned (as far as we know) components of feminine behavior include body language, mannerisms, and personal taste in clothing, and even the way vocabulary is employed. These learned behaviors come more naturally to some transgender individuals than to others. Examples would include knowing how to choose a style of dress that conceals masculine-shaped or bowed legs, or remembering not to sit like a sumo wrestler. Other examples might include holding a door open for another woman (which women often do, but in a slightly different way than men) or waiting for the other person to sit before being seated (usually masculine), being observant of details, and being solicitous about another person's comfort (usually feminine, except in courting situations). This may include the use of an authoritarian, competitive (masculine), or collaborative (feminine) approach in interpersonal relationships. Some MTF transgender people might be considered naturals in that they never adopted masculine mannerisms in the first place and have little relearning to do insofar as socially stereotypical female body language and behaviors are concerned.

Other Subtleties of Speech

Speech styles also include examples of learned gender-related behaviors. Although most of us take these subtle things for granted, we tend to notice incongruencies when they present themselves. There are words, inflections, and ways of phrasing that are more characteristic of males or females. The person who enters therapy with a natural female style of speech has less to learn and unlearn and can more easily go out and interact with others in public and may be more readily accepted as female. This type of person appears to gain more ready acceptance among family, friends, and co-workers. After transition, those who do not know that this person is transgender will be unlikely to question her femininity. If and when others do find out, it may be hard for them to imagine her having ever been male. Even family members and friends who have known the person since before transition seem to find it easier to let go of the transgender person's former masculine image when masculinity was never pronounced.

Sexual Fantasies and Partner Preference

When a participant reported fantasizing about both self as male and self as female, this was defined as being at ease in both gender roles. Similarly, when someone reported fantasies where either a male or a female sex partner was an option, this was defined as being at ease with both genders for sex partners. When one of the above categories is not mentioned in this discussion or in the associated table, it is because the category contained no data. This occurred when no one self-reported as fitting in these categories or when a case record did not contain the data.

As can be seen in Tables D.6 and D.11, change in sexual orientation was exclusively and significantly in the direction of becoming more interested in a male sex partner as the person was more able to imagine herself as female.

At the start of therapy, 36 participants had acted on their fantasies of self with a male partner, as compared to 42 who had done so by the most recent point in contact. Although this is an increase, it still represents fewer than half of the participants. This may be accounted for in part by the fact that most of them had not progressed in therapy or in the transition process to a degree in which they could readily support acting on these feelings. This is not to imply that GRS was the goal of all participants, nor to suggest that the goal of therapy was for them to become more open to having a male sex partner, but rather to say that many participants had not yet reached a point in their therapy at which they would have felt sufficiently at ease with themselves in the female role to act on their fantasies with any other person—whatever these fantasies may have been.

Many participants reported they felt the need to have a feminized body before they would be willing to act on fantasies of sex with a male partner. The degree to which this was true was subjective and varied from individual to individual, some defining it more as a need to really "feel like a woman," others saying it would require the feminizing effects of hormones, and yet others saying GRS would first be necessary. For this reason, it is important to examine the numbers of people who did or did not want or were not able to have GRS, as well as those who might want GRS at some future point but had not yet resolved this question or reached a point in their journey at which they would be ready to go forward with GRS. Although at the latest point of contact only 17% had decided they did not want GRS, another 4% had not yet given it consideration. Twenty-four percent wanted GRS at the latest point in contact but were unable to have it because of contravening medical problems or lack of funds. Another 11% were as yet undecided about GRS at the latest point in contact, while 28% were planning to have surgery eventually, but had not yet reached that point in their journeys. At the most recent point of contact, there was a combined total of 76% in which the primary fantasy included self as female, whether with a male or female partner.

It should be kept in mind that many people have fantasies they enjoy only as fantasies. They have no desire to experience them in reality. However, the fantasies used when collecting the data for this research were only those that were spoken of by the participants as something they actually would like to experience at some point in time.

Only 17% of the participants had had genital reconstruction surgery at the most recent point in therapy. Of these, the majority were in the initial postsurgical adjustment phase, during which one would not expect them to necessarily be ready to act on their sexual fantasies—in part because of the physical healing process, and in part due to the process of psychosocial adjustment to the surgical outcome and the new anatomy.

In the initial postsurgical period, the transgender person may understandably lack confidence in the appearance of her new genitals and the ability to "pass" sexually. She may be undecided as yet about whether or when to be truthful about her transgender status with a potential sex partner. There may simply be no potential sex partner available. She may be fearful of rejection or of possible violence from a potential sex partner if she is truthful, or conversely if not truthful and later discovered. She simply may be reacting to her somewhat unique circumstance of being a "virgin" all over again (assuming that the person was not a virgin when formerly in the male role—a situation that, as far as I know, is unique to transsexuals: to have a second chance at virginity), and having to make difficult decisions about once more becoming sexually active with another person, this time as a woman, and perhaps for the first time with a man.

If she does begin to experiment sexually by dating men who prefer female sex partners, the postoperative woman is often self-conscious and unsure of herself, and may look for clues to suggest whether the man finds her attractive. This is similarly true for most young teenaged girls; the analogy of reexperiencing some aspects of adolescence is useful. If the man does not call for a second date, the transsexual woman may be quick to assume it is due in some way to her sexual or social inadequacy, that he did not find her physically appealing or sexually attractive, or did not enjoy her companionship and conversation. In other words, like most young females just beginning to date, she has to develop confidence in her role as a woman and accumulate some experience in dealing with men in a dating situation—not to mention a sexual situation. These are issues that should be routinely discussed with clients, when appropriate, in the course of therapy.

How Gender Identity Influenced Sexual Orientation

As shown in Table D.6 in Appendix D, even at the beginning of therapy, the vast majority of people who participated in this research defined themselves as female in one way or another. One simply identified herself as female. Some preferred the term *transgender woman* or *transwoman*, and some defined themselves as MTF crossdressers. At the beginning of therapy, individuals were often reluctant to step across the gender threshold far enough to verbally define themselves as women. Saying these words out loud for the first time was (and is) a powerful experience for many transgender people, enhancing the reality of their transgender identity. This phenomenon is common for people in general when saying out loud any challenging reality they are faced with in life. For example, when someone close to a person dies, the first time, and for a while thereafter, that person tells someone else the death has occurred, it can seem as if the words make the death more real. It plays a part in the person coming to terms with the death of the loved one. The same concept is behind the practice in Alcoholics Anonymous meetings to introduce oneself by saying one's name, followed by the statement "and I am an alcoholic." It clarifies and reinforces the reality in one's own mind. It is a way of taking ownership of that reality.

There are many possible reasons that some transgender people might be reluctant to claim their female identity, especially early in their process, even when that is the identity that feels most true to them. This may be based on a lack of sense of entitlement, since they were not born female. It could be due to the fear of offending natal females. They may even fear the possibility of having their right to claim their female identity challenged. If they do not feel confident in their female identity, they may not feel adequately prepared to defend it to others. Certainly, some of the participants in the research study felt all of those things.

The Importance (or Lack Thereof) of Outward Appearance

Twenty-two of the research participants expressed confusion about their gender at the time of initial therapy contact with me. They indicated that they had male bodies, and they did not understand why they felt the way they did. Only one person identified himself as male at the beginning of therapy, and even he may have done so based on the socialized belief that gender was defined solely by genitals at birth, and by the way male hormones had masculinized his body. He may have felt this was the only valid criterion and that his feelings were not relevant when answering this question. Some of the participants believed these factors would forever prohibit them from becoming fully female. Others stated that they were fearful of appearing presumptuous or of being challenged if they dared to call themselves women, even though this was how they thought about themselves. They felt as if they were not entitled to call themselves women and experienced guilt if they did so, in spite of their inner feelings about themselves. While this might be the case with any transgender person early in the process of addressing her gender feelings, it was especially true of those whose bodies were the most masculine in appearance. While some had unrealistic hopes of looking like their ideal woman, others doubted that they would ever be able to look like anything but "a man in a dress." Even when the potential existed for them to blend in easily as female, they were afraid they would look ridiculous and become a laughing stock to others, and may even have been told that this would happen. Little wonder they were fearful!

Some of the participants stated the belief that their female gender identity was based on prenatal hormonal sexualizing of the brain, and that they had been female or partly female all their lives, regardless of genitals of birth. Although we have no definitive answer to the question of causation, this is the essence of a theory that seems to be the most supported by recent research. It is the theory base from which many professionals who specialize in gender identity issues, including myself, approach treatment. This is because it seems to fit best with our clinical observations, with patterns observed in other parts of nature (Roughgarden, 2004), and is also the theory that is least likely to do harm to the client. There are exceptions to this, and skilled therapists will use differential assessment and treatment planning, adapting their approach to the needs of the individual client.

There was one individual in this study who identified as male at the beginning of therapy, but it is essential to avoid the assumption that this was the same one who identified as male at the end of the study. We must also avoid the assumption that the single individual who identified as female at the start of therapy is the same individual who identified as female at last contact.

Forty-five of the participants identified themselves as transgender females at the start of therapy and 62 at last contact. None identified as bigendered or as transgenderists at either point in contact. Twelve identified themselves as transgender at both the start and end of contact. Twenty-two of them were unsure or confused about how to define their gender identity at the start of therapy, while only six of them reported feeling this way at the most recent contact. This represents a significant change over the course of contact (Table D.11, Appendix D).

Cultural Influences

Once an individual laid claim to her female identity, she would often become aggressive in proclaiming her right to it, much like someone who has just been freed from oppression might initially go to an extreme, indulging in the newfound freedom, perhaps even becoming highly sensitive and vocal in the extreme in defending it. Observations from the interviewing process confirmed that semantics and beliefs about causation definitely played a part in the choice of the words these individuals used to define themselves.

The process through which individuals defined or redefined their sexual orientation was both complicated and fascinating to observe. It was unavoidable that individuals were influenced by the culture in which they had been socialized and in which they would be required to continue to function. In reviewing these many influences, we must acknowledge that American society has been profoundly shaped by religion, especially by Judeo-Christian beliefs and traditions. We must assume that these research participants were impacted and shaped by these prevailing religious and social influences to varying degrees. Similarly, these influences would have affected most of those who comprise the social support system of the individual, the people to whom she had emotional or economic connections, or both.

To one degree or another, these same influences had an impact on every one of the other categories discussed above. Most obvious was the category of religious background of the person herself. However, there were several other ways in which this influence manifested itself in the lives of these individuals. For example, prevailing cultural and religious beliefs would have influenced the length of time it took each person to become willing to examine the issue of her own unique transgender identity. When participants were married, the marital status of an individual sometimes represented an attempt by the person to conform to social expectations, which were, in turn, shaped by religious influences. When participants were unmarried, the marital status of an individual sometimes represented an attempt to avoid the risk of intimacy or marital involvement in the face of uncertainty about gender identity.

The impossibility of being able to give separate specific weights to the various social influences was an unavoidable shortcoming of this study. Ultimately, these social influences had an impact on the ability of the individual to think objectively about sexual orientation.

First Awareness of Being Different

Although the people who participated in this study usually reported transgender awareness at an early age (26% by age 3 years), many did not understand what they were experiencing when they were young. Even when they began to figure it out, most didn't have a name for what they felt. They had to wait until they were older to discover the words for what they felt, to learn that there were others like themselves, and that there was something they could do to resolve their transgender conflicts and make their gender role conform more closely to their core gender identity. This gradually emerging awareness tended to be a lengthy process, sometimes not coalescing until the onset of puberty, and sometimes even much later than that.

When asking a person about her age at first awareness, it was necessary to clarify the question so the person could understand exactly what was being asked. If simply asked, "When did you first know you were transgender?" the person might give an answer based on when she first knew what "it" was called. If, however, she was asked, "How old were you when you first became aware of things that you now recognize as indications of being transgender?" the person might say, "When I was 4, I knew I fit in better with girls than with boys. I knew I preferred to play with girls and play at the things girls played more than I liked to do the things most boys liked to do. Even other children seemed to make assumptions about me fitting in better with the girls than with the boys, but I didn't know why until much later." Others might say they remembered playing dress-up with their sisters, or perhaps with a neighbor girl, but only later discovered that not everyone did this. Some even reported that they were convinced from earliest memory that they actually were girls or would somehow magically grow up to be girls, despite any evidence to the contrary.

Because of the usually gradual nature of gaining awareness, some exploration of this question needed to take place in therapy before the person could designate an age of first memory related to being transgender. While doing this, a therapist would need to exercise due caution not to lead the client, but simply to assist in examining the question.

The age at first memory related to feeling transgender, whatever that first memory might have been, may actually have been more a function of when the person recognized that what she was experiencing was something out of the ordinary for natal males. This realization may have been the actual reason the activity or feeling was impressed upon the memory of the child, whereas other indicators may have occurred earlier, but nothing may have happened to impress them on her memory.

As may be seen in Table D.6 in Appendix D, by the most recent point in therapy fully 75 (77%) of the participants defined their gender identity as entirely or nearly entirely female. This acceptance of the femme self could be viewed as a point at which their perceptions of their sexual orientations could also begin shifting, or at least could undergo reevaluation, since many of the participants fantasized about themselves as female with a male partner, though few had acted on these fantasies. It was common for a person to report that the fantasy of self with a male partner could not be acted upon for the time being because it would not feel right until she had the body of a woman (i.e., was feminized with hormones or GRS), as it would only feel right when the two sex partners were of opposite sexes.

Some reported an occasional fantasy of self as female with a male partner, but would still firmly define themselves as oriented to females. To understand this, it is essential to keep in mind that most people have sexual fantasies they have no desire and no intention of acting upon. For example, being taken forcibly is a fairly common sexual fantasy of females, and sometimes of males, but does not mean that the person wishes to be raped. S&M activity is typically engaged in as a role-play of a fantasy, taking the fantasy out of the realm of pure imagination, and yet keeping it out of actual reality. Most of us rehearse new behaviors in our imagination as a means of helping ourselves evaluate what it would be like to engage in that behavior, to help us decide whether to act on it, and to prepare ourselves to act, if that is the eventual choice. For many of the people who participated in this research, the fantasy of self as female with a male partner seemed like a matter of curiosity as to what that would be like, a further attempt to explore how it feels to be a woman. In such a case, the fantasy of sex with a male would not be indicative of sexual orientation, but rather part of the process of consolidating a female gender identity. For others, the fantasies were probably more like rehearsal in preparation for experimenting with this behavior. In each case it could be viewed as part of the process of reconsidering sexual orientation, a process that would be a necessary step in undergoing a change in sexual orientation.

Sexual Orientation Begins With "Who Am I?"

Table D.7 in Appendix D shows that at the start of therapy, 18% of participants preferred a male sexual partner (whether or not they had acted upon it). By the most recent point in therapy this figure had risen to 27 participants. Conversely, at the start of therapy, 61 participants reported the desire or the actual experience of having a female sex partner. By the most recent point in therapy this figure had decreased to 48. These figures show significant change in partner preference over time, as also may be seen in Tables D.9 and D.11 (Appendix D).

Smaller groups of participants were either unsure (five) or had no preference (five) with regard to sexual orientation at the start of therapy. The same number reported being unsure about partner preference (five) at the latest point in therapy, but these were not necessarily the same people who reported being unsure at the start. In other words, some who were at first unsure moved on to more certainty about a male preference, while others who initially considered themselves attracted exclusively to females began to question this preference and felt unsure about it.

Those who could be defined as bisexual increased from five to nine by most recent contact. Two reported interest in another transgender person as a sex partner, but this was readily explained as being a safe way to experiment with sex in the female role, and therefore not expected to be a lasting preference. There was a combined category of asexual and autosexual, with asexual being defined by the person reporting a long-standing history of little or no interest in sexual activity of any kind, and autosexual being defined as a long-standing history of little or no interest in sex with a partner, while the person did enjoy masturbation. These categories were combined for the purpose of this study because neither group was interested in partnered sex, which was the focus of this study. The lack of interest in sex with a partner, as reported by these individuals, appeared to remain fairly consistent throughout the course of therapy, with a slight decrease from 10% to 9%.

To Enjoy One's Own Gender Is Normal

None of the participants in this study identified their sexual orientation as autogynephilic. This may be partially attributable to a bias of this research. I would remind the reader that, as an integral part of therapy, all participants were given information about the wide range of normal human sexual behavior and erotic responses. Although there are instances of pathology that occur in all populations, in my opinion the term *autogynephilia*, in the vast majority of cases, tends to needlessly pathologize what might better be viewed as a normal human sexual response. The transgender population has already been overly pathologized, and to define a behavior as paraphilic only when it is engaged in by a transgender person, but not when other people do it, is unfair and inaccurate. It is natural and healthy for human beings to enjoy their own bodies. Most men and women find it sensual when they think of their bodies as looking attractive. Many of us dress and groom ourselves in specific ways for the erotic feelings this creates in us. These are the very same behaviors that have been labeled autogynephilic in transgender people when they find the exploration of their female identity to be erotic.

To illustrate this point, I often cite two examples from theater and film. One is from the movie *Flower Drum Song*, lately experiencing a revival on stage, but made memorable in the film starring Nancy Kwan (Directed by Henry Koster, 1961), in which she portrays an erotic boudoir scene, grooming herself and singing the Rodgers and Hammerstein song "I Enjoy Being a Girl." The other example is a scene from *West Side Story*, in which the character Maria sings "I Feel Pretty" (Robbins & Wise, 1961). Both of these are examples of females grooming and enjoying their own female bodies in an erotic manner to which most females can relate.

Rather than giving this response a pejorative label, it seems to serve the transgender individual better to encourage self-acceptance of commonly occurring, normal, and harmless sexual behaviors and responses. This is not to say there is no such thing as autogynephilia, but only to say that it does not appear to be common but, because of loosely defined criteria, is at high risk of being overidentified.

Neither are these statements intended to deny or ignore the fact that MTF transgender people are at times sexually aroused by the thought or sight of their own bodies en femme, because participants in this research certainly did report this experience. They reported that this response occurred most frequently under certain specific circumstances, such as during adolescence and young adulthood, when their libido was at its highest, or when crossdressing was fairly new and novel, or when it was done furtively and therefore fraught with anxiety and excitement related to taboo behaviors or guilt or fear of possible discovery.

For some people, crossdressing was sometimes engaged in specifi-cally for sexual arousal during those certain times in their lives, and it did, for some, have a transient paraphilic quality. However, as the individual matured out of adolescence, or at a later time became more at ease with the female role, this response tended to diminish until it fell within the more normal range of responses. Dressing en femme then appeared to be primarily a source of self-comfort, relegating the use of crossdressing for erotic enjoyment to a transient artifact of the transgender journey, not at all unlike the experience of many nontransgender people in adolescence and young adulthood, when self-pleasuring tends to be most frequent and fantasizing about self as flawlessly attractive and sensual is common. During those times, this kind of fantasy may be a normal part of the arousal template of the individual, unworthy of being labeled autogynephilic.

The Desire to Be Pretty

Even after the transgender individual has become comfortable in the female role, the fantasy of self as an attractive and sensual female may be used for sexual pleasure, in much the same way it may be used by nontransgender females, such as in the examples from theater cited above. Especially in the absence of a sex partner, this type of fantasy may play a significant part in sexual gratification. Moreover, since transgender people often report having used fantasy of self as female to help themselves function sexually in the male role, it is hardly surprising that vestiges of that pattern would remain for at least a period of time through the transition process. As long as this is not causing a problem for the individual, it seems to serve no constructive purpose to pathologize it by labeling it a paraphilia. No one who participated in this research study considered autogynephilia to be a sexual orientation, but only one of many possibilities for a rich fantasy life.

Most interesting of all was the fact that when change in self-reported sexual orientation did occur, it was consistently toward greater interest in a male partner, never the other way around. While those few people who began with a preference for a male partner did not change their preference, many of those who began with a preference for a female partner did. Some of these people reported changing from a preference for a female sex partner to preferring a male partner, and some only expressed a less exclusive attraction to females, but the change was always in the same direction.

It could be argued that a repressed desire for a male partner existed all along, and simply emerged in the course of therapy. However, if we rely on the self-reports of the people involved and look at their own ways of explaining the changes they reported, then we would have to accept that the consolidation of female gender identity was the decisive factor in the changes that occurred. Since no other person can know a person as well as that individual is capable of knowing herself, regardless of her imperfections, and since such broad permission was given to the participants to openly express a range of feelings about sexuality, this seems to be the most reliable source available.

Puberty Revisited

The ways MTF transgender people sort out their sexual orientation, in the face of a changing gender role and consolidation of a female gender identity, have components that would be familiar to most parents of adolescent girls. When a young girl first begins to discover her sexuality, the realization that it gives her power in her relationships with boys may surprise her. She may find it hard to believe. She may test this newly discovered power to see what happens when she flirts or dresses seductively. For this woman child, it may be like a newly discovered toy, and she enjoys playing with it. She does not mean it maliciously, nor is it simply a power trip. It is part of the joy of discovering one's own sexuality. When she finds that some boys pay more attention to her or appear to be charmed by her, or if she finds she is more able to influence their behavior, it may feel so euphoric that she cannot make the distinction between whether she is attracted to a particular boy or whether she is simply enjoying the affirmation of herself as a sexually attractive young woman, experienced through his attraction to her. Does she like him for himself or because he flatters her newly discovered womanhood? Both feel good to her.

In just this way, early in her transition the transgender woman can become confused because, when a man indicates that he is attracted to her, she finds the affirmation of her femininity so euphoric that she cannot be sure whether she is attracted to this man or just to the realization that he is attracted to her.

In exactly this way, there appears to be a strong interaction between the developing gender identity and the resultant reevaluation of sexual orientation in the transgender person that is analogous to the self-discovery of both adult gender role and sexual orientation in the developing adolescent (Grinder, 1969). In the transgender person, this could be viewed as a return to the maturation and socialization process that typically occurs during adolescence, which, for the transgender person, was first experienced in the male gender role, and is now being revisited in the female gender role.

Intentions Regarding Genital Reconstruction Surgery

The fact that many of the people in this study had considered GRS is not surprising, since even crossdressers, who may never choose to entirely give up their male role and do not have serious intentions to have GRS, may still fantasize about what it would be like to have a female body. They wonder what it would be like to live entirely as female, and may fantasize about how this change might affect their lives. In fact, it seems possible, perhaps even likely, that a large percentage of nontransgender individuals have wondered at one time or another what it would be like to be the other sex. They simply are not preoccupied with the idea to the same degree as a person who is transgender.

Eleven of the people who participated in this research study did not want GRS at the start of therapy. This number increased to 16 at the most recent point of contact. Although these numbers do not necessarily represent the same individuals, it may be possible to explain this change by the fact that it is an integral part of the therapy process to encourage each person to slow down and consider carefully the magnitude of this decision. This is done because many transgender people initially go from the extreme of being closeted to the other extreme of wanting to come out too fast, putting themselves at risk of harming their lives with precipitous or premature actions, of going farther than they would later be happy to have done, or going forward before they have sufficiently prepared their lives for the changes they are making.

At the start of therapy, 32 people said they were undecided about GRS; by the most recent point, only 11 said they were undecided. Clearly, a few of these may have moved into the category "does not want." Again, there is no way to know if these positions would change with additional time to monitor their process.

Medical Contraindications for GRS

At the start of therapy, there were five people who wanted but could not have GRS. By the most recent point of contact, there were 23. There are a number of reasons why any transgender person might want but be unable to have GRS. These fall into the categories of medical, psychological, financial, and social.

Weighing the Risk Factors

Medical reasons that could preclude GRS include a chronic health condition that prevents a person from being a good candidate for surgery. This could be due to diabetes or other medical conditions that make surgery too risky, although this must be decided on a case-by-case basis. There might also be an obesity problem that the person has not been able to bring under control. Obesity makes any surgery more difficult, increases the risk of complications, and tends to make the recovery more difficult. Most surgeons consider this risk factor when evaluating a surgical candidate. Some require the person to reach a reduced weight goal. Others simply charge more because of the additional care required. Smoking cigarettes also falls into this risk category, but people usually find it easier to quit smoking, however difficult it may be, than to lose weight.

No Immunity for Transgender People

Tragically, there are also transsexual individuals who are mentally ill, independent of their transgender, or who are of marginal IQs, or who may be too emotionally unstable or too lacking in coping skills to be good surgical candidates for GRS. This would be especially problematic if the person lacked the ability to follow instructions for pre- and postsurgical self-care (especially as the latter includes a somewhat demanding regimen of vaginal dilation). The person may not have the emotional stability to cope with the possible social repercussions that transition could precipitate, such as loss of job and social support. Such psychological factors do not necessarily rule out the person as a candidate for GRS, but they certainly do require more careful evaluation and more watchful care on the part of providers. Usually, this becomes apparent to everyone involved, including the transgender person herself, during the RLE (real-life experience).

Cost Versus Benefit

Some individuals who are otherwise clearly good candidates for GRS may still opt to forgo it, although this may be done with deep regret. Life circumstances may be such that the person simply has too much to lose by giving up the male social role, and cannot bear the prospect of these losses. Often such individuals live with the fantasy of a day when these circumstances will change and living as a woman will become feasible. Life may give any of us lifelong reasons for regret, so the transgender person is not alone in such circumstances. Healthy individuals learn to find rewards in life to accompany the regrets and to make life worth living, even though it may never be what it might otherwise have been. In this situation, the transgender person may use a variety of coping mechanisms. These could include becoming intensely involved in some project or endeavor that would help with suppression. It might also include making many opportunities for some level of femme expression.

I can readily think of two examples of this from life. One is a person who travels alone on frequent occasions, and during those times lives almost exclusively in the female role. Another person, someone who can afford the cost, attends several transgender community conventions or gatherings per year and also attends a support group on a regular basis, all of which offer outlets for femme expression. What works well for one person may not work so well for another. With enough diversion, some people can keep their transgender feelings in check. For others, if they try to provide outlets for female expression it only intensifies their feelings and makes it harder to manage them. For some individuals, suppression simply will not work, and providing outlets works better. Each person who finds herself in this dilemma of not being able to transition must work out her own solution. Unfortunately, there are a few for whom nothing seems to work. They live unhappy lives and may be at chronic risk for suicide.

An Unanticipated Reaction to Genital Surgery

Genital surgery itself can precipitate emotional upheaval. This is a manageable occurrence in an otherwise emotionally stable person, but could result in a crisis for someone who is not. First, because of risks related to blood clotting and excessive bleeding, the person must stop taking her hormone supplements two to three weeks prior to having surgery. This can make the person's moods more labile than they would ordinarily be. This is not a serious problem for most people, but requires more careful attention in the person who is less emotionally stable and who may become fearful and needy. On the other hand, for many transgender people, GRS is almost a nonevent. They get it over with and feel better, and they go on with their lives. Often, taking hormones, coming out to important people, and starting the RLE with the concomitant concern about loss of job are more dramatic events than GRS for the transgender person who is well prepared for it.

There is another factor that could contribute to emotional volatility immediately after GRS. The person cannot return to her former hormone regimen because the gonads that were manufacturing most of the testosterone in her body are now gone, and this changes the level of what is needed from external sources. As a result, she will need to return to the doctor who is prescribing her hormones, get her hormone levels reevaluated, and allow her body to adapt to a new hormone regimen. It is wise for the person to consult the prescribing physician prior to surgery and to have an interim plan in place for resuming hormones until the reevaluation occurs.

In addition, the body does not know that the surgery was chosen and deliberate. It only knows it has been assaulted and reacts in ways that can impact mood. An additional complicating factor is the fact that the person has been anesthetized and has been taking pain medication. These also affect mood and psychological ability to function smoothly, and the body will take several weeks to fully recover and restabilize itself from these medications alone.

Furthermore, because GRS has usually been a major life goal, there can be a sense of letdown and loss of focus that can accompany the achievement of such a major goal. The person may be left feeling adrift, with no new defined goals and no sense of direction in her life. This is an issue that can be anticipated in therapy, and the client can be prepared to avoid this occurrence.

In even the most emotionally healthy individual, the above-mentioned factors can combine to create a sort of postsurgical depression. I think of this as somewhat analogous to postpartum depression in that they both relate to major hormonal upheavals in the body and the impact these have on overall body chemistry and mood. However, in the healthy individual, this is usually fleeting and low in intensity. When the individual is not so healthy, either physically or mentally, extra care is required, and in extreme situations, surgery may be contraindicated.

Cause-and-Effect Relationships

Although it could be argued that a transgender person may be severely depressed precisely because of her transgender condition, and that surgery would be part of the solution, most transgender people who are severely depressed as a direct result of their transgender feelings will respond well just by coming to terms with it and having a plan to deal with it, either while remaining in the male role or by taking hormones, or at least by living as female. When this does not happen prior to genital surgery, there is reason to believe the depression is co-occurring rather than secondary to the transgender. In some, but not all, cases, this condition can make a person at least temporarily ineligible for GRS for psychological reasons. If the depression is treated successfully, she would then become eligible.

The Relationship to Finances

Sometimes, but not always, this type of condition (e.g., major depression) coincides with the person being unable to afford the cost of the surgery. Few health insurance plans will cover the cost of GRS. Persons whose mental or social functioning is marginal would probably not be able to secure the level of employment that would offer a benefit package that includes the premier health insurance that would cover some of these costs.

Even when the individual has insurance that will pay for GRS, the majority of surgeons who do this kind of procedure are out-of-panel providers. This means that the surgeon does not want to be in the middle between the patient and the patient's insurance company, or that the insurance company will not pay the surgeon directly. The surgeon will not or cannot bill the insurance himself. Instead, the patient is required to first pay the surgeon, and then seek reimbursement from her insurance provider. This can present a cash flow problem for the patient, who will usually need to have in the neighborhood of $20,000 available up front, independent of any travel costs associated with going to a surgeon far away from the transgender person's home.

When insurance coverage is available, it will usually reimburse about 80% of the direct medical costs. But most insurance companies specifically exclude GRS and other transgender-related treatments. The individual would have the ongoing out-of-pocket expense of prescriptions for hormones and the especially costly lab testing, while at the same time trying to save money for GRS. Clearly, many individuals would find it impossible to afford the out-of-pocket cost of GRS. If eligible, some people obtain loans to pay for surgery or charge it to their credit cards and pay it off over time, which is not the most economical way but is doable.

Which Reasons for GRS Are Valid?

Some MTF transgender people have GRS to feel whole and congruent. Some do so because they feel compelled to in order to validate their feminine identities in their own eyes or the eyes of others. If transition is the bridge, GRS is the burning of the bridge that tells everyone concerned that the transition is complete and settled with finality. Besides the reasons already mentioned, there are also legal reasons that a transgender person might want to have GRS. An individual who lives as female without GRS assumes the constant risk of arrest for using women's public restrooms and cannot obtain a passport that says female because that requires a letter from the surgeon attesting to the GRS. Having a passport that says male would make it risky for the transwoman to travel outside the United States.

While not exactly a legal matter, the transgender person must also consider how she might be treated if her genitals did not match her social gender role in a situation where she had to depend on the physical care of others at some point in her life. This could occur if she was sick or injured in an accident and taken to the hospital emergency room, or if she required hospitalization for some reason. It could also occur in her declining years if she had to live in a nursing home. These are very real issues for the transgender person to consider in making a decision about GRS.

In a more accepting social environment, some people might find themselves comfortable enough to forgo GRS while still living as women. Conversely, it is also possible that more people would choose to live openly with some lesser form of transgender expression short of transition were they not concerned with the social pressure to fit within society's strict binary definitions of male and female.

In a more perfect world, the only valid reason for having GRS would be to achieve a sense of wholeness. But we do not yet have that world, and sadly, we must still consider these other reasons as valid. Quality of life is the most significant consideration, and all of these reasons are contributing factors. If GRS helps a person fit in better in our less than perfect world, then one would have to say that any of those reasons are valid.

These ideas are only sources of speculation for now, but the speculation is an interesting exercise. When one considers how much the world has changed in the past 20 years, with the advent of a widely available Internet and related technological advances, there is good reason to believe the world of the future will result in remarkable advances that are hard for us to foresee.

At this point, with regard to making a decision about GRS, it is at least possible to say that whether or not a person has had GRS, whether she has given it thought, or whether she will ultimately act upon her thoughts, the majority of the people who participated in this study have at least given serious consideration to GRS.

Beginning to Notice Attractive Men

At some point in the transition process it is fairly common for a transwoman to begin to notice men in a new way. Often it comes as a surprise to her and may confuse or amuse her. In the case of my clients, we have usually already discussed this possibility, so she would be a little prepared, and the ice would already have been broken for us to discuss this reaction. Even then, for any transgender person, it takes time to decide if this is a true change in sexual orientation. It may be experimental behavior that will pass or a euphoric reaction to the realization that men are noticing her in a new way.

As may be seen in Appendix D, and based only on the results of this one study, it appears there was a statistically significant change in the sexual orientation among the members of this group of MTF people: From experiencing exclusive preference for a female sex partner, those who reported change consistently moved in the direction of increased preference for a male sex partner (Table D.11). No one moved from being attracted to males to becoming attracted to female sex partners. Long-term studies that follow subjects through therapy and several years postsurgery, or at least posttransition, would be especially valuable in illuminating MTF sexual orientation after the participants had a longer period of adjustment to their new female social role or new female genitals.

I emphasize the importance of the female genitals because they play such an important part in the availability and type of sex partners with whom the transgender person can interact sexually. The reader should keep in mind that statistics telling us who transgender people have as sex partners also reflect the willingness of a partner to accept the transgender person as a sex partner. Partner choice is a reciprocal process. If the MTF transwoman were attracted to females and viewed herself as a lesbian, some, although not all, lesbian females would probably reject her as a partner because of her male history. A gay man would also want a male-bodied partner, so a post-GRS transwoman would not be attractive to him.

Heterosexual females might not accept a transwoman as a partner because they do not consider themselves to be lesbians, as such a relationship would imply. There are exceptions wherein the female partner is able to see herself as bisexual. Whether lesbian or heterosexual, she might then be able to sustain or engage in a relationship with a transwoman partner despite this partner's history. In some other cases a woman may find ways to reconcile this conflict while still viewing her own sexual orientation as unchanged. She could do this by using fantasy to conceptualize her partner during sex in the way that works best for her. This is almost the converse of what a MTF person does prior to transition, when "he" might use a fantasy

of himself as female or vicariously put himself in the place of his
female partner when engaging in sexual activity with her.

After she has had genital surgery, if the MTF transwoman is
attracted to males, a gay man would probably consider her too female.
And as a heterosexual female, she might not be attracted to gay men,
but only to straight men. She can only hope that a heterosexual male
will appreciate her femaleness enough that this will outweigh her
male genital history. With a longitudinal study, a more reliable picture could be obtained of the long-term incidence of change in sexual orientation with all of its varied implications. At least this study
indicates that many MTF transgender people undergo a change in
sexual orientation in the course of transition, and that this change
is from preference for a female sex partner to an increased interest
in a male sex partner. But the original question remains a point of
confusion for transgender people, as well as for the rest of us: Exactly
who is the opposite sex?

9

Where Do We Go From Here?

A New Beginning

Finding or creating a neutral environment in which to study the MTF population is impossible in today's world because of the lack of social and societal neutrality. Little is actually known about their sexual orientation, specifically what happens as they become more comfortable with their transgender identity and as they decide and then perhaps go about transitioning from living in the social role of the male to living full-time or nearly full-time in the female role. The study presented here certainly has its shortcomings, but it is nevertheless one of the few available windows through which to examine the topic of sexual orientation in transgender people as they explored their options and made difficult decisions about how to integrate their core gender identity into their daily lives. It has been my privilege to have so many transgender people place their trust in me and share their lives and struggles with me, making it possible to document the information presented herein. I sincerely hope that I have represented them well and accurately.

Essentially, a researcher seeking to explore this topic further will only be able to find subjects by using some means of attracting them to her, as I have done, by going where they are, or by casting a wide net. In going to places frequented by transgender people, this might include transgender community conventions, support groups, or certain bars that are known to be hangouts for transgender people. A request for volunteers to participate in a study can be publicized through a variety of venues, such as an ad in a newsletter, a magazine, or a website targeted to the population from which the researcher is seeking subjects, asking people to come to the researcher. The researcher can also make use of a variety of services (such as therapy, electrolysis, or certain types of surgery) that attract transgender people, and ask there for people to participate in a research project.

In any case, the subject pool would be self-selected by the environment in which the subjects are found or by the individuals who come forward to participate. We have discussed how this limits the validity of the conclusions, since they would apply only to that specific subgroup of the larger population being studied. In addition, individuals who seek to mainstream their lives and simply blend in to the general population would not be found in the places mentioned and would not come forward to participate in a research study, and so would be excluded from such a research project.

Geographical differences would certainly be present in a similar study, regardless of where it was conducted. A massive survey could be undertaken, such as was done in the Kinsey study (Kinsey, Pomeroy, & Martin, 1948), and covering a range of geographic locations and economic strata. Using this "casting a wide net" approach for studying transgender people would require that the participants not be limited to transgender subjects, but rather, the researcher(s) would try to identify these subjects as they were caught in the net along with others who were not transgender. Although it would be a fascinating study (and enormously expensive and time-consuming), it would probably be more accurate than any other research method, but this approach would have limitations of its own. For example, in any approach, there would be deeply closeted transgender people who would be unwilling or unable to identify themselves as such even when they were caught in the net. Neither is it likely that it would be possible in such a large study to examine the lives of the participants in as much depth as was done in the current study.

It is my sincere hope that this preliminary work will inspire others to pursue this topic further. It would contribute to the entire fund of knowledge about gender identity and sexual orientation in transgender people, helping both transgender people and the professionals who serve them gain greater insight and sensitivity about the widely ranging manifestations of gender identity and expression. Beyond that, from such research we would inevitably learn more about gender identity and sexual orientation in all human beings.

Although, in some ways, access to in-depth information about transgender people may be more readily available in a therapy setting, we see only those people who seek therapeutic support. As I have already pointed out, many transgender people never seek therapy.

Some MTF transgender people might be left out because they had been successful in suppressing their transgender urges. Also left out would be MTF transgender people who commit suicide because they could not accept their transgender feelings, or because they had been unsuccessful in finding help, individuals who could not bear to continue living in what seemed to them like a hostile world, and who would take their secret feelings with them to the grave. Some others would have resigned themselves to live with feelings of futility and unhappiness.

There are numerous MTF transgender individuals who live and express their transgender feelings privately or openly—some to a limited extent, and others who successfully transitioned to live as female without therapeutic assistance. This would probably be especially true for those who transitioned early in life. These individuals may have sought out GRS from a surgeon who is not known for this specialty, or from a surgeon who was willing to perform the surgery without the recommended mental health letters. Others may have sought GRS from surgeons outside the United States.

Although WPATH is an international organization and many providers throughout the world participate in it, there are some providers who either do not know about it or simply choose not to participate. While compliance with the SOCs is recommended for the benefit of both patient and provider, there is no law that says they must do so. And of course, some transgender people obtain false documentation of mental health letters as a means of obtaining GRS.

Since it would be impossible to conduct a truly controlled study of this population and the sexual orientations of its members, we must rely on repeated studies of smaller subgroups of the larger transgender population in less controlled settings, or in very large population samples, with ongoing comparison of results.

Tracking When There Is No Paper Trail

Because this population is often so closeted—both early in the transgender process and even after GRS—conducting a study that requires follow-up at a later time is and will probably remain problematic for the foreseeable future. For example, at transgender conventions, one can find a large number of individuals who would gladly participate in a survey that requires only a single contact with the researcher. As a whole, this population is interested in promoting a better understanding of transgender and in contributing to any research that would forward this cause. They are full of questions about how they came to be this way and also how to explain the differences in gender identity and expression that exists among individual transgender people. It usually seems to them that they were born this way, but they would like to know for certain if this is true. They want to know if parenting practices or critical events in early life have played a part in the formation of their gender identities. They would like to have answers for themselves and their loved ones. They will support research efforts, and will be helpful and generous with their time and in sharing their personal stories at a single point of contact.

The people who attend these conventions are sometimes closeted in one or more domains of their personal lives and may not consider it safe to give out personal contact information, such as their legal names, home or work addresses, or phone numbers, for follow-up purposes. Such a contact could create a paper trail or could lead to questions being raised by family or co-workers about the nature of the contact—questions that could be destructive to the life of an individual. The slightest indiscretion on the part of a caller could be disastrous for a transgender person. Bitter experience and oral tradition have taught them that well-meaning people sometimes make human errors that can destroy lives.

Living in Stealth

Postsurgical transsexuals, and sometimes even those who do not have genital surgery but are living full-time as female, often disappear into the general population, keeping their transgender status a secret in an effort to live an ordinary life. In a sense, this could be viewed as trading one closet for another, but it can also be viewed as a matter of personal privacy, or even a practical matter of survival, or the only way to have an acceptable quality of life, free from fear of harassment. In my mind, the distinction lies in whether the decision is or is not shame based, but in either case, living a secret life is not healthy for the individual. The ability to be intimate with another person has limitations when there is a secret of this magnitude that cannot be shared. Still, in some situations, it may be the lesser of two evils. This choice to live without disclosing a transgender history is referred to within the transgender community as living in stealth. Even if a researcher could find these individuals, understandably they would be extremely cautious about making themselves available for a long-term research study.

The Diversity of Crossdressers

"How can I tell you who I am if I don't know myself?" This is a good way to think about what it might mean to a crossdresser if you asked if he is male or female. And how can he be clear about his sexual orientation under these circumstances? Once, when attending a seminar that included a panel presentation by a group of transgender people, there was a person who disclosed that he was both biracial and a crossdresser. He was asked that very question: "Do you consider yourself male or female?" He answered that he could no more choose a gender than he could choose a race. He could only say, "I am both," while at times he felt as if he were neither. At other times he felt more as one or the other, but only for isolated periods.

Based on this question, another worthwhile research contribution would be a specific study of sexual orientation among male crossdressers. This, too, would require a researcher who likes a challenge because, as valuable as this kind of study would be, there are several reasons why it would be difficult to conduct. Significant variation in self-identity and expression of gender exists even within this subgroup of the transgender population. It would be difficult to find a pool of subjects that represented a broad spectrum of this population and who would be willing to participate over a span of time, people who would have reached a point of personal insight and self-acceptance that would allow them to provide reliable information.

This diversity among male crossdressers exists even in social and support groups such as Tri-Ess (shorthand for SSS, which in turn stands for the Society for the Second Self), a peer organization with chapters in many major cities throughout the United States. This group has bylaws specifically limiting full membership to heterosexual male crossdressers and their natal female partners. One might think this would be a fairly homogeneous group, but it is not. Considerable diversity exists even there.

The shortcoming of the Tri-Ess membership position, which is broadly recognized by its own members, is that, initially, many transgender people simply do not know where they fit into the spectrum of gender identity. They join Tri-Ess in good faith and later realize their transgender feelings go beyond occasional crossdressing. Some may recognize their desire to live more fully as female from the beginning, but hold themselves in check because they anticipate potential losses associated with going further and are too fearful or unwilling to risk incurring these losses. And, of course, I am not even mentioning that such a person may reevaluate his or her feelings about gender identity and sexual attraction over time.

Since an individual may not be able to accurately define his or her gender identity early in the process of self-exploration, or may choose to publicly self-define in a different way than is consistent with his or her internal reality, even seeking out a group such as Tri-Ess would not offer a researcher a simple solution to accessing the crossdressing population separately from the broader transgender population. And as we know, the above factors pertain not only to gender identity; they include a possible change in sexual orientation. It was for these reasons that the present study included all forms of MTF transgender expression and identity.

Discovering the Real Truth

I have mentioned these things, not to discourage an aspiring researcher, but only to highlight the pitfalls so the researcher can avoid or compensate for them. And there is yet another problem. Because of the common misconception within the general population that associates crossdressing with being gay, great care has been taken by heterosexual crossdressers to emphasize their heterosexuality in order to debunk this misconception. When the wives of crossdressers first learn about their husband's gender identity issues, the question "Are you gay?" is one that comes immediately to mind (Boyd, 2003). The husband is usually quick to reassure the wife that he is not. He is usually being truthful, but is also trying to preserve peace, and the marriage itself.

If there is any doubt in his mind about his sexual orientation, the crossdresser may reject and suppress any questions that even he may have about it, keeping them hidden deep within himself. This is not meant to imply that many crossdressers are secretly gay or bisexual. I clearly do not believe that to be the case. I only wish to highlight that those few who may be so may also be reluctant to face it within themselves or to be straightforward with others about it due to the enormous investment of the entire group in making the distinction between crossdressing as a form of gender expression and being sexually attracted to men, and thus being identified as gay.

Furthermore, it is readily recognized that some segments of American society remain exceedingly uncomfortable with people who identify as gay. It is therefore predictable that same-sex attraction may be even more taboo among some groups of crossdressers or other transgender individuals who are members of that segment of society than is typical of the wider general population. Since a transgender person who is first entering therapy may not yet recognize his internalized social homophobia, he would only be able to answer truthfully about himself as far as he knows the truth to be. Anyone who is attempting to research the topic of sexual orientation in crossdressers will have to take all of this into account in order to obtain truthful and reliable answers from research subjects and to achieve reliable results.

More Limitations

Earlier, I pointed out the limitations in our vocabulary and in our perceptions related to sex and gender as circumscribed by social expectations and binary definitions. Some crossdressers might provide an example of how these perceptions are limiting. Suppose it were possible that a small number of crossdressers were oriented exclusively to females while in the male mode, but while in female mode, and only then, were also attracted to men. I do not know that this is the case—I'm only speculating—but it is noteworthy that we do not have room for this kind of variation of sexual orientation in our vocabulary or in our social expectations, as this would not fit the usual definition of bisexuality. Instead, we get all hung up on our concerns about who is attracted to whom, when in the final analysis it probably does not make very much difference, except only to the specific individuals involved, and is then more a matter of honesty and fidelity between people who are in a relationship with each other than it is a question of sexual orientation.

Anecdotally, some crossdressers have told me that they are attracted to males when en femme, or have at least become curious about what it would be like to be with a man sexually, but report this happening only and exclusively when en femme. For some of these people, it seems to be an actual sexual attraction, and for others, it seems to be more an extension of wanting to feel more fully female. We know very little about what happens to the sexual orientations of crossdressers while in the female role—and this could be fascinating information if it could be obtained, albeit possibly unnerving for the wives of crossdressers.

Trust and fidelity do matter, but these are different from attraction. It is normal for us to notice other people who we find attractive. Noticing another attractive person besides the one with whom we are in an exclusive committed relationship does not mean we will break that commitment. It only means we are not blind. We can and do control our impulses on a daily basis. If humans all lacked impulse control and could not suppress the urge to jump the bones of everyone we found attractive, no one would ever dare walk down Main Street, USA, and the entire world would be in chaos!

Waiting Until One's Body Is "Right"

Many MTF individuals do not consider the possibility of sexual attraction to males until they reach a point in transition or therapy at which a male sex partner would seem a more acceptable option. This may be because of greater acceptance of themselves as female, or because their bodies have become feminized with hormones or surgery. Many others, when first examining their transgender issues and while yet poorly informed, may experience confusion between the concepts of sexual orientation and gender identity and may wonder if their feminine feelings mean they are gay. For some, being gay would be preferable—less disruptive to their lives than being transgender. For others it might be just the opposite. In either case, it is necessary for individuals to reexamine and hopefully overcome their own attitudes if they are driven by prejudice and misconceptions.

Any research related to transgender has implications far beyond this specific focus. When we have a better understanding of transgender people, how their gender identities and sexual orientations came to be what they are, we'll be able to do a better job of helping them live comfortably in the world. But even more importantly, society as a whole will benefit because any improvement in our ability to understand the sexual orientation or gender identity of any one person or group of people will add to our knowledge about sexual orientation or gender identity in all of us. As we gain a better understanding of gender identity and sexual orientation in all people, the world as a whole will benefit in ways that may be beyond our present ability to imagine.

Beyond Semantics

There is an important philosophical consideration in forming conclusions from this research or any other research related to this topic, a consideration that has to do with the question: When is change really change? There's no absolutely reliable way for us to know if the changes observed here were true or whether they represent the uncovering of sexual orientations that were present all along in the participants—orientations that were initially masked with layers of defenses. Neither do we know if the alleged changes we observed are transient.

This point is important because it speaks to the larger question of whether sexual orientation in any person is subject to modification or outright change, and, if so, under what circumstances. This question is already hotly debated between the gay community and the religious right. Although the American Psychiatric Association has labeled the practice of conversion (sometimes also known as reparative) therapy ineffective and potentially harmful (American Psychiatric Association, 2000; Besen, 2003), it is still being used by some fundamentalist Christian counselors and others. In some other cultures, as well as in some parts of our own, sexual orientation is viewed as a moral issue. This way of defining sexual orientation can lead to hate crimes against sexual minorities.

The argument about the genesis of sexual orientation, which has been debated over an extended period of time, seems to be based on the question of whether sexual orientation is chosen and whether it can be changed (Leland & Miller, 1998; Peyser, 1998; Humphreys, 1972), the usual assumption being that if it is not chosen, it cannot be changed. Most research into sexual orientation is focused on the causes of homosexuality (rather than trying to understand the causes of heterosexuality), but it is easy to see the implications for sexual orientation in transgender people, and for transgender identity itself.

Avoiding Misinterpretation

It may be interesting for us to speculate about the possibility that sexual orientation does not become fixed in any person until gender identity is consolidated. Thus, it would remain more fluid for a longer time in transgender people than in other people. As more is learned about how sexual orientation is formed and how amenable it is to change, the information we gain will contribute to our ability to understand the possible changes in the sexual orientations of transgender people and the implications this has for all human beings. Based on my observations thus far, I would have to say that I believe sexual orientation does change under various specific circumstances, but I do not believe this change is a matter of choice or decision, but rather that it happens spontaneously, on its own, under these specific conditions that are not yet well recognized or understood.

I cannot emphasize too strongly, and I believe it to be of critical importance, that the information presented here not be misconstrued or used inappropriately to support an argument that sexual orientation can be changed at will or that homosexuality can be "cured." I do not believe that for even a minute, nor do I believe that this would be an appropriate course of action even if it were possible. I do not believe that the changes that I have observed and reported here were chosen by the participants in my research. Until we have conclusive information from well-grounded research on the human brain, human genes, the influence of hormones, and interpersonal dynamics of the body and mind at work together at different points in life, we can in all honesty and fairness only reserve judgment and, as mental health professionals, function under the edict "Do no harm." This means it is incumbent upon us not to try to get people to change something over which they may well have no control, and regardless of whether they themselves would prefer to change. We would doom them to failure and force them to carry an unfair burden of guilt. I would view this course of action as unprofessional conduct in a mental health practitioner.

Kinsey, in his groundbreaking study of sexuality in the human male, reached the conclusion:

> Only 50% of the population is exclusively heterosexual throughout its adult life, and since only 4% of the population is exclusively homosexual throughout its life, it appears that nearly half (46%) of the population engages in both heterosexual and homosexual activities, or reacts to persons of both sexes, in the course of their adult lives. (Kinsey, 1948, p. 656)

While the present study used a different means of obtaining information than did Kinsey with his much larger sample, and while this study had a much narrower focus than his, some rough comparisons can be made. As can be seen in Table D.7 (Appendix D), at the beginning of my study the largest proportion (61%) of participants identified themselves as having a preference for a female sexual partner, while only 19% reported preferring a male partner. At the latest point in contact, an increased proportion of these MTF people identified themselves as having a preference for a male sexual partner (28%), while only 50% continued to report a preference for a female partner.

At the time of my initial contact with these people, many were attempting to conform to social expectations of traditional gender identity and behavior and expectations for heterosexual preference in sexual partners. They were not as yet accepting of their femme selves. It appears that the transgender person who reaches a point of being comfortable with herself as a woman, or at least as a transgender person, may be more at ease with exploring options in sexual behavior, including the testing of her own validity in the female role, and the reevaluation of the confusing question of "Who is the opposite sex?"

In the final analysis, it appears that in their variations in sexual orientation, the participants in this research study really were not so very different from Kinsey's subjects. Kinsey's findings, indicating a wide range of variation in sexual orientation in the general population, have been largely ignored in both modern lay and academic circles. But scientific research should be examined objectively and dispassionately for what it can teach us. We cannot simply disregard those parts that make us feel uncomfortable. How can we learn and grow if we do not allow ourselves to move beyond our comfort zones and allow our minds to explore new territory? We need to question and ponder everything, gleaning as many new truths as possible for whatever new information is presented.

I am deeply troubled by recent attempts to discredit Kinsey's research by besmirching his character and personal life. This is a tactic we've seen many times before, this focusing of attention away from findings that make some people uncomfortable—in this case, findings on human sexuality, findings that remain controversial more than 50 years after their initial publication. It would be interesting to know if any of these naysayers have actually read Kinsey's books and if they know how earnest and thoughtful he was in his approach.

I have asked the reader to please keep in mind that without further study there is no way to know if my findings can be replicated in other subgroups within the larger population of transgender individuals, or even in a study of a similar subgroup. Still, the people who were the subjects of this research were given broad permission for self-definition of gender identity, individual choices in expression of gender role, and in questioning and expressing their preferences for sexual partners. While there are limitations to this study, there would be corresponding limitations to other approaches. The choices were provided out of respect for the individuals and in the belief that each person has the potential to know herself better than anyone else could ever know her. But these people could know themselves only up to a given time. When you were 16, could you have imagined where and who you would be at age 40? Just as we cannot know about the permanence of the reported changes in sexual orientation toward preference for male partners, we also cannot know how many of these people, the ones who had experienced no change in sexual orientation, might eventually experience such a change.

In the course of this study and in the conduct of my clinical practice, I have tried and continue to try to treat clients with respect. I point this out because there have been times when I have been disappointed with a few of my colleagues—some of whom were in clinical practice and some of whom were in academic research circles—who did not seem to feel or show respect for their clients and for the people who were the subjects of their research, colleagues whose attitudes and behaviors did not reflect respect, although they gave lip service to it. Not only am I concerned about the questionable ethics of such attitudes and the resulting way clients and subjects are treated, but I also believe this approach to people undermines the therapy process and the validity of any research the academic person may do. Regardless of professing political correctness, clients and research subjects are usually quick to pick up on subtle cues, and they do know the underlying truth.

In any population, it can be difficult to obtain truthful answers from people. To obtain truthful answers to the best of the ability of a person to know the truth, there must be a foundation of trust between the research subject and the researcher. Subtle and sometimes not so subtle hints and behaviors will unmask a pretense of respect. The researcher or therapist can expect, and deserves to get, as much respect as he or she is willing to give. It is my opinion that therapists and researchers should excuse themselves from working with any individual or population if and when they find themselves unable to give this respect. They should simply go find something else to do.

I will repeat—and please assume that each reiteration is directed toward an ever-deeper layer of understanding—that in a study that relies on self-report, the possibility for valid responses has limitations. Although a person may answer truthfully to the best of her knowledge, all people have their own perspectives, social biases, blind spots, private agendas, and distorted perceptions that limit their ability to be objective about themselves. This is an unavoidable limitation of any study based on individual self-report—and such a study can only be conducted in a manner designed to minimize reporting bias. Researchers unavoidably have their own biases too, so a good research study should be designed to minimize the effect of biases in the researcher as well as the subjects.

I made an effort to minimize reporting bias when interviewing the people in this study. I made a conscious and deliberate effort to present questions in as neutral a manner as possible. The initial hypothesis of this study stated that while there were some transgender individuals who remained constant in their sexual orientation regardless of which gender role they were functioning in at a given time, there were a significant number of individuals who experienced a shift in sexual orientation concurrent with their gender role transition (Table D.11, Appendix D). Based on these findings, this hypothesis was borne out by the results of this study. Without drawing conclusions that may be unwarranted by these tentative results, I hope this work leads the reader to ponder the complexities inherent in gender identity and sexual orientation.

In conclusion, I would like to state once more that I do not want anything I have said here to be twisted into an attempt to support the position that sexual orientation is chosen. That is not my belief, nor is it a valid interpretation of the results of my research. I would also like to say that diversity makes the world more interesting and beautiful. Everything in nature supports the existence of diversity. We would not want to be confined to basic colors, when we can have infinite shades of each. I look out my window and it feeds my spirit to see so many shades of green that I cannot count them all. We appreciate the varieties of flowers and trees. We respect and recognize the contributions of many other cultures to our American culture. One example of this is in our language, which has words derived from many other languages, and we appreciate that this makes our own language richer and more colorful. So, would we really want to live in a world of clones, where all people are alike? I doubt it. There is no reason for us to feel threatened by others who are different from us. That's how we tell each other apart! Without differences in personality and appearance, there would be no drama on TV (or anywhere else), which we often find so entertaining. As long as no one is truly threatening you, just relax and let others be who they are. It's not your problem! And please remember one of my favorite quotes, which I shared with you earlier and repeat here as a reminder:

Without deviation from the norm, progress is not possible.

Appendix A: Mental Health Evaluation Checklist for Transgender Clients

Rule Out: Vegetative Signs of Depression/ Anxiety Whenever Indicated*

Persistent sad, anxious, or empty mood or excessive anxiety most of the day, nearly every day, especially for over past 6 months

Lack of interest in daily activities, loss of pleasure in hobbies or social/leisure activities, including sex, difficulty controlling worry, apprehensive expectation

Significant changes in weight or appetite

Trouble sleeping, sleeping too much or too little, difficulty falling or staying asleep

Being hyperactive, restless, keyed up or on edge, muscle tension, irritability

Fatigue, lack of energy or feeling slowed down

Feelings of worthlessness, helplessness, hopelessness, pessimism, or excessive guilt

Difficulty thinking, remembering, concentrating or making decisions, mind going blank

Persistent physical symptoms such as headaches, digestive upsets, or chronic pain that does not respond to medical treatment

Family history of depression, other mental health conditions, suicide

Recurrent thoughts of death or suicide, morbid or negative preoccupation

Symptoms of Panic Disorder*

Racing or pounding heartbeat

Chest pains

---

*Adapted from DSM-IV.

Difficulty breathing
Fear of dying
Sweating
Flushes or chills
Tingling or numbness in hands
Nausea
Dizziness
Derealization or depersonalization
Fear of loss of control and doing something embarrassing
Persistent concern about having another panic attack
Significant changes in behavior related to the attacks
Worrying about what the attacks mean, for example, having heart attack, going crazy
Rule out medical or substance abuse causation

Topics to Cover in Comprehensive Transgender History

Vital statistics: Legal name, alternate or preferred name, address, home phone number, who else lives in home, date of birth, Social Security number (optional except when using insurance), place of employment, how long, job title, work phone number, cell phone number when available. Level of discretion needed when calling client.

Precipitants to requesting therapy, expectations of treatment.

Need for crisis intervention.

Genogram-ecogram (family constellation, significant others, including significant past relationships, support systems, and strained relationships, words to describe, and significant facts about most important people). Pets. Who knows about client's transgender? How long? How found out? Attitude?

Medications, current and of note in past, including hormones, OTC, and dietary supplements. If on hormones, put start date on genogram and how obtained.

Health history of self and family, client hospitalizations (of any kind), surgeries, traumatic brain injuries (TBIs). Primary care physician. Most recent checkup. Incidence and attitudes about homosexuality, history of nontypical hormonal symptoms, nontypical gender expression/sexual behavior.

Previous mental health therapy for self and family, attitudes, quality of experience. Family violence, ever give or receive abuse, hit, kicked, shoved, choked, or otherwise hurt? Suicide or attempts in self, family, or other close person? Childhood traumas, abuse, any sexual activity against your wishes, fire starting, bed wetting? Any other mental health provider currently involved?

Substance use/abuse; current use (how much, how often, most at one time, negative consequences of use), history in self and family; nicotine, caffeine, alcohol, pot, other.

Legal history: Represented by an attorney or appeared in (juvenile) court, family legal history. Any case currently pending?

Religious history, self, family and significant others. Current role.

Employment and military history, type of discharge from military, occupations of self and family, current financial stability, sources of income, current career and financial goals.

Childhood history, family life, education. Special education classes? Repeat a grade? Quality of educational experience from kindergarten on up, academic and social. Quality of home life during those years. Include number of times family moved, number of times client changed schools, significant events.

Chronology of transgender and sex awareness and behavior, childhood history of transgender-related feelings, including first memory, behaviors. Family life, critical incidents and responses of others. Fantasies, past and present. History of tucking, body enhancement/adornment/mutilation. History of sexual activity, number and sex of partners and significant relationships. Current sexual activity, including masturbation. STIs and HIV. Define sexual orientation and arousal template.

Social life and leisure activities: Hobbies/interests (pets, childhood relationships with animals), past and present. Interpersonal relationships in family, work, and social life.

Gender community awareness, contacts, responses, involvement.

Electrolysis/laser therapy status.

Is there anything else I should know about you or your world that might help me understand you better?

Meeting with family member if appropriate: who and when?

Add all pertinent info to genogram.

Conclusions regarding comorbid or secondary diagnoses, need for professional consultation, discuss with client.

Life goals and initial mutually agreed upon therapy goals.

Note: Discuss and explain possible implications to client as needed for each set of questions, such as:

1. Rule out areas of potential concern or that could complicate ability to achieve goals.
2. Identify possible topics for further discussion (goal identification).

3. Safety issues associated with risk of incarceration.
4. Role of caffeine in depression, and of nicotine use regarding hormones and surgery.
5. Knowing about family and friends as related to planning for coming out.
6. Avoid redundancy where client has already volunteered certain information.

Appendix B: Basic Data Sheet

1. Age at start of treatment:
2. File reference #:
3. Stated reason for seeking treatment:
4. Highest grade completed in school?
   - ☐ 8th grade or less
   - ☐ Some high school
   - ☐ High school graduate
   - ☐ Some college
   - ☐ College graduate (4-year degree)
   - ☐ Some graduate school
   - ☐ Graduate degree obtained
5. Occupation:
   At start of therapy _____
   At most recent contact _____   ☐ No change
6. What is subject's religious background?
   - ☐ Catholic
   - ☐ Protestant
   - ☐ Jewish
   - ☐ None
   - ☐ Other
7. Was religion an important part of subject's life?
   At start of treatment: At most recent date of treatment:
                                                       ☐ No change
   - ☐ Yes—somewhat
   - ☐ Yes—very
   - ☐ No

   - ☐ Yes—somewhat
   - ☐ Yes—very
   - ☐ No
8. Living situation of subject:
   At start of treatment: At most recent date of treatment:
   - ☐ Alone
   - ☐ With biological female lover

   - ☐ Alone   ☐ No change
   - ☐ With biological female lover
                                        ☐ No change
   - ☐ With biological male lover
   - ☐ With biological male lover
                                        ☐ No change
   - ☐ With MTF trans lover
   - ☐ With MTF trans lover
                                        ☐ No change
   - ☐ With FTM trans lover
   - ☐ With FTM trans lover
                                        ☐ No change
   - ☐ With parent(s)
   - ☐ With parent(s)   ☐ No change

☐ With spouse (with or   ☐ With spouse (with or
   without children)   without children)
                                            ☐ No change

☐ With child (children)   ☐ With child (children)
                                            ☐ No change

☐ With sibling or family   ☐ With sibling or family
   member   member
                                            ☐ No change

☐ With nonrelation   ☐ With nonrelation
   roommate(s)   roommate(s)
                                            ☐ No change

9. At start of treatment, has subject been married, or cohabited with
   the same person for 1 year or more (in subject's lifetime)?
   How many times?_____   Married _____   Cohabited _____
10. Of the people referred to in number 9, how many were:
    Heterosexual   Heterosexual   Gay male _____
    male _____   female _____
    Lesbian _____   Bisexual male _____
    Bisexual female _____ Another transperson _____
11. How many consensual sex partners does subject report in total?
    At start of treatment _____   At most recent date
                                     of treatment _____
12. Of the above-mentioned people, how many were:
    Heterosexual male _____   Heterosexual female _____
    Gay male _____   Lesbian _____
    Bisexual male _____   Bisexual female _____
    Another transperson _____

    Note: Although the above is the format I used at the time of the
    study, in retrospect I would change this, replacing the category
    "another transperson" with the two categories of "transman" and
    "transwoman."

13. Does the person report being the object of sexual abuse as a child?
    ☐ Yes   ☐ No
    If yes, how many perpetrators were:
    Male _____   Female _____
14. At what age does subject report first having consensual genital
    intercourse?
    Age: _____   (NA if never)
15. At what age does subject report self as being in first memory
    related to being transgender?
    Age: _____

16. Length of time in treatment to date:
No. of sessions _____ No. of months _____

17. How does subject prefer to be perceived by others when crossdressed at start (S) of treatment and at most recent (R) date in treatment?
   a. Prefers to present self androgynously ☐ S ☐ R
   b. Prefers others to perceive self as a masculine-looking biological female ☐ S ☐ R
   c. Prefers others to perceive self as an average-looking biological female ☐ S ☐ R
   d. Subject is indifferent to how she is perceived by others ☐ S ☐ R
   e. Is inexperienced in how to dress en femme ☐ S ☐ R
   f. Fearful of being read ☐ S ☐ R
   g. Chooses androgynous look for safety ☐ S ☐ R
   h. Tends to overdo dress and makeup, cannot seem to judge appropriate dress for occasion, lacking objectivity ☐ S ☐ R
   i. Prefers a seductive or flamboyant look ☐ S ☐ R
   j. Has body type that makes it possible for subject to pass as female ☐ S ☐ R
   k. Dresses well ☐ S ☐ R
   l. Lacks awareness that body type makes passing unlikely ☐ S ☐ R
   m. Aware that body type makes passing unlikely ☐ S ☐ R
   n. Unaware that masculine mannerisms make passing unlikely ☐ S ☐ R
   o. Recognizes that masculine mannerisms make passing unlikely ☐ S ☐ R
   p. Voice is androgynous enough that it does not preclude passing ☐ S ☐ R
   q. Voice is too masculine to pass even when appropriately groomed as female ☐ S ☐ R

18. What is the extent of subject's transgender experience at start (S) of treatment and at most recent (R) date in treatment?
   a. Has never experimented with dress or makeup ☐ S ☐ R
   b. Is only vaguely aware that there are others with transgender issues ☐ S ☐ R
   c. Never talked with anyone about his transgender feelings/behavior before ☐ S ☐ R
   d. Has some limited experience with dress, make-up, or both, but only in private ☐ S ☐ R
   e. Feels fear, shame, or both about being transgender ☐ S ☐ R

   f. Has fair amount of knowledge of transgender   □ S   □ R
   g. Is very closeted   □ S   □ R
   h. Has Internet contact with other transgender
       individuals   □ S   □ R
   i. Has given self a female name for informal use   □ S   □ R
   j. Has gone out in public dressed as a woman
       1–2 times   □ S   □ R
   k. Has gone out in public dressed as a woman
       3–10 times   □ S   □ R
   l. Has gone out in public dressed as a woman 11
       or more times   □ S   □ R
   m. Has had verbal interaction with others
       while dressed as a woman in public   □ S   □ R
   n. Has had face-to-face interaction with other
       transgender individuals   □ S   □ R
   o. Goes out freely while crossdressed   □ S   □ R
   p. Is closeted with family   □ S   □ R
   q. Is out to one or more people in personal
       life (not another transperson)   □ S   □ R
   r. Has had beard (entirely or nearly) removed
       by laser or electrolysis   □ S   □ R
   s. Is out to most or all family and close friends,
       goes freely in public as female   □ S   □ R
   t. Spends most or all of time outside of work in
       female role   □ S   □ R
   u. Has never taken female hormones   □ S   □ R
   v. Has experimented with female hormones,
       but does not take them regularly   □ S   □ R
   w. Takes female hormones on a regular basis   □ S   □ R
   x. Plans to have a legal name change   □ S   □ R
   y. Has legal name change to female name   □ S   □ R
   z. Lives full-time as female   □ S   □ R
   aa. Undecided about or does not want genital
       surgery   □ S   □ R
   bb. Plans to have genital surgery   □ S   □ R
   cc. Is not medically able to have genital surgery
       at this time   □ S   □ R
   dd. Lives full-time as female, has already
       had genital surgery   □ S   □ R

19. What does subject report as primary sexual fantasy?

    S: _____

    R: _____   □ No change

20. Regarding the fantasies listed in number 19, has subject acted on these?

    S: ☐ Y   ☐ N
    R: ☐ Y   ☐ N

21. How does subject define his or her own gender identity?

    At start of treatment: _____
    At most recent date of treatment: _____   ☐ No change

☐ Male	☐ Male	☐ No change
☐ Female	☐ Female	☐ No change
☐ Transsexual female	☐ Transsexual female	☐ No change
☐ Crossdresser	☐ Crossdresser	☐ No change
☐ Bigendered	☐ Bigendered	☐ No change
☐ Uncertain	☐ Uncertain	☐ No change
☐ Transgenderist	☐ Transgenderist	☐ No change
☐ Transgender	☐ Transgender	☐ No change

22. Using the options below, how does subject define his or her sexual orientation?

At start of treatment:	At most recent date of treatment:
☐ Asexual, or nearly so	☐ Asexual, or nearly so
	☐ No change
☐ Autogynephilic	☐ Autogynephilic
	☐ No change
☐ Prefers masturbation fantasy	☐ Prefers masturbation fantasy
	☐ No change
☐ Self as M without partner	☐ Self as M without partner
	☐ No change
☐ Self as M with M partner	☐ Self as M with M partner
☐ Self as M with F partner	☐ Self as M with F partner
☐ Self as M with either M or F partner	☐ Self as M with either M or F partner
	☐ No change
☐ Self as either M or F without partner	☐ Self as either M or F without partner
☐ Self as either M or F with M partner	☐ Self as either M or F with M partner
☐ Self as either M or F with F partner	☐ Self as either M or F with F partner
☐ Self as either M or F with M or F partner	☐ Self as either M or F with M or F partner
	☐ No change
☐ Self as F without partner	☐ Self as F without partner
☐ Self as F with M partner	☐ Self as F with M partner
☐ Self as F with F partner	☐ Self as F with F partner

    ☐ Self as F with either M or   ☐ Self as F with either M or
        F partner   F partner

                                                    ☐ No change

☐ Prefers sexual partner where partner is:

    ☐ Male   ☐ Male
    ☐ Female   ☐ Female
    ☐ Transsexual female   ☐ Transsexual female
       (post-op)   (post-op)

* Note: While the format shown here is what I used at the time of this study, in retrospect I would add the category of "transmale" to both "At start of treatment" and "At most recent date of treatment" columns.

    ☐ Uncertain/confused   ☐ Uncertain/confused
    ☐ Transgenderist   ☐ Transgenderist
    ☐ Transgender   ☐ Transgender
    ☐ Preference not based   ☐ Preference not based
       on gender   on gender

23. If suject reports change in perception of own sexual orientation, to what does subject attribute this change? (Indicate NC if no change.)

Appendix C: More About Methods

To elaborate on the information presented in Chapter 3 regarding research methods, the people who became the subjects in this research were seen for various lengths of time ranging from four or five sessions to as long as several years. Files of clients who were seen for less than three sessions contained insufficient data and were excluded. There were no other exclusions.

In spite of their concerns about their gender identities, the vast majority of the subjects in this study were functioning reasonably well in all other domains of their lives. The initial case files that provided data that were used in this research dated from the time when I was just beginning to work with transgender clients. Gradually my client base came from a wider range of sources. Gradually, too, the Internet became more widely available, and as information about my practice became available on the Internet, this also contributed to how clients found their way to me. These "grapevine" factors contributed to the characteristics of the subject sample for this research.

The case records used in this study represent a range of outcomes. Some subjects chose only to become more at ease with occasional crossdressing. Others opted for or were only able to manage partial gender role transition during the time they were seen. Still others elected to pursue complete gender role transition. For some, this included genital reconstruction surgery. Some cases were still open, while others were closed at the time the study ended, but either way, that does not tell us what these people will do about their transgender at some future time.

The subjects who were studied here sought therapy for a variety of reasons. Some wanted to gain a better understanding of their transgender feelings, including what made them feel and behave this way. Others came in order to comply with the WPATH protocols. Some came with the hope that I could "cure" or rid them of their transgender feelings. During the course of therapy, some continued to function for a part of their lives as male, whereas others fully transitioned to live as female, utilizing every means available to create congruency within their bodies and minds.

At the time of our initial contact, individuals were at various points in the transgender self-discovery process. Some were novices who had almost no knowledge of transgender, while others were already well informed. Some were closeted, while others had already begun living full-time as female. The majority were somewhere between these extremes. The sample included people who were married, others who were single, some who were virgins, and some who were sexually experienced with multiple partners of one or both sexes. Included were young adults, and those who were well beyond the middle years in life.

The complete spectrum of transgender would extend beyond all of the intermediate forms mentioned here to include the most complete forms of transgender, that is, extended periods of living full-time across natal gender lines, living well-adjusted lives with all the changes that hormones could provide and with surgical reconstruction of the genitals to match the new gender role. All of the manifestations of transgender I have mentioned exist in most parts of the world, but not all are represented in this study.

How This Research Was Carried Out

For each person, I gathered a complete psychosocial and sexual history, just as I do for any other client. In Appendix A you will find the checklist that I routinely use as a tool for this purpose. I now use a modified form of this checklist, which includes the same major points but in a more efficient format. I do not adhere to it rigidly, as my first priority is the needs of the individual client. But I do use it as a guide to help me obtain uniform information and also to help me refer back when I need to review a client's history or locate information. The purpose of this history and evaluation is to develop recommendations and establish mutually agreed-upon therapy goals for each client. In other words, we need a plan. These goals were (and are) always defined as tentative and short term, with provision for review and revision. I avoid placing a client in the position of making an initial commitment to an outcome from which, in the course of therapy, she might want to retreat. I emphasize the importance of keeping one's options open while examining feelings, giving careful consideration to the possible outcomes of various courses of action, and of testing reality. I discourage clients from taking actions that would burn bridges until these things have been carefully considered, although ultimately the decisions are the client's to make, and bridges must be burned if forward movement is chosen. Just telling another person about one's transgender feelings is burning a bridge because that other person will never forget what was said. A client may make different decisions than a therapist would recommend, but it is the client who must live her life. We all have to walk around in our own shoes.

The Measuring Tools

For the purpose of my study, I developed a data sheet (see Appendix B) to gather information from the client file of each participant. The selection of questions was based on my clinical observations of the influences that might shed the most light on or have the most significant impact on sexual orientation. Most difficult, and probably most arbitrary, was the selection of indicators to assess where a subject was in the process of transgender self-discovery and level of cross-gender experience. I did ask for input from others, including clients and colleagues, but ultimately the choices were my own. I can only say that I did my best to choose valid indicators.

For purposes of my research, I made no attempt to distinguish between the occasional crossdresser at one end of a continuum and the postoperative transsexual at the other. I considered categories such as crossdresser, transgenderist, and transsexualism unreliable because there was no way of knowing or being able to predict at the start of therapy where a client would be at the end of therapy, or to know where a client might go in her transgender journey at some later point in life, long after she was no longer my client. I based this decision largely on the personal stories of clients who were already far along in their process of gender discovery, as they often told me how they could not have predicted early on that they would be where they were now. Based on their histories, I was humbly forced to say that I could not have predicted this in any reliable or consistent manner myself.

From the time when I first began working with the transgender population, I have attempted to use a uniform process for interviewing new clients (thanks to the example of Alfred Kinsey). This format, which became my evaluation checklist, evolved as I gained insight about the questions that needed to be asked in order to have a well-rounded picture of the individual and her social context. However, this did not lead me to change the basic format so much as I learned to fine-tune the wording of the questions that I asked within the format of my checklist. This was because the format was based on what would be a good basic guide to evaluating any client, regardless of presenting problems or gender identity. The only other changes I have made to this checklist over time were to reorganize it for increased efficiency rather than making significant alterations in content.

Clients often volunteered information that made it unnecessary to ask some of the questions, so the checklist was used as a tool, to make sure important information was not overlooked. As might be expected, there were exceptions. For example, if a client entered therapy in crisis or on the brink of crisis, this situation was dealt with before the more extensive evaluation process was undertaken. The answers to some questions made it unnecessary to pursue that topic further, whereas certain other answers were indicative of the need for further exploration.

Some case files lacked specific data on occasion, although this was rare; questions that could not be answered were left blank. As I have already noted, the data presented here are based entirely on client self-report and perception.

Since the files used were part of my confidential case records, I gathered all the data myself, unassisted. I assigned each case file a reference number and used this number to track the corresponding data sheet. The key was available only to me, as was the case file of each subject. After the data had been collected and analyzed and there was clearly no further need to verify information, the key was destroyed.

While I had assistance in the development of the raw data once it had been collected, the confidentiality of the client files was in no way violated or compromised.

The data were analyzed to show the characteristics of the population being studied and to examine the relationship between these characteristics and the self-reported sexual orientations of the subjects. Appendix B shows what was included in the data sheets.

Comparisons were made between the subject's reported sexual behaviors and sexual fantasies at the beginning and most recent point in therapy. I noted the numbers of sexual partners, the preference of the subject with regard to gender of sex partners, and the predominance of particular types of fantasies, as well as self-reports of lack of interest in partnered sex or lack of interest in sexual activity of any kind, both in the past and at our most recent point of contact. This information and more of how the data were developed and what they showed can be found in Appendix D.

Appendix D: More About Data and Findings

Overview of Subject Pool

As mentioned in Appendix C, all subjects of the present research were MTF transgender people. All data came from the author's private clinical files. The total number of subjects was 97. Their ages ranged from 26 to 68 years at start of therapy. The mean was 41 years. Several categories were compared with reported sexual orientation to see if there was a significant correlation between them. The categories were chosen because they appeared to be the ones most likely to have potential relevance to sexual orientation.

These categories were:

- Religious background and status
- Marital status and living situation
- Age at first memory related to being transgender
- Age at start of therapy
- Length of time in therapy
- Experience with transgender expression
- Primary sexual fantasy
- How subject defined own gender identity
- How subject defined own sexual orientation
- Use of feminizing hormones
- Status with regard to genital reconstruction surgery

Religion

A standard 5-point Likert-type continuum ranging from *not at all* to *very important* was used to measure the importance of religious beliefs. Only 16% of subjects defined religion as very important. However, for even the most religious subjects, any religious concerns the person may once have had about sexual orientation gradually melted away as the person became more comfortable with her gender identity. Typically, the individual was able to find a way to make transgender identity fit into her system of religious beliefs without abandoning religion altogether.

Table D.1 shows the religious background of the subjects. Of the pool of subjects, 56% identified as Protestant, 3% as Jewish, 28% as Catholic, and 1% as other. Eleven percent of subjects had no identified religion, and 1% was of unknown religion because I did not obtain the information from the client.

As may be seen in Table D.2, the level of importance of religion in the lives of the subjects was essentially the same at both points of comparison. Sixteen percent defined religion as very important in their lives, both at the beginning and at the most recent point in therapy; 40% reported it as somewhat important at the start, and 41% at the most recent point in therapy. Forty-three percent defined

TABLE D.1   Religious Background of Subjects

Religion	Number of Subjects	Percent of Subjects
Protestant	54	56
Jewish	3	3
Catholic	27	28
Other	1	1
None	11	11
Unknown	1	1
Total	97	100

TABLE D.2   Religious Status of Subjects at Start and Most Recent Point in Therapy

Importance of Religion	At Start	At Most Recent
Very important	15 (16%)	15 (16%)
Somewhat important	39 (40%)	40 (41%)
Not important	42 (43%)	41 (42%)
Unknown	1 (1%)	1 (1%)
Number of subjects who did not change status		95 (98%)
Number of subjects who did change status		1 (1%)

religion as not important at the start of therapy, and 42% reported it was not important at the most recent point in therapy.

Marital Status and Living Situation

Information was gathered about the number of times a subject had been married or had cohabited for more than one year, and how many subjects were living with a spouse at the start and most recent point in therapy. Figure D.1 illustrates the range in number of times married (0–3, with a mean of 0.80) and the range in number of times for cohabitation (0–8, with a mean of 0.36). Thirty-three subjects were living with a spouse or cohabiting in a committed relationship at the start of therapy, and 28 at the most recent point in therapy. There is no category of "male lover" in Figure D.1 because it was known to be an empty category.

Age at First Memory Related to Being Transgender

The age range for this category was 3–14 years old. The median was 5 years (Figure D.2). All of the subjects were well into adulthood when they sought therapy, between the ages of 26 and 68.

Figure D.3 illustrates the relationship between first awareness of transgender in self and age at start of therapy. When awareness of being transgender was described as "from earliest memory," it was counted as age 3, making this age group better described as "3 or under."

Age at Start of Therapy

Ninety percent of subjects reported awareness of their transgender identity well before reaching their teen years. The few remaining subjects came trickling in at a rate of one or two per year until age 14, by which time 100% had awareness of being transgender.

The contrast between the earliest awareness of transgender and the age of the subject when the subject first seeks therapy becomes evident when examining Table D.3B and Figures D.3 and D.4.

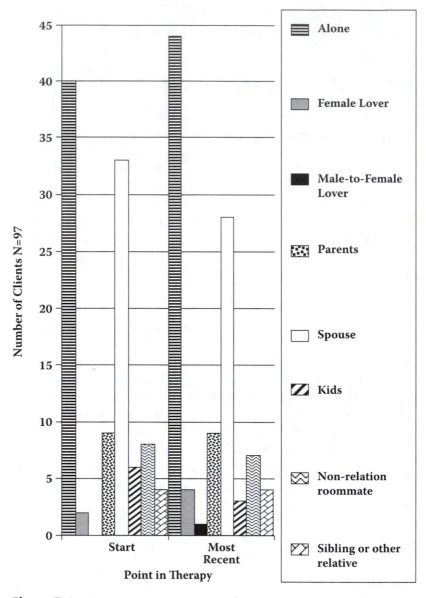

Figure D.1   Living situation at start and most recent point in therapy.

Length of Time in Therapy

This was measured in both the number of 50-minute therapy sessions and the number of months between each subject's initial session and most recent point in therapy. The mean number of sessions was 25.

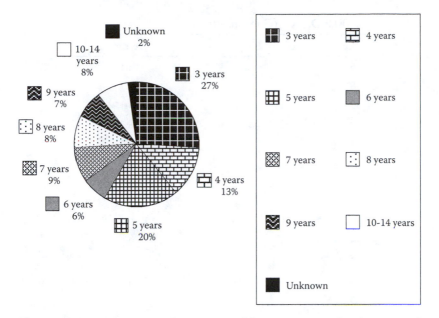

Figure D.2 First reported memory of being transgender (percent of participants).

TABLE D.3A   Age at Start of Therapy (N = 97)

Age	Frequency	Percent
20	1	1.0
21	1	1.0
22	2	2.1
23	1	1.0
24	1	1.0
26	2	2.1
27	1	1.0
28	3	3.1
29	3	3.1
30	2	2.1
31	1	1.0
33	2	2.1
34	4	4.1
35	3	3.1

(Continued)

TABLE D.3A   (Continued)

Age	Frequency	Percent
36	2	2.1
38	2	2.1
39	3	3.1
40	8	8.2
41	7	7.2
42	3	3.1
43	4	4.1
44	4	4.1
45	5	5.2
46	9	9.3
47	1	1.0
48	8	8.2
49	4	4.1
50	1	1.0
53	1	1.0
54	1	1.0
56	1	1.0
57	1	1.0
59	2	2.1
62	1	1.0
65	1	1.0
68	1	1.0
Total	97	100.0

The mean number of months was 24. This included periods of time when contact with the subject was interrupted because the subject came for one to four sessions, obtained information and withdrew from therapy, but then returned at a later time and engaged in sessions on a more regular basis.

To compensate for the fact that there were occasional interruptions in therapy and the frequency of sessions was titrated over time, both the number of sessions attended and the number of months between entering therapy and the most recent contact were measured. No correlation was found to exist between the age at first

TABLE D.3B   Age of First Awareness of Being Transgender (N = 94)

Age	Frequency	Percent
3	24	24.7
4	13	13.4
5	19	19.6
6	6	6.2
7	9	9.3
8	8	8.2
9	7	7.2
10	1	1.0
11	2	2.1
12	2	2.1
13	1	1.0
14	2	2.1
Total (N)	94	96.9

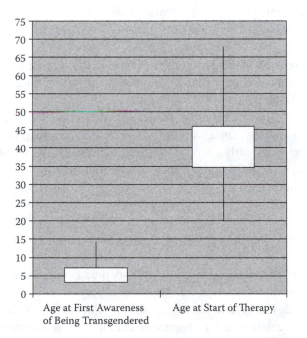

Figure D.3   Box plots comparing age at first awareness of being transgender (N = 94) with age at start of therapy (N = 97).

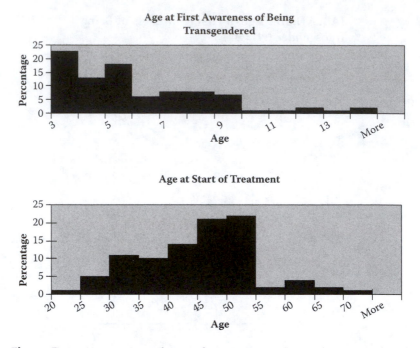

Figure D.4   Histograms of age at first awareness (N = 94) compared with age at start of therapy (N = 97).

memory related to being transgender and the age when entering therapy (Pearson correlation = −.059). A summary of findings is presented in Table D.11.

The range for number of sessions was 4–125. For number of months in therapy, the range was 1–76. With the mean number of months being 24, only a few of the subjects reached the point of having genital reconstruction surgery within that time period, if indeed that was their goal.

Experience With Transgender Expression

Specific questions were developed (see Appendix B, questions 17 and 18) to assess the subject's level of transgender experience, the subject's preferred female image, and the degree of the subject's objectivity regarding self-presentation as a transgender female at start and most recent point of contact. For each subject, the responses were used as benchmarks on a cross-gender continuum, as illustrated in Figure D.5.

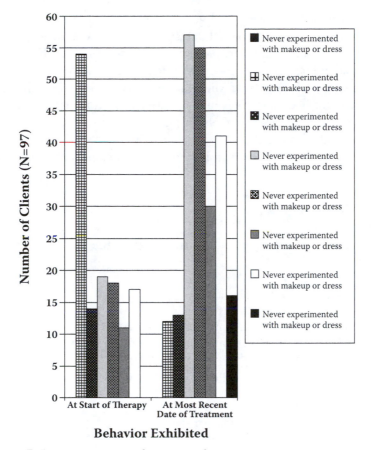

Figure D.5   Experience with transgender expression.

Based on the characteristics described in the combined 49 questions, subjects were assigned places on the continuum at both the start and most recent time of contact, so changes could be looked at over time in relation to changes in a subject's perception of his or her sexual orientation, that is, was there an identifiable cross-gender change or behavior that correlated with becoming sexually attracted to a male partner?

At the beginning, 0 subjects reported never having experimented with dress or makeup, while 54 subjects reported that they had experimented only in private. An overview of the other criteria used to gauge degrees of cross-gender experience shows that there was a range of 11–19 subjects who had engaged in some of the other various behaviors on the list of criteria at the start of therapy, with the exception that 0 subjects had genital reconstruction surgery at the start. At most recent contact, 11 subjects had experimented with dress and makeup only in private, but these were largely subjects who had entered therapy the most recently and had been in therapy for shorter periods of time when the data were collected. At the most recent point of contact, 56 subjects were out to most of their friends and family, and 55 went freely in public as female. Thirty subjects were spending most of the time outside of work in the female role, 41 lived full-time as female, and 16 had genital reconstruction surgery.

Primary Sexual Fantasy

For recording subject self-report in this area, the following categories were used:

- Self as male with male partner
- Self as male with female partner
- Self as male with either male or female partner
- Self as either male or female with male or female partner
- Self as either male or female with male partner
- Self as either male or female with female partner
- Self as female with either male or female partner
- Self as female with male partner
- Self as female with female partner
- Unknown
- Other
- None (meaning the subject does not report fantasizing)

As shown in Table D.4, there were two people with unknown fantasies at start of therapy and two with unknown fantasies at most recent contact. The category of "other" was used as a catchall category that included clients who said their fantasies were variable, including several of the above choices or changing frequently; those who fantasized about being with another transgender person; and so forth. There were 10 subjects in this category at start, which was down to 5 by most recent contact.

The number of subjects whose primary fantasy was of self as female with a female partner was 35 at start of therapy and 31 at most recent contact. Those who fantasized about self as female with either a male or a female partner was 7 at start and 13 at the most recent point, possibly the first indication of a shift.

TABLE D.4   Primary Sexual Fantasy of Subjects at Start and Most Recent Point in Therapy

Primary Sexual Fantasy	Number of Subjects (N = 97)	
	At Start (%)	Most Recently (%)
Self as female with:		
Female partner	35 (36)	31 (32)
Male or female partner	7 (7)	13 (13)
Male partner	17 (18)	30 (31)
Self as female or male with:		
Female partner	9 (9)	2 (2)
Male or female partner	2 (2)	0
Male partner	0	0
Self as male with:		
Female partner	2 (2)	0
Male or female partner	0	0
Male partner	0	0
Unknown fantasy	2 (2)	2 (2)
Other fantasies not listed	10 (10)	5 (5)
None (no reported fantasy)	13 (13)	14 (14)
Total number of subjects who changed primary sexual fantasy		30 (31)

The number who fantasized about self as female with a male partner was 17 at the beginning and 30 at the end. There were a total of nine at the start and two at the most recent contact who reported fantasizing about self as either male or female with a female partner. Subjects who said they fantasized about self as either male or female with either a male or a female partner numbered two at the start and zero at the most recent contact. This implies that even those subjects who may have been bisexual had a dominant preference for either a male or a female sex partner.

Those who reported fantasies about self as male with a female partner numbered two at start and zero at the end of the study. There were 13 subjects who reported having no sexual fantasies at the start, and 14 at the most recent point in therapy. Thirty-six subjects had acted upon their fantasies at the start of therapy, and 42 at most recent time. Of those who did not act on their fantasies, there were 56 at the start and 51 at most recent point of contact. The unknowns were

TABLE D.5   Number of Subjects Acting on Sexual Fantasies at Start and Most Recent Point in Therapy

Action Taken	At Start	At Most Recent
Acted on fantasies	36 (37%)	42 (43%)
Didn't act on them	58 (60%)	53 (55%)
Unknown	3 (3%)	2 (2%)
Number of subjects who did not change status		72 (74%)
Number of subjects who did change status		22 (23%)
Number of subjects whose status change is unknown		3 (3%)

three at the start and two at the most recent contact. Two subjects fell in the category of not applicable because they reported not having fantasies at the start or at the end point of contact. Table D.5 shows the pattern of behavior of subjects with regard to acting on their fantasies. However, since subjects often reported unwillingness to act on their fantasies until their bodies were "right for this" (i.e., sufficiently feminized, with "sufficiently" being a highly subjective concept), the infrequency of acting on these fantasies is to be expected where large numbers of subjects had not (yet) had GRS.

There was a significant overall change in primary sexual fantasies in the direction of increased sexual attraction to male-bodied partners. This change was not limited to subjects who planned to or already had GRS (Table D.11). This suggests that these changes were related more to subject self-acceptance as a transgender person than to changing one's body to become more female.

How Subjects Defined Their Gender Identity

The subjects were divided into eight self-identified categories of gender identity:

- Male
- Female
- Transsexual female/woman
- Crossdresser
- Bigendered
- Transgenderist
- Transgender
- Unsure/confused

As shown in Table D.6, there was only one subject at the start and two at the most recent contact who defined their gender identity simply as male. There was also only one subject who identified as female at the start and one at the end point of contact. There were 45 who identified as transsexual females at the start of therapy and 62 who did so at last contact. At both the start and end of contact there were 12 who identified as transgender. There were 22 who were unsure or confused at the start of therapy, and only 6 at most recent contact.

Among those subjects who planned to have or already did have GRS at the time of most recent contact, there was a significant change in how these subjects defined their gender identity (Table D.11).

How Subjects Defined Their Sexual Orientation

Regarding this question, the following categories and subcategories were used:

- Asexual (entirely or nearly)
- Autogynephilic
- Prefers masturbation fantasy of self as female:
  - With male partner
  - With female partner
- Prefers sexual partner who is:
  - Male
  - Female

TABLE D.6   Subjects' Self-Defined Gender Identity at Start and Most Recent Point in Therapy

	Number of Subjects (N = 97)	
Gender Identity	At Start (%)	Most Recently (%)
Male	1 (1)	2 (2)
Female	1 (1)	1 (1)
Transgender female	45 (46)	62 (64)
Crossdresser	16 (17)	14 (14)
Bigendered	0	0
Transgenderists	0	0
Transgender	12 (12)	12 (12)
Unsure/confused	22 (23)	6 (6)
Total number of subjects who changed gender identity		25 (26)

- Transgender female (MTF who has had GRS)
- Transgender (in any way other than immediately above)
- Unsure/confused
- No preference

As shown in Table D.7, there were nine subjects who described self as asexual at the start, and eight at most recent contact. There was only one self-defined autogynephilic at both the start and end point of contact. For clarification, it should be noted that the latter subject was not the same individual who did so at the start of the study, but rather was someone who was newer in the therapy

TABLE D.7   Sexual Orientation of Subjects at Start and Most Recent Point in Therapy

	Number of Subjects (N = 97)	
Sexual Orientation	At Start (%)	Most Recently (%)
Asexual or nearly so	9 (9)	8 (8)
Autogynephilic	1 (1)	1 (1)
Prefers masturbation fantasy:		
Self as female with male partner	0	0
Self as female with female partner	0	0
Prefers sexual partner who is:		
Male	18 (19)	27 (28)
Female	59 (61)	48 (50)
Transgender female	1 (1)	1 (1)
Transgender	0	1 (1)
Unsure/confused	4 (4)	4 (4)
No preference	5 (5)	7 (7)
Totals	97 (100%)	97 (100%)
Total number of subjects who changed sexual orientation		16 (17)

Note: 17% of subjects (N = 16) changed from one orientation to another as follows:
   1 subject changed from asexual to preferring females
   2 subjects changed from preferring females to no preference
   1 subject changed from preferring males to unsure/confused
   8 subjects changed from preferring females to preferring males
   2 subjects changed from unsure/confused to preferring males
   1 subject changed from preferring females to unsure/confused
   1 subject changed from preferring females to preferring transgendered
     partners

process. No one who was in the therapy process for a lengthy period of time remained self-identified as, or appeared to be, autogynephilic.

No subject preferred a masturbation fantasy to partnered sex (with either a male or female partner), at either start or end point of contact. There were 18 at the start and 27 at most recent contact who preferred a male sexual partner. None of these identified as gay males, but instead consistently identified themselves as heterosexual females in their sexual relationships with male partners. Those who preferred a female partner numbered 59 at the start and 48 at most recent contact. There was only one subject who preferred a transgender female partner at the start and one at the time of most recent contact.

Hormones

There were 38 subjects who never took feminizing hormones during their time in therapy. Of these 38 subjects, 7 reported change in sexual orientation at most recent point of contact, a significant number (see Table D.11 for summary of findings). There were 35 subjects who were not taking hormones at the start of therapy but began taking them during the course of therapy and continued to do so at most recent contact. Table D.8 illustrates the pattern of use.

Of these, five reported change in sexual orientation at most recent contact, a significant number. Another 14 were already taking hormones when they entered therapy and continued at most recent contact. Of these 14 subjects, 3 reported change in sexual orientation, also a significant number. Since the change was consistent among those who did and those who did not take hormones, it does not appear that hormones caused the change in sexual orientation. Table D.9 compares changes in sexual orientation to hormone use,

TABLE D.8   Pattern of Subject Use of Feminizing Hormones

Hormone Status	Number of Subjects
Did not take hormones regularly during course of therapy	44 (45%)
Took hormones at most recent point, but not at start of therapy	38 (39%)
Took hormones throughout course of therapy	15 (15%)

TABLE D.9   Relationship Between Use of Feminizing Hormones and Changes in Sexual Orientation

Sexual Orientation	At Start	At Most Recent
Subjects Who Did Not Take Hormones Regularly During Therapy (N = 38)		
Female partner	29 (76%)	24 (63%)
Unsure/confused	3 (8%)	4 (11%)
No preference	3 (8%)	4 (11%)
Transgender female partner	0	0
Transgender partner	0	0
Male partner	3 (8%)	6 (16%)
Number of subjects who changed sexual orientation		7 (18%)
Subjects Not Taking Hormones at Start, but Taking Hormones at Most Recent Point (N = 35)		
Female partner	23 (66%)	19 (54%)
Unsure/confused	1 (3%)	0
No preference	2 (6%)	3 (9%)
Transgender female partner	0	0
Transgender partner	0	1 (3%)
Male partner	8 (23%)	12 (34%)
Number of subjects who changed sexual orientation		5 (14%)
Subjects on Hormones at Both Start and Most Recent Points in Therapy (N = 14)		
Female partner	7 (50%)	4 (29%)
Unsure/confused	0	0
No preference	0	0
Transgender female partner	1 (7%)	1 (7%)
Transgender partner	0	0
Male partner	6 (43%)	9 (64%)
Number of subjects who changed sexual orientation		3 (21%)

and the results indicate that hormone use does not appear to cause these changes in sexual orientation.

The relationship between sexual orientation and both the number of therapy sessions and the number of months in therapy was also examined. Figures D.6 and D.7 illustrate this relationship.

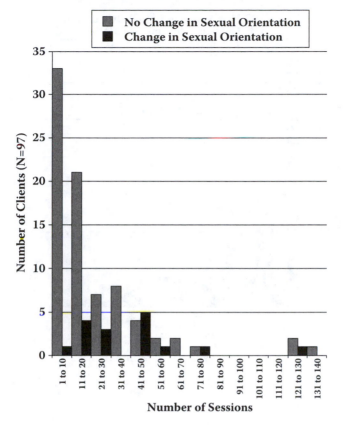

Figure D.6   Number of months in therapy compared to changes in sexual orientation.

Subject Intentions With Regard to Genital Reconstruction Surgery

A 6-point scale was used to assess subject status with regard to GRS at both the start and most recent points of contact. These included:

1. Has not considered GRS
2. Does not want GRS
3. Undecided
4. Wants but cannot have GRS
5. Plans to have GRS
6. Has already had GRS

As shown in Table D.10, at the start of therapy, 7% of subjects had not yet considered GRS, while this changed to 4% by most recent

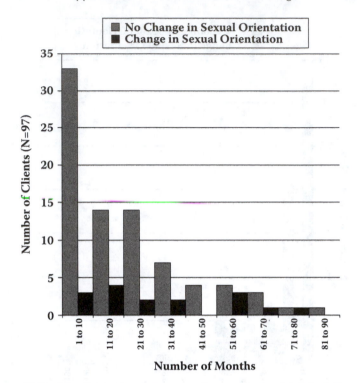

Figure D.7   Months in therapy versus changes in sexual orientation.

TABLE D.10   Subject Status Regarding Genital Reconstruction Surgery at Start and Most Recent Point in Therapy

Genital Reconstruction Surgery	At Start	At Most Recent
Has not yet considered	7 (7%)	4 (4%)
Does not want	11 (11%)	16 (17%)
Undecided	32 (33%)	11 (11%)
Wants to, but cannot	5 (5%)	23 (24%)
Plans to have	42 (43%)	27 (28%)
Already had	0	16 (17%)
Total number of subjects who did not change view about genital reconstruction surgery		48 (50%)
Total number of subjects who changed view about genital reconstruction surgery		49 (51%)

TABLE D.11   Summary of Statistical Findings: Independent Z-Tests, T-Tests, and Correlations

Category	N	Test Value	1-Sided or 2-Sided
Importance of religion	96	Z = −1.0*	2-sided
Importance of religion to those who plan to have or have already had genital reconstruction surgery at most recent point in therapy	43	Z = undefined	1-sided
Age of therapy versus age of first memory of being transgender	94	Pearson = −0.06	—
Sexual fantasy	73	Z = 4.61*	1-sided
Sexual fantasy of those who plan to have or have already had genital reconstruction surgery at most recent point in therapy	38	Z = 2.90*	1-sided
Action taken on sexual fantasy	94	Z = −1.25*	1-sided
Gender identity	97	Z = 4.87*	1-sided
Sexual orientation	87	Z = 3.40*	1-sided
Gender reconstruction surgery	97	Z = 3.59*	1-sided
Sexual orientation versus hormones:			
Subjects who never took hormones	38	Z = 10.76*	1-sided
Subjects who took hormones at most recent point, but not at start	35	Z = 110.83*	1-sided
Subjects who took hormones at both start and most recent point	14	T = 1.88*	1-sided

*$p \leq .05$ (significant change in subjects over time spent in therapy).

contact. These figures indicate that the majority of this subject pool had at least given some thought to genital surgery. The difference between 7% and 4% is small, indicating a consistent pattern of giving thought to GRS. The 7% of subjects at start and the 4% at most recent point of contact were not necessarily the same people. This slight difference (7% compared to 4%) could be explained by the presence of more subjects who were earlier in their transgender journey at the beginning of the study than they were at the end.

Eleven percent of the subjects did not want GRS at the start of therapy, and 17% at the most recent point. At the start of therapy, 33% were undecided about GRS, and by the most recent point only

11% remained undecided. Clearly, a few of these may have moved into the category of "Does not want." Eleven percent of the subjects fell into this category at the start of therapy, whereas there were 17% in that category at the most recent contact.

At start of therapy 5% of subjects wanted but could not have GRS, with 24% in this position at most recent point of contact.

Summary

An overview of comparisons, including statistical analyses, is shown in Table D.11. The summary of findings and comparisons shown in this table provides the reader with a quick reference for overall results.

Appendix E: Internet Resources

Professional Websites

- American Association of Sex Educators, Counselors and Therapists (AASECT): <http://www.aasect.org>
- Gender Identity Research and Education Society (GIRES): <http://www.gires.org.uk>
- Harry Benjamin International Gender Dysphoria Association (HBIGDA): <http://www.hbigda.org>; new name: World Professional Association for Transgender Health (WPATH)
- International Journal of Transgenderism: <http://www.symposion.com/ijt>
- Intersex Society of North America (ISNA): <http://www.isna.org>
- Kinsey Institute at Indiana University: <http://www.indiana.edu/~kinsey>
- Magnus Herschel Archive of Sexology: <http://www2.hu-berlin.de/sexology>
- Parents and Friends of Lesbians and Gays (PFLAG): <http://www.pflag.org>; use search engine using keyword *transgender* and look at the bottom of the page.
- Society for the Scientific Study of Sexuality: <http://www.sex-science.org>
- Society for Sex Therapy and Research: <http://www.sstarnet.org>

Trans Community Websites

- Andrea James' TS Roadmap: <http://www.tsroadmap.com>
- Children of Lesbians and Gays Everywhere (COLAGE; has information for trans children too): <http://www.colage.org>; use the search engine using the keyword *transgender*.
- Children of Transsexuals (COT): <http://www.geocities.com/reneelind>

- Chrysalis (for transgender children, teens, and their families): <http://www.tgchrysalis.com>
- GenderTalk: <http://www.gendertalk.com>
- Gender Education and Advocacy: <http://www.gender.org>
- Gender Public Advocacy Coalition (GenderPAC): <http://www.gpac.org>
- Lynn Conway: <http://www.lynnconway.com>
- National Transgender Advocacy Coalition: <http://www.ntac.org>
- Rebecca Allison, MD: <http://www.drbecky.com>; for a direct link to therapist resources, <http://www.drbecky.com/therapists.html>
- Renaissance Transgender Association (for transgender people and their family members): <http://www.ren.org>
- Society for the Second Self, Inc. (Tri-Ess; an organization for heterosexual crossdressers and their family members): <http://www.tri-ess.org>
- Susan's Place for Transgender Resources: <http://www.susans.org>
- Transgender Family: <http://www.transfamily.org>
- Transgender Forum: <http://www.tgforum.com>
- Transgender Law and Policy Institute: <http://www.transgenderlaw.org>

Advocacy/Activist Groups

- FTM International (Female to Male): <http://www.FTMi.org>
- GID Reform: <http://www.transgender.org/gidr/index.html>
- International Foundation for Gender Education (IFGE): <http://www.ifge.org>
- Intersex Society of North America (ISNA): <http://www.isna.org>
- National Center for Transgender Equity (NCTE): <http://www.pfc.org.uk>
- National Transgender Advocacy Coalition (NTAC): <http://www.ntac.org>
- Press for Change (PFC): <http://www.pfc.org.uk>
- Transgender Law and Policy Institute: <http://www.transgenderlaw.org>

Annotated Bibliography

Allen, J. J. (1996). *The man in the red velvet dress: Inside the world of cross-dressing*. New York: Birch Lane Press, Carol Publishing Group. A well-educated and articulate crossdresser researches the world of crossdressing and writes about it from the perspective of a cross-dresser. The author discovers more diversity than he was originally aware existed, but also offers a unique perspective, including aspects of sexuality.

Allison, R. (1999). Reply to Dr. Anne Lawrence. *Transgender Tapestry, 87,* 50–51 (published by the International Foundation for Gender Education). Another transgender physician challenges the position of Anne Lawrence regarding autogynephilia, as presented in an earlier article. This ongoing journalistic debate highlights the fact that even among highly educated and well-informed transgender individuals, there is no consensus as to the origins of transgender and its associated sexuality.

Amato, T., & Davies, M. (Eds.). (2004). *Pinned down by pronouns* (2nd ed.). Boston: Conviction Books. This is a collection of personal stories written by 75 gender-variant individuals in the Boston area, many of them youthful, discussing the impact on their lives of the gender binary and traditional use of pronouns. This lively discussion includes several points of view about what needs to change. It offers a window of insight into the thinking of younger transpeople.

American Psychiatric Association. (1980). *Diagnostic and statistical manual of mental disorders* (DSM-III) (3rd ed.). Washington, DC: Author. Uses diagnoses of (1) transvestic fetishism, which most transgender people see as a phase that occurs early in the experience of crossdressing for most individuals, and (2) gender identity disorder, which is essentially transsexualism. Divides transsexuals into three types: heterosexual, homosexual, and asexual. Biological sex is reference point for these. Would have to use (3) not otherwise specified diagnosis to denote the individual who shifts sexual orientation as gender role changes.

American Psychiatric Association. (2000). *Diagnostic and statistical manual of mental disorders* (DSM-IV) (4th ed.). Washington, DC: Author. Most recent revision of the primary diagnostic manual for mental disorders and source of diagnostic codes used by mental health professionals in the United States.

Beach, F. A. (Ed.). (1976). *Human sexuality in four perspectives*. Baltimore: Johns Hopkins University Press. Drawing on the work of several noted authors, this book examines human sexuality from the developmental, sociological, physiological, and evolutionary perspectives. The contrast among the perspectives is challenging and thought-provoking.

Bem, S. L. (1993). *The lenses of gender*. New York: Yale University Press. Focuses on gender roles and how they develop. Discusses male and female differences and the perpetuation of male social power. Using the concept of social lenses, present from birth, shaping perceptions, and deeply embedded in culture, the author identifies components that influence gender roles. She examines the theories of gender identity development and issues inherent in establishing equal rights for women and sexual minorities. Discusses whether or not males and females are fundamentally different, and whether it is better to reduce or eliminate the differences or celebrate them. Bem does an excellent job of setting forth the social issues and provoking thought about the existing social structure and possible directions for change.

Benjamin, H. (1966). *The transsexual phenomenon*. New York: Julian Press. A pioneer in the field of transgender writes about his findings and observations.

Bentler, P. M. (1976). A typology of transsexualism: Gender identity theory and data. *Archives of Sexual Behavior, 5*, 567–84. Divides transsexuals into three types: heterosexual, homosexual, and asexual. Biological sex is the reference point for these. Does not address sexual orientation.

Berkovitz, I. H. (Ed.). (1972). *Adolescents grow in groups*. New York: Brunner/Mazel. Studies in adolescent development, including sexuality.

Besen, W. B. (2003). *Anything but straight: Unmasking the scandals and lies behind the ex-gay myth*. New York: Harrington Park Press. As the title implies, this is an exposé of the ex-gay movement and the fundamentalist ministries behind it. However, do not be quick to dismiss it as lacking in credibility just because it is an exposé. It is well written, well researched, and very readable. Most importantly for the focus of this book, it speaks to the nature of sexual orientation, albeit in the gay population.

Blanchard, R. (1985). Typology of male-to-female transsexualism. *Archives of Sexual Behavior, 14*, 247–61. Report on a study testing the hypothesis that male transsexuals are either heterosexual or homosexual, that there are no intermediate categories. What may appear as such are actually subtypes of heterosexual transsexuality. Blanchard uses natal biological gender as the point of reference for these labels. He studied 163 MTF transsexuals and believes his findings support this view.

Blanchard, R., Clemmensen, L. H., & Steiner, B. W. (1987). Heterosexual and homosexual gender dysphoria. *Archives of Sexual Behavior, 16*, 139–52. The authors write about sexual orientation with the assumption that it remains constant throughout the sex reassignment process.

Bockting, W. (1999). From construction to context: Gender through the eyes of the transgendered. *SIECUS Report, 28*, 3–7. This article points out that transgender identity may fluctuate over time and circumstance, recognizing that this may represent a process of self-discovery. Bockting goes on to challenge existing theories of transgender as not fitting with the experience reported by MTF transgender individuals themselves with regard to sexual orientation, reporting that some remain attracted to males, some to females, and some report shifting attraction as gender role shifts.

Bockting, W. O., & Coleman, E. (1992). *Gender dysphoria: Interdisciplinary approaches in clinical management.* Binghamton, NY: Haworth Press. As the title indicates, this book offers a summarized model for assessment and treatment of the transgender client. Included are comments about the currently used DSM classification in relation to sexual orientation (p. 149).

Bolin, A., & Wheleban, P. (1999). *Perspectives on human sexuality.* New York: State University of New York Press. Textbook study of human sexuality covering anthropological and biological perspectives as well as anatomy and physiology, life stages of sexual development and expression, gender and sexual identity, sexual behaviors and HIV. Included is a section on transgender that is well presented. However, the question of the effect of transition of gender role on sexual orientation is not addressed.

Boyd, H. (2003). *My husband Betty: Love, sex, and life with a crossdresser.* New York: Thunder's Mouth Press. Written by the wife of a crossdresser, I consider this to be the best book available for and about the wives of crossdressers, and perhaps about crossdressers themselves. Boyd did not settle for drawing upon her own personal experience, but interviewed many other wives of crossdressers and many other crossdressers themselves. She has captured a broad cross section of the world of crossdressing and tells us about it in a compassionate and nonjudgmental way. Neither does she shy away from the tough issues, such as the initial negative feelings that many wives have when they find out about a husband's crossdressing, or the sensitive issue of sex both inside and outside of the marriage.

Boylan, J. F. (2003). *She's not there: A life in two genders.* New York: Broadway Books. An autobiographical memoir of a gender role transition by an author and Colby (Maine) college professor. Articulate and comprehensive, giving insights into many aspects of the transition process, including the struggles of family and friends, the hurdles of coming out, how children can be included, and how they respond when the situation is handled with maturity and mutual respect. Included is an afterword by Jennifer's friend and 2001 Pulitzer prize-winning author Richard Russo, discussing the impact of transition on friendship.

Brown, G. R. (1987). The transsexual in the military: Flight into hypermasculinity. *Archives of Sexual Behavior, 17,* 527–37.

Brown, M. L., & Rounsley, C. A. (1996). *True selves: Understanding transsexualism—For families, friends, coworkers, and helping professionals.* San Francisco: Jossey-Bass Publishers. Using Brown's years of clinical experience, the authors have presented the transsexual experience with sensitivity and insight for the benefit of isolated transgender people, those close to them, and the professional who faces working with such a client but lacks experience and resources. Some of the most common questions are answered. A little of the history of treating transsexualism, including theories, is provided, and important names in the field are identified. The role of therapy is explained, as well as the process of transition, how to deal with issues related to job and career, and telling important people in one's life.

Bullough, V. L., & Bullough, B. (1993). *Cross dressing, sex and gender.* Philadelphia: University of Pennsylvania Press. A comprehensive historical and cultural overview of transgender in the Western world. Also examines transgender in its various forms. Does not address sexual orientation in relation to a shifting gender role.

Burke, P. (1996). *Gender shock, exploring the myths of male and female.* New York: Anchor Books, Doubleday. Discusses the concepts of gender prevalent in our society and the cost to individuals and society as a whole for rigidly adhering to the associated behavioral definitions. Examines abuses to individuals, especially children. Identifies historically harmful responses of therapists and researchers. Attributes all gender-related behavior to learning; denies any of it is innate. Roundly condemns most of the people who are considered leaders in the field for their research, teaching, writing, and therapy, on the basis of perpetuating these restrictive and stifling concepts.

Burr, C. (1996). *A separate creation: The search for the biological origins of sexual orientation.* New York: Hyperion. As implied in the title, this work reviews and critiques the research into the biological origins of sexual orientation, examining the biases and belief systems that obstruct objectivity. The author also provides the reader with a basic and clear lesson in biology and the world of research. The writing style makes the review of the research seem more like a detective story, thus making it palatable to the lay reader.

Cohen-Kettenis, P., & Pfafflin, F. (2003). *Transgenderism and intersexuality in childhood and adolescence making choices.* (Developmental Psychology and Psychiatry Series, Book 46). Thousand Oaks, CA: Sage Publications. This wonderfully forward-looking work sets forth for the reader the range of conditions and issues related to sexual differentiation and gender identity variation. It explores the clinical and ethical issues inherent in the treatment of children who present with these conditions, including theories and treatment options. It is enlivened with numerous case histories that illustrate the points under discussion.

Colapinto, J. (2000). *As nature made him: The boy who was raised as a girl.* New York: Harper-Collins Publishing. Recounting of a landmark case that began in 1967 when a baby boy suffered the loss of his penis in the process of circumcision and was subsequently raised as a girl. This case set the stage for the feminist movement position that gender was a social construct and was learned. It has also forced social scientists to reexamine this construct in light of new information that, in this case, the individual was not happy as a female and has since reclaimed his male identity.

Cole, S. S., Denny, D., Eyler, A. E., & Samons, S. L. (2000). Issues of transgender. In L. T. Szuchman & F. Muscarella (Eds.), *Psychological perspectives on human sexuality* (pp. 149–95). New York: John Wiley & Sons. Chapter 4 provides a broad overview of some depth on medical, psychological, social, and political issues as they relate to transgender persons and their family members. Written by co-authors of diverse disciplines, all with expertise in transgender issues. Does not address the impact of gender role transition on sexual orientation.

Coleman, E. (1987). Assessment of sexual orientation. *Journal of Homosexuality, 14,* 10–24. This article specifically addresses the question of how sexual orientation is defined and offers suggestions for alternative ways to view this complex concept.

Coleman, E., & Bockting, W. O. (1988). "Heterosexual" prior to sex reassignment—"homosexual afterwards": A case study of a female-to-male transsexual. *Journal of Psychology & Human Sexuality, 1,* 69–82. While this article specifically offers a case study of a FTM person, it is relevant to a discussion of MTF sexual orientation, as it illustrates the unconventional way this subject defined his sexual orientation, and the discussion has implications for the sexual orientation of MTFs as well.

Coleman, E., Bockting, W. O., & Gooren, L. (1993). Homosexual and bisexual identity in sex-reassigned female-to-male transsexuals. *Archives of Sexual Behavior, 22,* 37–49. This article is a report on nine FTMs who are sexually attracted to males. Although anecdotally the path of FTMs appears quite different from that of MTFs, the way these subjects view their sexual orientation is analogous to that of many of the MTFs in the study being reported upon in this book, and therefore provides an interesting contrast.

Coleman, E., Colgan, P., & Gooren, L. (1992). Male cross-gender behavior in Mayanmar (Burma): A description of the acault. *Archives of Sexual Behavior, 21,* 313–321. This article describes the Burmese belief system and social attitude toward the acault within their culture. There does not appear to be any distinction between MTF transgenders and effeminate male homosexuals, but the belief is that being this way is not chosen but is due to being visited by a female spirit, usually early in life. While sex between male partners is not accepted in this culture, the acault are viewed as female and it is expected that their sex partners will be male.

Daskalos, C. T. (1998, December). Changes in the sexual orientation of six heterosexual male-to-female transsexuals. *Archives of Sexual Behavior,* 605–14. The author states, "Such changes have rarely been investigated and present a challenge to current understandings of sexual orientation." His article reports on a study that included 20 transsexuals, 16 MTF and 4 FTM. All were living full-time in the gender role with which they identified. Only six reported a shift in sexual orientation, and these were all MTFs shifting away from orientation to females. Of these six, four were postoperative and two preoperative. Subjects explained the shift in various ways that correspond to what was found in the present study. The author does not believe that the concept of autogynephilia is sufficient to explain the shift in orientation.

Dennis, P. (1955). *Auntie Mame.* New York: Ballantine Books, a division of Random House, Inc. A fictionalized and humorous account of being raised by a flamboyant and eccentric but loving aunt.

Denny, D. (1999) Transgender in the United States: A brief discussion. *SIECUS Report, 8,* 8–13. In this overview article, the author devotes one small paragraph to sexual orientation in transgender people, but in that brief context, she states, "This orientation may or may not change after transition." Thus, without elaboration, she gives recognition to the reality of this aspect of transgender experience.

Denny, D., & Green, J. (1996). Gender identity and bisexuality. In B. A. Firestein (Ed.), *Bisexuality: The psychology and politics of an invisible minority* (pp. 84–102). Thousand Oaks, CA: Sage Publications. Chapter 3 offers a concise summary of the transgender dilemma, along

with a review of some of the recent literature relating to sexual orientation in both MTF and FTM transgender individuals. The authors
make a strong case for the fluidity of sexual orientation within the
transgender population and possibly within the larger general population that includes nontransgender people. They propose terminology that would be less pejorative and less limiting in the way we view
sexual orientation.

Devor, H. (1989). *Gender blending*. Indianapolis: Indiana University Press.
The author discusses the genetic, biological, and social influences that
combine to support her theory of gender as a social construct distinct
from biological sex. Her specific focus is on biological females who
live so close to the male-female gender line as to be mistaken at times
for men. She specifically presents for the reader the lives of 15 females
who represent a spectrum of gender blending.

Diamond, L. M. (2000). Sexual identity, attractions, and behavior among
young sexual-minority women over a two-year period. *Developmental Psychology, 36*, 241–250. An early report on a longitudinal study
of female sexual orientation, now nearly in its 10th year. For more
information, see Diamond, L. M., & Hicks, A. M. (2005). Attachment
style, current relationship security, and negative emotions: The medi-
ating role of physiological regulation. *Journal of Social and Personal
Relationships, 22*, 499–518.

Diamond, M., & Sigmundson, H. K. (1997). Sex reassignment at birth:
Long term review and clinical implications. *Archives of Pediatrics
and Adolescent Medicine, 151*, 298–304. Assumes sexual orientation
is constant and independent of gender role.

Docter, R. F. (1988). *Transvestites and transsexuals: Toward a theory of
cross-gender behavior*. New York: Plenum Press. Reports the results
of the largest survey to date on transgender behavior, and proposes a
theory, including what the author identifies as secondary transsexualism, with Docter's concept being that there are early- and late-onset
transsexuals, and they are clinically different in several primary ways.
The study is based on the initial 110 responses from people who identify themselves as heterosexual crossdressers. Several of their wives
are also included. Docter has been (and is) a well-known figure in the
transgender community, often speaking at transgender community
conventions, and thus having extensive opportunity to mingle and
interact with hundreds of subjects. He talks about the many manifestations of cross-gender behavior and goes over some of the early
theories of causation.

Docter, R. F. (2004). *From man to woman: The transgender journey of Virginia Prince*. Northridge, CA: Docter Press. Based on a long-standing
friendship and a series of interviews, Docter tells the story of

Virginia Prince, born in 1912 and long considered by many as the Grande Dame of the transgender community. Inseparable from Virginia's story is the story of the early development of the transgender community.

Doorn, C. D. (1997). Towards a gender identity theory of transsexualism. Unpublished dissertation, Vrije Universiteit, Amsterdam, The Netherlands. This is a work that I very much regret is not more widely available. It is the best source I have found for both a comprehensive review of the literature and a truly objective look at the question of sexual orientation in relation to transsexualism.

Dreger, A. D. (1998). *Hermaphrodites and the medical invention of sex.* Cambridge, MA: Harvard University Press. This book examines the history of the biomedical treatment of intersexed humans or hermaphrodites in France and Britain in the late 19th and early 20th centuries. It was during this time that the foundation was laid for the modern medical treatment of intersex, an approach to treatment that is now being criticized by the intersex community and reviewed by many medical centers.

Dreger, A. D. (Ed.). (1999). *Intersex in the age of ethics.* Hagerstown, MD: University Publishing Group. The author is a medical historian and medical ethicist. Through this collection of essays, she traces the history of the medical perception of intersexuality and how that thinking has evolved. Included are some writings of personal experience by people who are intersexed, as well as how thinking about intersex has evolved, and some of the more prominent schools of thought as to whether change in the way the medical profession addresses intersex conditions in infants is indicated, and how families can be helped to deal with intersexuality in a loved one.

Ebershoff, D. (2000). *The Danish girl.* New York: Viking Press. This story is a fictionalized account of the true story of an early sex change surgery and the transsexual person upon whom it was performed. Taken from the nonfictional account *Man Into Woman* by Niels Hoyer in the early 1930s, this story describes the emerging female identity, how the spousal relationship evolved, and one of the earliest known sex change surgeries.

Ekins, R., & King, D. (1997). Blending genders: Contributions to the emerging field of transgender studies. *International Journal of Transgenderism, 1*(1), <http://www.symposion.com/ijt/ijtc0101.htm>. The authors discuss the current classification system for types of transgender and the limitations it imposes for social scientists and the medical profession. This paper also includes the experiences of transgender people, ranging from crossdressers through those who have sex change surgeries; examines social patterns with regard to transgender over the past few decades, the emergence of gender blending as a popular social phenomenon, and the medicalization of gender blending; and discusses debates about the political significance of gender blending.

Epstein, R. (2006). Do gays have a choice? *Scientific American Mind, 17,* 50–57. Although this article does not address transgender at all, it is a fascinating discussion of sexual orientation in gays that has implications for transgenders as well.

Ettner, R. (1996). *Confessions of a gender defender.* Chicago: Spectrum Press. An unaffected and readable autobiographical account of how a psychologist was first introduced to the world of transgender and how it affected some of her own perceptions of clients, her work, and the world. She intersperses vignettes with information and her own interpretations to help the reader better understand what it is like for a transgender person to navigate through life in a world that is at best indifferent and often hostile, judgmental, and unaccepting. She describes how the transgender person often faces life with some of the same attitudes and mistaken beliefs as the larger society of which he is a member. She describes medical procedures that are commonly needed and sought by transgender persons, and how these procedures impact lives. Ettner goes on to describe some of her own frustrations as she tries to offer education to her own profession, especially as she has encountered disinterest from the people she had most expected to show a sympathetic interest.

Ettner, R. (1999). *Gender loving care, a guide to counseling gender-variant clients.* New York: W.W. Norton & Co. Ettner draws from many resources to provide a brief overview of historical views of transsexualism, from a historical, social, and clinical perspective, with theories of gender identity development and suggestions for diagnosis and therapy. This book, together with the work of Mildred Brown, is essential reading for the mental health professional beginning to work with the transgender population.

Eugenides, J. (2002). *Middlesex.* New York: Farrar, Straus and Giroux. This is a fictionalized account of the life of a young person with the intersex condition known as 5-alpha-reductase. For this work, the author became the recipient of a Pulitzer Prize. But while dramatically portraying the effects of this condition on this young person and the family of that person, this is also an epoch story of a family over many generations and of a couple of pivotal points in history, in the Mediterranean area of the family's origin, and in Detroit, Michigan, where they ultimately settled. The characters are memorable and the description of the effects of this intersex condition are accurate. There is one troubling point, and that is the implication that a family history of incest was a causative factor in the occurrence of the intersex condition. I do not believe that there is any scientific evidence to support this idea.

Fausto-Sterling, A. (2000, July/August). The five sexes, revisited. *The Sciences*, pp. 20–25. With primary focus on intersexuality, this article discusses the dramatic changes that have occurred in the past seven years with regard to the concept of gender. Fausto-Sterling briefly touches on the role of transgender in this process and recognizes the diversity in sexual orientation, but does not address shift in orientation.

Feinberg, L. (1996). *Transgender warriors: Making history from Joan of Arc to RuPaul*. Boston: Beacon Press. This is an account of the author's personal experience that also breaks new ground in both history and theory. The author demonstrates that the historical suppression of transgender has rendered invisible the links between class and gender oppression. She calls on all of us to wield the emerging recognition of transgender warriors throughout history as a weapon in the struggle to make the world a safer and better place for people of all sexes, genders, and desires.

Fraiberg, S. H. (1959). *The magic years*. New York: Charles Scribner's Sons. Understanding and handling the problems of early childhood through age 6, including sense of self, sense of reality, and learning about sex.

Freund, K., Steiner, B. W., & Chan, S. (1982). Two types of cross-gender identity. *Archives of Sexual Behavior, 11*, 49–63. Describes transvestites as heterosexual males who engage in contragender behavior or fantasy only when erotically aroused, as distinguished from male-to-female transsexuals who are biological males who have a long-standing and consistent desire to have a female body and live entirely as females.

Garber, M. (1992). *Vested interests: Crossdressing & cultural anxiety*. New York: Routledge Press. The author traces the role and importance of crossdressing in Western culture, as manifested in art, social practice, and public scandal. She asserts that Western culture would have been altered completely without the influence of crossdressing.

Gore, A. Jr. (1998, March). The genetic moral code. *The Advocate, 31*, 9. Even the vice president of the United States gets into the debate about sexual orientation. Of course, until the debate is settled for the larger minority we refer to as homosexuality, the focus on transgender and sexual orientation is not likely to get much attention.

Green, R. (Ed.). (1974). *Sexual identity conflict in children and adults*. New York: Basic Books. A collection of articles on this subject, all viewed from the pathologizing perspective that the individual who does not conform to the binary norm of male or female is suffering from a psychological illness that requires treatment and correction for the individual to be able to live easily within society.

Grinder, R. E. (Ed.). (1969). *Studies in adolescence*. London: The Macmillan Co., Collier-Macmillan Ltd. Readings in adolescent development, including various aspects of socialization, physical and cognitive growth, and sexual development and learning.

Haeberle, E. J. (1978). *The sex atlas: A new illustrated guide*. New York: The Seabury Press. This is a comprehensive reference book, including sections on the human body, human sexual behavior, and sex in society.

Hamer, D., & Copeland, P. (1994). *The science of desire: The search for the gay gene and the biology of behavior*. New York: Simon & Schuster. Describes the groundbreaking research that raised such controversy about the origins of sexual orientation as well as some other behaviors. Written in part like a detective story, this fascinating work leaves the reader with the author's opinion but no definitive answers.

Hammerstein, O., II, & Fields, J. (Screenplay writers). (1961). *Flower drum song* (Directed by Henry Koster). Based on the novel of the same name by C. Y. Lee (1957).

Harry Benjamin International Gender Dysphoria Association (HBIGDA). (1998). *Standards of care for gender identity disorders* (5th ed.), Minneapolis: Author. Also see <http://www.hbigda.org>.

Harry Benjamin International Gender Dysphoria Association (HBIGDA). (2000). *Standards of care for gender identity disorders* (6th ed.), Minneapolis: Author. Also sees: <http://www.hbigda.org>.

Hirschfeld, M. (1922). *Sexualpathologie* [Sexual pathology]. Bonn, France: Marcus & Weber. Defined four types of gender disturbance in males: heterosexual, homosexual, bisexual, and narcissistic or automonosexual. The latter is distinguished from asexuality in that the individual does have a sexual interest in self, but lacks sexual interest in others.

Hirschfeld, M. (1991). In M. A. Lombardi-Nash (Trans.), *Transvestites: The erotic drive to cross-dress*. Buffalo, NY: Prometheus Books. This translation of a pioneering work of Magnus Hirschfeld (1868–1935), much of whose work was lost during the rise to power of Adolph Hitler, provides the reader with a window to the early thought about a segment of the transgender population. In this work, divided into three parts, Hirschfeld first addresses some ethical questions in serving this population. He goes on to discuss diagnosis from many different perspectives, including sexual expression in its various forms, of which homosexuality is but one. He also offers historical and ethnological perspectives.

Humphreys, L. (1972). *Out of the closet: The sociology of homosexual liberation*. Englewood, CA: Prentice-Hall. Discuses homophobia and the question of whether a homosexual orientation can be changed.

Hunt, S., & Main, T. L. (1997). Sexual orientation confusion among spouses of transvestites and transsexuals following disclosure of spouse's gender dysphoria. *Journal of Psychology and Human Sexuality, 9,* 39–51.

Hunter, R. (Producer) & Rodgers, R., & Hammerstein, O. II (Music/lyrics). (1961). *Flower drum song* [Motion picture]. Universal Pictures Company, Inc. & Ross Hunter Productions, Inc. Nancy Kwan sings the song "I Enjoy Being a Girl."

Hutchins, L., & Kaahumanu, L. (Eds.). (1991). *Bi any other name: Bisexual people speak out.* Boston: Alyson Publications. This work is a collection of personal stories and essays on relevant topics written by over 100 bisexual males and females. Organized into categories of reaching self-acceptance, finding spiritual healing, the community of bisexuals, and the politics of being different even among other sexual minorities, this work presents a broad view of bisexuality and supports the earlier work of Kinsey that suggests that the lines between heterosexuality and homosexuality, especially over time, are human fabrications that do not reflect the reality of human sexuality.

Israel, G. E., & Tarver, D. E., II. (1997). *Transgender care: Recommended guidelines, practical information & personal accounts.* Philadelphia: Temple University Press. This is one of the better written books about the clinical treatment of transsexualism. Covering a comprehensive array of issues from diagnosis through surgery, and including common clinical problems and suggestions for addressing them. While the authors make clear the distinction between gender identity and sexual orientation, like other authors, they do not speak to the question of what often appears to be change in sexual orientation that can occur as the shift in gender role takes place.

Kessler, S. J. (1998). *Lessons from the intersexed.* New Brunswick, NJ: Rutgers University Press. This work offers a thorough examination of the traditional medical and surgical treatment of intersexed infants and children. It challenges Western culture's medicalization of this condition, raises ethical questions to the narrow definition of "normal" that is in current use, and suggests alternatives that may be somewhat idealistic in today's world, but a vision of the future that may be possible to achieve.

Kinsey, A., Pomeroy, W., & Martin, C. (1948). *Sexual behavior in the human male.* Philadelphia: W. B. Saunders Co. Coupled with the authors' following work on the human female, this is unquestionably the single most important study of human sexuality of the 20th century. Kinsey and his associates devoted many years of their lives to interviewing thousands of subjects in depth about their sexual histories and practices, then performed a comprehensive analysis of the data. In a time when scientific methods of studying large populations were as yet not well defined, Kinsey discusses the methods he used at length, explaining the drawbacks of various possible approaches and his reasons for using the approach he elected. Even with its limitations, this work provides the baseline against which most other researchers who followed him compared their own results.

Kirby, D. (2000, November). After the fall. *The Advocate, 21*, 41–44. John Paulk had been considered the poster boy for Christian right-wing conversion therapy, in which gays could be treated and made straight. His marriage in 1992 was highly publicized. Gay activists considered him a traitor of sorts. So, in 2000, when he was discovered hanging out in a gay bar, this too was highly publicized and added fuel to the conversion controversy.

Klein, Fritz. (1993). *The bisexual option*. New York: The Harrington Park Press. The author presents a study of 144 bisexual males and females, obtaining a general profile and discussing factors that influenced how socially well adjusted these individuals had become. Also discusses the place of bisexuality in today's society.

Lawrence, A. (1998, Winter). Men trapped in men's bodies. *Transgender Tapestry*, 65–68. Published by the International Foundation for Gender Education. Lawrence sets forth her view of the concept of autogynephilia, which she believes to explain transgender from a different perspective, one that makes such perfect sense to her that she cannot understand why everyone is not agreeing with her. She does address openly the range of sexual expression in transgender in a positive way when too many have tried to flavor transgender sexuality vanilla in order to make it more palatable to the general population. However, in the process, she discounts any other perspectives, whether competing or simply broadening the view. This includes discounting the experience of many of her transgender sisters, characterizing them as "troublesome people" when they report differing self-perceptions.

Lawrence, A. (1999, August). Autogynephilia: Frequently asked questions. *Transsexual Women's Resources*, 65–68. Published on author's website: <http://www.annelawrence.com/agfaqs.html>. Using question-and-answer format, Lawrence elucidates the theory of autogynephilia. In essence, this corresponds very closely to Docter's concept of primary and secondary transsexualism, with the defining characteristic being eroticized crossdressing in reality or fantasy.

Leland, J., & Miller, M. (1998, August 17). Can gays convert? *Newsweek*, pp. 47–50. Cover story regarding the controversy about homosexual conversion therapy.

Lev, A. I. (2004). *Transgender emergence: Therapeutic guidelines for working with gender-variant people and their families*. Binghamton, NY: Haworth Clinical Practice Press.

LeVay, S. (1996). *Queer science: The use and abuse of research into homosexuality*. Cambridge, MA: MIT Press. Brings together the research to date, along with the social and political ramifications of the search for the "gay gene." The author also reviews other prominently considered causative theories of homosexuality and critiques each.

Meyerowitz, J. (2002). *How sex changed: A history of transsexuality in the United States*. Cambridge, MA: Harvard University Press. This book combines an amazing amount of well-documented information with a readable style to provide the reader with not only a detailed early history of transsexuality and the social and medical responses to it, but also the preliminary history in Western Europe that provides the backdrop to what was happening in the United States. It is an excellent resource, but it does not address what might be termed modern times, that is, the last two decades of the 20th century and beyond.

Money, J. (1986). *Lovemaps*. New York: Irvington Publishers. Money sets forth his clinical concepts of sexual and erotic health and pathology. He describes his theories of gender identity and transposition in childhood, adolescence and adulthood, including the development of sexual and psychosexual disorders. Included are indexes and a glossary of terms relating to sex characteristics, paraphilias, and disorders.

Money, J. (1995). *Gendermaps*. New York: Continuum Publishing Co. This work is where Money focuses specifically on his theory of gender in its many aspects. He discusses how the term *gender* came into use and elaborates on the concept of gender role. He discusses gender differentiation and his concept of nature/critical period/nurture.

Money, J., & Ehrhardt, A. A. (1973). *Man & woman, boy & girl*. Northvale, NJ: Jason Aronson. This is the groundbreaking work in which Money and Ehrhardt set forth their theory of gender identity as a social construct, learned in subtle and not so subtle ways from the moment of birth, but not fully set for the first few months of life. Although this theory is now in serious question, the work of these authors did open up the topic for discussion, and the ensuing social and scientific dialog has transformed our society.

Nichols, M. (Director). (1996). *The birdcage* [Motion picture]. United Artists. A movie staring Robin Williams, Nathan Lane, Gene Hackman, and Diane Wiest. A remake of the classic film *La Cage aux Folles*. A comedy based on the dilemma of a young man needing to introduce his fiancée and her parents to his gay father and his partner, the ones who raised him.

O'Keefe, T., & Fox, K. (1996). *Trans-x-u-all: The naked difference*. London: Extraordinary People Press. Co-authored by a transsexual woman who is also a therapist, and her natal female partner, this work offers a comprehensive overview of the transsexual experience. It begins with the author's theory about "pansexuality," which includes the various combinations and manifestations of gender identity and sexual orientation. It discusses many possible causative factors, describes diagnosis and treatment, and includes some social, legal, and political considerations and several personal stories of transsexuals and their family members and friends.

Pauly, I. B. (1992). Terminology and classification of gender identity disorders. In W. O. Bockting & E. Coleman (Eds.), *Gender dysphoria: Interdisciplinary approaches in clinical management* (pp. 1–14). Binghamton, NY: Hayworth Press. Raises the question of the role of age of onset as it relates to sexual orientation in transgender people, and also challenges the prevailing method of using the terms *homosexual* and *heterosexual* based on natal gender assignment. Does not address shift in sexual orientation.

Person, E., & Ovesey, L. (1974a). The transsexual syndrome in males: Part I: Primary transsexualism. *American Journal of Psychotherapy, 28,* 4–20. Part I of a two-part series. Used three categories for transsexuals: primary, transvestic, and homosexual. The latter two were viewed as secondary developments to transvestism and to effeminate homosexuality, respectively. Primary transsexuals were thought to be asexual. As such, these categories are very similar to those of Bentler and the DSM-III, both above.

Person, E., & Ovesey, L. (1974b). The transsexual syndrome in males: Part II: Secondary transsexualism. *American Journal of Psychotherapy, 28,* 174–93. Part II of a two-part series (see the above article), with focus on transgender persons whose transsexuality appears to evolve rather than being present from early childhood.

Peyser, M. (1998, August 17). Battling backlash. *Newsweek*, pp. 50–52. Story regarding the controversy about homosexual conversion therapy.

Ramsey, G. (1996). *Transsexuals, candid answers to private questions*. Freedom, CA: The Crossing Press. Written in a question-and-answer format. Much good information but tends to perpetuate the stereotype of the transsexual as an entity that is separate from other forms of transgender. Strongly supports professional involvement in irreversible and life-transforming decisions while the concept of self-determination is gaining strength in the transgender world. Retains the idea that transsexuals tend to be hyposexual, a concept no longer widely accepted and belied in clinical practice, except where the client might be inclined to dissemble to gain the desired medical and surgical treatment. Ramsey is so clinical in approach that he fails to speak to the human side. It appears that he had so far made up his mind academically that even clinical observations to the contrary were not enough to alter his opinions.

Regan, Melissa (Producer). (2001). *No dumb questions*. A privately pro-
    duced short (25-minute) video (VHS). Winner of a Sundance Film
    Festival award. A delightful documentary following parents and their
    three young children as they face the fact that the paternal uncle of
    the children is becoming a woman. Available online at <http://www.
    nodumbquestions.com/>.

Rekers, G. A. (1988). Psychosexual assessment of gender identity disorders.
    In R. J. Prinz (Ed.), *Advances in behavioral assessment of children and
    families* (Vol. 4, pp. 33–71), Greenwich, CN: JAI Press. Discussion of
    assessment of a number of challenging clinical presentations.

Robbins, J., & Wise, R. (Directors), & Bernstein, L., & Laurents, A. (Writ-
    ers). (1961). *West side story* [Motion picture]. Mirish Pictures. Movie
    in which the character Maria, played by Natalie Wood, sings "I Feel
    Pretty." According to the October 17, 2004, edition of *Parade*, Natalie
    Wood's vocals were dubbed and were actually sung by Marni Nixon.

Rottnek, M. (Ed.). (1999). *Sissies and tomboys: Gender nonconformity and
    homosexual childhood*. New York: New York University Press. A
    collection of essays on the subject of gender roles and identity, and
    gender nonconformity, examining social attitudes and perceptions
    dating from the 1960s' sexual revolution through the continuing
    changes in how gender is defined. It presents and challenges current
    theories of gender identity formation, our current use of the diagnosis
    of gender identity disorder, and even our current definition of *gender*.
    Ultimately, it challenges the current social definition of normal and
    who has the right to decide personal gender.

Roughgarden, J. (2004). *Evolution's rainbow: Diversity, gender, and sexual-
    ity in nature and people*. Berkeley: University of California Press. This
    is a broad and fascinating study of diversity, especially sex and gender
    diversity, in animals and humans, and in some cultures, illustrating
    that variation is the norm and probably more common than most of
    us imagined.

Samons, S. L. (2001). Building your own prison: The use of external struc-
    ture to reinforce suppression of transgender feelings and behaviors.
    Gender and Psychoanalysis: An Interdisciplinary Journal, 6, 143–57.
    Describes a common dynamic in transgender individuals of invest-
    ment in secrecy, factors in the inability to sustain it, and the dilem-
    mas associated with making changes.

Savage, D. (2000, December). Ex-ex marks the spot. *OUT Magazine*. See
    Kirby (2000).

Steiner, B. W. (Ed.). (1985). *Gender dysphoria: Development, research, man-
    agement*. New York: Plenum Press. Introduction written by Steiner,
    R., Blanchard, R., and Zucker, K. J., in which they agree that there are
    only two categories of MTFs: transvestites and transsexuals.

Stone, A. R. (as Sandy Stone). (1991). The empire strikes back: A post-transsexual manifesto. In J. Epstein & K. Straub (Eds.), *Body guards: The cultural politics of gender ambiguity* (pp. 280–304). New York: Routledge Press. The author, a postoperative transsexual woman and a sociologist, frankly discusses transsexualism, cutting through misconceptions perpetuated by the medical community (e.g., all transsexual persons are "confused and bizarre"), as well as those perpetuated by transsexual persons themselves (e.g., the "I'm a woman/man trapped in a man's/woman's body" argument). Stone suggests that transsexuals, rather than assimilating, take responsibility for all their history, "to begin to rearticulate their lives not as a series of erasures … but as a political action begun by reappropriating difference and reclaiming the power of the refigured and reinscribed body." Annotation by D. Denny.

Stuart, K. E. (1991). *The uninvited dilemma.* Portland, OR: Metamorphous Press. Based on interviews with 75 transsexuals, their family members, and their medical and mental health providers, this book looks broadly at the transgender condition. It recognizes that transgender people may shift sexual orientation with shift in gender role, and identifies some of the factors that may influence this shift. It also identifies the need for additional research in this area of study.

Tully, B. (1992). *Accounting for transsexualism and transhomosexuality.* London: Whiting and Birch. Points to the need to investigate sexual orientation in transgender people over time.

University of Michigan Office of the Provost. (2004). *From inclusion to acceptance: Report of the Task Force on the Campus Climate for Transgender, Bisexual, Lesbian and Gay (TBLG) Faculty, Staff and Students.* Ann Arbor, MI: Author. If fully implemented, this report and its recommendations will be a model for the nation on the needs of this population in an academic setting (and elsewhere). It can be found in its entirety online at <http://www.umich.edu/~provost/reports/tblg/>.

Wallerstein, J. S., Lewis, J. M., & Blakeslee, S. (2000). *The unexpected legacy of divorce: A 25 year landmark study.* New York: Hyperion Press. This is a controversial, groundbreaking work that reports the results of the most definitive study to date of the impact of divorce on children. A sample of 131 children were followed for a 25-year period. The authors found that the conventional wisdom simply does not hold true, that is, that a good divorce is better than a bad marriage. While the young children in her study clearly exhibited adjustment and behavior problems, the authors found that the most distressing effects do not surface until young adulthood, when these individuals set about forming families of their own. The social and psychological impact and typical behavioral and personality manifestations are described, including the implication that these children are at higher than average risk to have their own marriages end in divorce, thus perpetuating the unhealthy dynamic through generations.

Weinberg, S. (2007, May). Affirmative practice with LGBT folks; reaching the margins of the margin. Paper presented at the National Association of Social Workers NASW-MI annual convention. The author does an excellent job of identifying the subgroups of this larger marginalized population, the members of which are so much further marginalized as to be unlikely to be included in any research.

Weiss, J. T. (2001). The gender caste system: Identity, privacy, and heteronormativity. *Law & Sexuality, 10,* 123–86. The author states, "This article examines the incongruity of the heteronormative standard, proposing a legal theory of gender which accommodates the new reality of transsexuality." The author discusses the basis for her claims about the existence of a caste system, the difficulty and legal inconsistencies in attempts to define sex and gender, the existing legal issues that circumscribe and also contradict each other in defining individual rights to privacy and self-determination, and the parameters of legal intrusion into private lives. She brings this all together with constructive suggestions for making the law more consistent and respectful of individual citizens while continuing to protect the common good.

White, Mel. (1994). *Stranger at the gate: To be gay and Christian in America.* New York: Simon & Schuster. Autobiographical story of a gay man who has had a long career as a writer and video producer for the Christian religious right, including noted televangelists such as Pat Robertson and Jerry Falwell. He spent many years struggling with his homosexuality and went through several intensive Christian "cures," in which he desperately wanted to succeed. In this book, he also addresses the beliefs within the religious right and gives some sense of the veritable trap some of these people are in, noting that they may have their heart in the right place but dare not make a controversial stand. He explains how he was able to realign his belief system to resolve his own Christian conflict. This book is a powerful rebuttal for the conservative religious antigay position.

Williams, W. L. (1986). *The spirit and the flesh: Sexual diversity in American Indian culture.* Boston: Beacon Press. Williams has written an in-depth anthropological study of sexual diversity among Native American tribal cultures. This includes variations of transgender as they are manifested in these various groups. While sex in general tends to be viewed with humor, couplings that are somewhat out of the ordinary are the object of greater humor. However, this is done for the most part without malice. Still, sexual orientation, even in all its diversity, is not seen as something that shifts, but rather that some individuals enjoy more diversity in their sex than do others.

Index